'Drawing on the concept of passive revolution, Kevin Gray successfully highlights the dialectical relationship between the subordination of labour and wider geo-political dynamics underpinning East Asian Development. A must read for political economists!'

Andreas Bieler, Professor of Political Economy,
University of Nottingham, UK

'Gray's account of unfolding tensions inherent in the political and ideological management of labour in China's capitalist revolution is theoretically sophisticated, compelling in argument and well written.'

Garry Rodan, Professor of Politics and International Studies,
Murdoch University, Australia

LABOUR AND DEVELOPMENT IN EAST ASIA

The Chinese Communist Party's response to the wave of factory strikes in the early summer of 2010 has raised important questions about the role that labour plays in the transformation of world orders. In contrast to previous policies of repression toward labour unrest, these recent disputes centring around wages and working conditions have been met with a more permissive response on the part of the state, as the Chinese Communist Party ostensibly seeks to facilitate a transition away from a model of political economy based on 'low-road' labour relations and export dependence.

Labour and Development in East Asia shows that such inter-linkages between labour, geopolitical transformations, and states' developmental strategies have been much more central to East Asia's development than has commonly been recognised. By adopting an explanatory framework of the labour–geopolitics–development nexus, the book theorises and provides an historical analysis of the formation and transformation of the East Asian regional political economy from the end of the Second World War to the present, with particular reference to Japan, South Korea, Taiwan, and China.

This book will be of interest to students and scholars of international relations, development studies, and comparative politics.

Kevin Gray is a Senior Lecturer in International Relations at the University of Sussex. He is author of *Korean Workers and Neoliberal Globalization*, and co-editor of *Rising Powers and the Future of Global Governance* (with Craig N. Murphy), and *People Power in an Era of Global Crisis* (with Barry Gills).

Rethinking Globalizations

Edited by Barry K. Gills, Newcastle University, UK

This series is designed to break new ground in the literature on globalization and its academic and popular understanding. Rather than perpetuating or simply reacting to the economic understanding of globalization, this series seeks to capture the term and broaden its meaning to encompass a wide range of issues and disciplines and convey a sense of alternative possibilities for the future.

1. Whither Globalization?
The vortex of knowledge and globalization
James H. Mittelman

2. Globalization and Global History
Edited by Barry K. Gills and William R. Thompson

3. Rethinking Civilization
Communication and terror in the global village
Majid Tehranian

4. Globalization and Contestation
The new great counter-movement
Ronaldo Munck

5. Global Activism
Ruth Reitan

6. Globalization, the City and Civil Society in Pacific Asia
Edited by Mike Douglass, K.C. Ho and Giok Ling Ooi

7. Challenging Euro-America's Politics of Identity
The return of the native
Jorge Luis Andrade Fernandes

8. The Global Politics of Globalization
"Empire" vs "Cosmopolis"
Edited by Barry K. Gills

9. The Globalization of Environmental Crisis
Edited by Jan Oosthoek and Barry K. Gills

10. Globalization as Evolutionary Process
Modeling global change
Edited by Geroge Modelski, Tessaleno Devezas and William R. Thompson

11. The Political Economy of Global Security
War, future crises and changes in global governance
Heikki Patomäki

12. Cultures of Globalization
Coherence, hybridity, contestation
Edited by Kevin Archer, M. Martin Bosman, M. Mark Amen and Ella Schmidt

13. Globalization and the Global Politics of Justice
Edited by Barry K. Gills

14. Global Economy Contested
Power and conflict across the international division of labor
Edited by Marcus Taylor

15. Rethinking Insecurity, War and Violence
Beyond savage globalization?
Edited by Damian Grenfell and Paul James

16. Recognition and Redistribution
Beyond international development
Edited by Heloise Weber and Mark T. Berger

17. The Social Economy
Working alternatives in a globalizing era
Edited by Hasmet M. Uluorta

18. The Global Governance of Food
Edited by Sara R. Curran, April Linton, Abigail Cooke and Andrew Schrank

19. Global Poverty, Ethics and Human Rights
The role of multilateral organisations
Desmond McNeill and Asunción Lera St. Clair

20. Globalization and Popular Sovereignty
Democracy's transnational dilemma
Adam Lupel

21. Limits to Globalization
North-South divergence
William R. Thompson and Rafael Reuveny

22. Globalisation, Knowledge and Labour
Education for solidarity within spaces of resistance
Edited by Mario Novelli and Anibel Ferus-Comelo

23. Dying Empire
U.S. imperialism and global resistance
Francis Shor

24. Alternative Globalizations
An integrative approach to studying dissident knowledge in the global justice movement
S. A. Hamed Hosseini

25. Global Restructuring, Labour and the Challenges for Transnational Solidarity
Edited by Andreas Bieler and Ingemar Lindberg

26. Global South to the Rescue
Emerging humanitarian superpowers and globalizing rescue industries
Edited by Paul Amar

27. Global Ideologies and Urban Landscapes
Edited by Manfred B. Steger and Anne McNevin

28. Power and Transnational Activism
Edited by Thomas Olesen

29. Globalization and Crisis
Edited by Barry K. Gills

30. Andre Gunder Frank and Global Development
Visions, remembrances and explorations
Edited by Patrick Manning and Barry K. Gills

31. Global Social Justice
Edited by Heather Widdows and Nicola J. Smith

32. Globalization, Labor Export and Resistance
A study of Filipino migrant domestic workers in global cities.
Ligaya Lindio-McGovern

33. Situating Global Resistance
Between Discipline and Dissent
Edited by Lara Montesinos Coleman and Karen Tucker

34. A History of World Order and Resistance
The Making and Unmaking of Global Subjects
André C. Drainville

35. Migration, Work and Citizenship in the New Global Order
Edited by Ronaldo Munck, Carl-Ulrik Schierup and Raúl Delgado Wise

36. Edges of Global Justice
The World Social Forum and Its 'Others'
Janet Conway

37. Land Grabbing and Global Governance
Edited by Matias E. Margulis, Nora McKeon and Saturnino Borras Jr.

38. Dialectics in World Politics
Edited by Shannon Brincat

39. Crisis, Movement, Management: Globalising Dynamics
Edited by James Goodman and Jonathan Paul Marshall

40. China's Development
Capitalism and Empire
Michel Aglietta and Guo Bai

41. Global Governance and NGO Participation
Charlotte Dany

42. Arab Revolutions and World Transformations
Edited by Anna M. Agathangelou and Nevzat Soguk

43. Global Movement
Edited by Ruth Reitan

44. Free Trade and the Transnational Labour Movement
Edited by Andreas Bieler, Bruno Ciccaglione, John Hilary and Ingemar Lindberg

45. Counter-Globalization and Socialism in the 21st Century
The Bolivarian Alliance for the Peoples of our America
Thomas Muhr

46. Global Civil Society and Transversal Hegemony
The Globalization-Contestation Nexus
Karen M. Buckley

47. Contentious Agency and Natural Resource Politics
Markus Kröger

48. Social Movements, the Poor and the New Politics of the Americas
Edited by Håvard Haarstad, Mark Amen and Asuncion Lera St Clair

49. Development in an Era of Neoliberal Globalization
Edited by Henry Veltmeyer

50. The State–Capital Nexus in the Global Crisis
Rebound of the Capitalist State
Edited by Bastiaan van Apeldoorn, Naná de Graaff and Henk W. Overbeek

51. From Empires to Imperialism
The State and the Rise of Bourgeois Civilisation
Boris Kagarlitsky, translated by Renfrey Clarke

52. Global Justice and the Politics of Information
The Struggle over Knowledge
Sky Croeser

53. Labour and Development in East Asia
Social Forces and Passive Revolution
Kevin Gray

54. Global Capitalism and Transnational Class Formation
Edited by Jason Struna

55. Rethinking Border Control for a Globalizing World
A Preferred Future
Edited by Leanne Weber

56. Global Governance, Legitimacy and Legitimation
Edited by Magdalena Bexell

57. Critical Rationalism and Globalisation
Towards the Sociology of the Open Global Society
Masoud Mohammadi Alamuti

LABOUR AND DEVELOPMENT IN EAST ASIA

Social forces and passive revolution

Kevin Gray

Routledge
Taylor & Francis Group
LONDON AND NEW YORK

First published 2015
by Routledge
2 Park Square, Milton Park, Abingdon, Oxon OX14 4RN

and by Routledge
711 Third Avenue, New York, NY 10017

Routledge is an imprint of the Taylor & Francis Group, an informa business

British Library Cataloguing in Publication Data
A catalogue record for this book is available from the British Library.

Library of Congress Cataloging-in-Publication Data
Gray, Kevin, 1973-
Labour and development in East Asia : social forces and passive revolution / Kevin Gray.
pages cm. – (Rethinking globalizations ; 53)
Includes bibliographical references and index.
1. Labor market–East Asia. 2. Economic development–East Asia.
3. East Asia–Foreign economic relations. I. Title.
HD5826.A6G73 2014
331.12095–dc23
2014013879

ISBN: 978-0-415-68184-1 (hbk)
ISBN: 978-0-415-68185-8 (pbk)
ISBN: 978-1-315-75075-0 (ebk)

Typeset in Bembo
by Cenveo Publisher Services

CONTENTS

ACKNOWLEDGEMENTS

This book is the product of a long process of research on East Asian labour, development, and state formation. Some of the key themes and arguments have been significantly developed from ideas found in earlier research publications, including my previous book, *Korean Workers and Neoliberal Globalization* (London: Routledge, 2008), as well as a number of journal articles including 'The Social and Geopolitical Origins of State Transformation: The Case of South Korea,' *New Political Economy*, 16(3), 2011; 'Labour and the State in China's Passive Revolution,' *Capital and Class*, 34(3), 2010; and 'Taiwan and the Geopolitics of Late Development,' *Third World Quarterly*, 24(5), 2011.

It is impossible to provide a comprehensive overview of all individuals who have influenced my own intellectual formation during the years spent preparing this manuscript. I would like, however, to express particular gratitude to a number of people who have provided crucial feedback on the chapters that underpin this book. Several of my colleagues at the Department of International Relations in the University of Sussex have provided constructive criticism on various parts of the text; these colleagues include Justin Rosenberg, Ben Selwyn, Kamran Matin, and Kees van der Pijl. More broadly, the intellectual culture provided by the faculty and students in the Department and in the Centre for Global Political Economy at Sussex has been central to the development of several of the key ideas underpinning this book. Further afield, particular thanks go to Jamie Doucette at the University of Manchester, Lin Chun at the London School of Economics, Chen Hsin-Hsing at Shih-Hsin University in Taipei, Huang Chenwei at National Cheng Kung University in Tainan, and Baek Seung-Wook of Chung-Ang University in Seoul.

I would also like to express my gratitude to the Democracy and Social Movements Institute at Sungkonghoe University in Seoul, and particularly to Cho Hee-Yeon, Jang Youngseok, Kim Dong-Choon, and Hur Sungwoo. It was during my time as a visiting researcher at Sungkonghoe University in the summer of 2008 that several of the key ideas for this book first began to take shape. I would also like to thank the Department of Sociology at Tsinghua University, Beijing, and in particular Prof. Shen Yuan. Preliminary research on the China case study was carried out whilst I was a visiting researcher at the department in the summer of 2007. I would also like to express my gratitude to Research Councils United Kingdom (RCUK). Early chapter drafts of the book were completed whilst I was holding a RCUK Postdoctoral Fellowship in Emerging Global Capitalisms at the University of Sussex. This fellowship was crucial in sparing me from many of the pressures faced by early career academics and gave me the space and time to begin work on this manuscript.

Finally, I would like to offer my greatest note of thanks to my wife, Han Yoojung. Without her generous support, patience, and relentless encouragement through numerous difficulties, this book would never have been completed. It is therefore to her that I dedicate this book.

ABBREVIATIONS

ACFTU	All China Federation of Trade Unions
AFL-CIO	American Federation of Labor - Congress of Industrial Organizations
CAL	Collective Action Law
CCP	Chinese Communist Party
CEPD	Council for Economic Planning and Development
CFL	Chinese Federation of Labour
CLA	Council for Labor Affairs
DPP	Democratic Progressive Party
DSP	Democratic Socialist Party
EOI	Export-oriented industrialisation
FDI	Foreign direct investment
FKTU	Federation of Korean Trade Unions
GSP	Generalised System of Preferences
HCI	Heavy and chemical industrialisation
IFI	International financial institution
IMF	International Monetary Fund
IPE	International political economy
ISI	Import substitution industrialisation
JCP	Japanese Communist Party
JNR	Japan National Railway
JSP	Japanese Socialist Party
KCIA	Korean Central Intelligence Agency
KCTU	Korean Confederation of Trade Unions
KDLP	Korean Democratic Labor Party
KMT	Kuomintang
KMWU	Korean Metal Workers' Union

LMDSL	Labour Management Dispute Settlement Law
LSL	Labour Standards Law
LUL	Labour Union Law
LUPR	Labour Union Policy Roundtable
MITI	Ministry of International Trade and Industry
MNC	Multinational Corporation
SCAP	Supreme Commander for the Allied Powers
SOE	State-owned enterprise
TCP	Taiwanese Communist Party
TCTU	Taiwan Confederation of Trade Unions
TLF	Taiwan Labor Front
TRLU	Taiwan Railway Labour Union
SME	Small and medium enterprise
UIM	Urban industrial mission
WTO	World Trade Organization

TABLES AND FIGURES

INTRODUCTION

In the summer of 2010, China witnessed an unprecedented outbreak of labour unrest. The spate of worker suicides at the Taiwanese-owned Foxconn plant in Shenzhen, Guangdong Province, perhaps attracted the most attention in the national and international media. Working conditions at the factory were reported to be so harsh that, in the first five months of the year, sixteen workers at the factory had taken their own lives. As tragic as these desperate actions were, it was the strike wave at a number of automobile part manufacturers elsewhere in the province that were arguably more indicative of a nascent yet profound transformation in the nature of Chinese labour relations. The significance of the strike wave was, paradoxically, its apparent 'normality.' The seventeen-day strike at Nanhai Honda in the city of Foshan, in particular, was centred not around the often desperate and defensive demands concerning the infringement of workers' rights by employers but on proactive demands for wage rises and for the democratisation of the company union. Furthermore, the strike served to spur similar struggles at other Honda suppliers in Guangdong province including Atsumitec and Ormon (a supplier to Honda, Ford, and BMW), as well as Honda Locks in neighbouring Zhongshan. A strike for higher wages at a Toyota-owned parts supplier, Denso Guangzhou Nansha, also halted production at the final assembly plant in the northern city of Tianjin. Whilst the strikes had primarily affected Japanese-invested companies and their suppliers, industrial unrest also broke out at the Korean-owned Hyundai car plant in Beijing.

The breadth of the strike wave and the nature of the demands made by workers appear to suggest that a qualitative shift is underway in China toward militant workers' consciousness, oriented against the comprehensive system of labour subordination that has underpinned the country's recent export-led growth. Given the reliance of China's industrialisation on the ready availability of cheap and exploitable labour, demands for higher wages and a more secure livelihood constitute a direct challenge to the government's developmental strategy. Furthermore, as a result of China's role in recent years as 'workshop of the world,' this heightened restiveness is likely to have implications far beyond the country's borders. China's 2010 strike wave took place amidst a longer-term upsurge of social restiveness that has compelled the country's political elites to rethink the viability of an export-oriented developmental model based on labour subordination. The passing of the Labour Contract Law in 2007, for example, was an attempt by the Chinese Communist Party (CCP) to reform the legal framework governing labour relations so as to provide more legal channels for the redress of individual worker grievances. Furthermore, in contrast to the more repressive policies of the past, the Chinese authorities adopted a more moderate response to the 2010 strike wave, thereby suggesting a nascent shift in the CCP's developmental strategy away from a model of political economy based on 'low-road' labour relations and export dependence. However, this tentative transformation in government's labour policies is also situated in a rapidly transformed global conjuncture in which the international underpinnings of China's export-oriented industrialisation (EOI) have been directly challenged by the recent global financial crisis. As part of a growing realisation of the heightened domestic and international vulnerabilities associated with export dependence, the CCP has, rhetorically at least, adopted an explicit policy of seeking to increase wages and facilitate a transition toward increased reliance on domestic consumption.

As this book seeks to argue, whilst often viewed as analytically separate, this confluence of and dynamic relationship between the 'threat' of domestic labour unrest and the broader contours of the international political economy is central to explaining the vicissitudes of national experiences of late development. This nexus between labour, the international political economy, and development is not limited to China's recent wave of labour unrest but is a broader constitutive element in the history of the region's developmental experience. Although theories of East Asian development have often focused on the relative roles of states and markets (or more accurately, the relationship between bureaucrats and businessmen), what has often been neglected is how labour subordination has formed a central underpinning of the symbiotic relationship between the export-oriented regional political economies of East Asia and the hitherto seemingly inexhaustible demand provided by the American market.

In seeking to explain East Asian development, therefore, the key questions that this study addresses are as follows: What are the origins of East Asia's labour subordination? More specifically, what role did the post-war geopolitical conjuncture play in making East Asia comparatively well placed to embark upon a project of EOI based on the political repression of labour? How did industrialisation under US auspices affect subsequent processes of working-class formation? What were the implications of such processes for East Asia's position within the international political economy? Notwithstanding a broader conception of regional labour subordination, how can the origins of divergent developmental outcomes across the individual countries of the region be explained? What role did the rise of labour subjectivities in the region play in the decline of national developmentalism and the transition toward more neoliberal strategies, and how has labour adapted to and resisted the challenges inherent in this transition? How did East Asia's economic rise, based as it was on the subordination of labour, subsequently impact upon the structure of post-war US hegemony itself? How have the specificities of each national labour regime enabled or hindered resistance to neoliberalism? Whilst detailed studies of East Asian labour regimes have tended to be left to the field of comparative sociology or political science, each question posed here reveals the shortcomings of the national-comparative approach that is dominant in the literature.

This neglect of labour is a serious shortcoming because, as I will argue, the basis of East Asian EOI upon the prior subordination of workers owes much to the specificities of the post-war geopolitical conjuncture. Whilst labour subordination in the region has pre-war antecedents, US intervention in the polities of Japan, South Korea (herein Korea), and Taiwan in the aftermath of the Second World War played a crucial role in the repression of labour militancy across the region and in securing the political primacy of anticommunist pro-US developmental elites. Indeed, this intervention by the US was explicitly directed at inducing economic growth in the region and reconstructing the broader global capitalist economy. The East Asian 'strong state,' based as it was on its superlative administrative and repressive capacity, was thus integral to the US-centred Cold War regional order.

East Asian labour subordination underpinned the region's remarkable economic growth yet was in turn a key component of the global overproduction that increasingly impinged upon capital profitability in the advanced industrialised countries of the West, eventually leading to what Duménil and Lévy (2004a) have termed 'the neoliberal counter-revolution.' Furthermore, East Asia's newly industrialising countries, such as Korea and Taiwan, were well placed to absorb internationally mobile capital searching for a 'fix' to ongoing problems of profitability, thereby underpinning much of the region's growth in the 1970s and 1980s. Deepening industrialisation from the 1970s led to the intensification of labour shortages and processes of working-class formation, and ultimately, to growing challenges by workers against their subordination under authoritarian developmentalism. Furthermore, the combination of rising labour costs and worker militancy with liberalising pressures from the United States led to the rise of neoliberalism as a political project within the East Asian states aimed at tackling both the internal (social) and external (geopolitical) contradictions of late development. These processes led to the subsequent emergence of China as a key site of production for East Asian capital. However, as the events outlined above have shown, China's role as a 'fix' for regional and global capital is likely to be only temporary in scope as a result of both domestic process of class formation within China and the unsustainability of US debt-financed consumerism.

The states and markets approach of conventional accounts of East Asian development have, for the most part, failed to adequately comprehend this dynamic relationship between labour and 'the international.' As is well known, the East Asian states of Japan, Korea, and Taiwan have played a central role in the theorisation of late development. Their rapid post-war economic growth gave rise to a longstanding debate surrounding the relative roles of the states and markets in facilitating catch-up industrialisation. Neoclassical economists argued that East Asia's post-war industrialisation was made possible by the fact that market forces were allowed to operate unhindered by excessive state intervention (Little *et al.* 1970, Patrick and Rosovsky 1976, Bhagwati 1978, Balassa 1988, Westphal 1990). Statist theorists, on the other hand, countered that East Asian development occurred as a result of a highly effective form of coordination between state and capital, though one in which the latter was clearly subjected to the directive capacities of the former. Chalmers Johnson, the originator of the concept of the developmental state, famously argued that the Japanese state's interventionist approach to economic development lay between the 'market ideological' state of Western liberal capitalism and the 'plan ideological' state of the communist bloc countries. The Japanese developmental state and, in particular, the bureaucracy's pilot agency known as the Ministry of International Trade and Industry (MITI), adopted a pragmatic approach of subjecting private capital to the guidance of the state in service of wider goals of catch-up industrialisation. Through its control over the distribution of foreign exchange, MITI was thereby able to strategically guide corporate investment throughout the entire economy in accordance with centrally devised industrial policy goals (Johnson 1982, pp. 22–25).

Following Johnson's study, Alice Amsden (1989) and Robert Wade (1990) subsequently produced studies of Korean and Taiwanese economic development, where they argued that the role of both states in facilitating industrialisation bore strong resemblances to the Japanese case. Both Amsden and Wade were, however, more explicit in terms of how their case studies challenged neoclassical exhortations for the government to step back and allow prices to find their own natural equilibrium. Amsden argued, for example, that a key feature of the Korean developmental state was its defiance of the logic of the market through deliberately 'getting the prices wrong.' In the context of a reciprocal relationship with large diversified business conglomerates (the *chaebŏl*), the Economic Planning Board set export targets, price controls, restrictions on capacity expansions, limits on market entry, prohibitions on capital flight, restraints on tax evasion, and control over the banking system. In exchange for subsidies, the *chaebŏl* were in turn expected to meet strict performance standards. Strict capital controls meant that the *chaebŏl* had little choice but to cooperate with the state's strategic direction; as such, Korea's developmental experience was characterised not by the 'invisible hand' of the free market but by the 'visible hand' of the strong state (Amsden 1989, pp. 141–147). Wade similarly argued that, in the Taiwanese context, the government owned and controlled the banks upon which large- and medium-sized businesses depended heavily for finance. As a result, the country's high savings were transferred through the banking system to investors in accordance with industrial policy (Wade 1990, pp. 159–172). Through this disciplining mechanism of state control over finance, the Taiwanese bureaucracy took a leading role in deciding what products or technologies should be encouraged, then provided the public resources to fund investment in those industries (Wade 1990, pp. 28–29).

Whilst Japan, Korea, and Taiwan were all, therefore, deemed as conforming to a broader state-led model of development, there was a key difference in how these respective authors viewed the policy implications of their arguments.

Johnson's (1999) analysis paid greater attention to the historical specificities of Japan's late-developmental experience and was consequently more sceptical about the applicability of the so-called 'Japanese model' elsewhere. Wade and Amsden, on the other hand, in line with their more explicit critique of neoclassical development economics, argued that the lessons learnt from East Asian industrialisation could be more widely applied in countries faced with the challenges of late development. As such, their approach to the developmental state involved the downplaying of historical and geopolitical contexts in order to construct a model more widely applicable across the Third World (Wade 1992, Amsden 1994, see also Chang 2007; Hayashi 2010). The irony was, however, that whilst this policy-driven approach to understanding the developmental state emerged as part of a debate with the increasingly dominant field of neoclassical development economics, the abstraction of the East Asian experience from its historical and geopolitical context meant that development state theorists largely failed to recognise how the rise of global neoliberalism was serving to transform actually existing East Asian developmental states, particularly from the 1990s onwards.

On the one hand, this failure stems from a constrained view of how post-war geopolitics have shaped East Asian experiences of late development. It is unfair, of course, to say that developmental state theorists have been completely oblivious to the constitutive role of the international in late development. Whilst their primary focus has been on domestic state institutions, Johnson, Amsden, and Wade all recognised the crucial role of the post-war intervention by the United States in laying the groundwork for the key developmental state institutions (Johnson 1982, pp. 173–197; Amsden 1989, pp. 35–38, 43–48; Wade 1990, pp. 82–83). They also saw that the political goals of national development were very much borne of geopolitical pressures and intense perceptions of external and, in most cases, internal vulnerability. As Johnson (1982, p. 25) has argued,

> [t]he need for economic growth in a developing country has few if any economic springs. It arises from a desire to assume full human status by taking part in an industrial civilization, participation in which *alone* enables a nation or an individual to compel others to treat it as an equal.

Indeed, the role of the international is implicit in how developmental state theorists deploy the notion of late development. In many respects, developmental state theorists have borrowed from Alexander Gerschenkron's (1962) understanding of how 'lateness' in world historical time shapes the nature and trajectory of industrialisation (Amsden 1989, p. 3; Wade 1990, p. 351; Shin 2002).

Against the neoclassical view that late-industrialising countries necessarily had to pass through stages of agrarian industrialisation and labour-intensive manufacturing, Alexander Gerschenkron argued that, given the prior existence of already-industrialised countries, late developers such as Germany and Russia would have access to the most advanced production techniques in some of the most rapidly expanding industries and were thereby able to skip intermediate stages of development

(Gerschenkron 1962, p. 32). However, this lateness in world-historical time also necessarily affected the kinds of institutions that would underpin the developmental effort. In Germany, for example, the greater scope of the industrialisation movement, the larger average size of plants, and the concentration of industrialisation in branches of relatively high ratios of capital to output meant that instead of a gradual accumulation of capital and its transfer to industry, there emerged large banks designed to finance the much longer-term investment in the construction of railways, mines, factories, canals, and ports (Gerschenkron 1962, p. 14). However, Russia's greater backwardness and scarcity of capital during its industrialisation drive in the 1890s meant that no bank could conceivably succeed in attracting sufficient funds to finance large-scale industrialisation. The state therefore stepped in to facilitate the supply of capital for industrialisation through its taxation policies, thereby directing incomes from consumption to investment (Gerschenkron 1962, pp. 19–20). In this sense, the developmental state can by no means be seen as unique to twentieth-century East Asia but rather as an extension of an institutional arrangement common to countries successfully responding to the imperatives of late development.

However, the role of the international here is only present in the a rather restrictive sense: the existence of already-industrialised states shapes the institutional arrangements within later developing states of East Asia, and the United States played a key role in the formation of these arrangements. The implicit rather than explicit treatment of international context is not accidental, however. A fully theorised account of the mutually constitutive relationship between the dynamics of the Cold War and domestic experiences of late development in East Asia would serve to challenge the overriding policy objective of establishing a more widely applicable model of development. Thus, as T. J. Pempel (1999, p. 146) is surely correct to argue, 'despite an agenda that concentrates on international catch-up, the developmental state is assessed largely in terms of its domestic context.' This failure to fully integrate the causal role of the international into analyses of East Asian development became increasingly apparent since the 1990s, as East Asian states appeared to confirm ongoing arguments surrounding global neoliberal convergence. Both within and beyond the developmental state approach, it has been argued, for example, that there have been marked transitions toward neoliberalism in Japan (Otake 1999, Hirashima 2004, Ikeda 2004, Reitan 2012) and Taiwan (Tsai 2001, Hsu 2009, Chen 2012).

Whilst mainland China has received less attention from within the developmental state approach (Baek 2005, Bolesta 2007, Appelbaum *et al.* 2011), a number of authors have seen Deng Xiaoping's post-1978 reforms as signifying a transition from state socialism toward neoliberalism (Harvey 2005, Petras 2006). Nowhere have these forces of convergence toward neoliberalism been more widely noted than in the case of Korea, however. The aftermath of the 1997 economic and financial crisis, in particular, led to a debate concerning not only the causes of the Korean crisis (Chang 1998a, Wade 1998, Shin 2000) but also the extent to which the International Monetary Fund (IMF) bailout and Washington Consensus conditionality had brought about the 'end of late development' (Cumings 1998). Indeed, the conditions attached to the IMF's bailout package clearly called for the dismantling of Korea's developmental state institutions and the imposition of an Anglo-American model of capitalism.

Critical responses to this alleged East Asian neoliberal transition have been varied, however. A number of developmental state theorists have argued that claims of neoliberal convergence notwithstanding, East Asian states have retained strong if somewhat transformed developmental capabilities (Weiss 1998, 2003; Amsden and Chu 2003; Dent 2003). Underpinning this argument is a relatively benign view of globalisation as a form of heightened international economic competition to which autonomous bureaucracies can respond, through a process of what Linda Weiss (2003, p. 259) has referred to as 'managed openness.' A key example of this alleged resilience in the face of such competitive conditions is precisely that of the Japanese MITI's active policy of encouraging the relocation of parts of the production process offshore, a process which is seen as constitutive of 'globalisation' itself (Weiss 1998, p. 204).

Taiwan has also been held up as an example of a developmental state that has both pursued liberalisation at the same time as facilitating a process of industrial upgrading. The continued directive capacity of the Taiwanese bureaucracy led to a more cautious process of financial liberalisation, whereby strong regulatory oversight enabled the country to escape the worst of the 1997 regional crisis (Thurbon 2001; Zhang 2002; Weiss 2003, pp. 258–266). Despite the debacle of the crisis, the Korean state too is seen by some as having regained much of its former governance capacity by having taken a proactive role in facilitating the restructuring of the country's *chaebŏl* conglomerates and preparing them to withstand the entry of foreign companies (Weiss 2003, pp. 249–258). According to this view, claims of 'neoliberalism everywhere' (Pieterse 2011, p. 32) thus tend to underestimate the resilience of East Asia's distinctive institutional forms. As Beeson argues, developmental states have persisted in East Asia as a consequence of path dependency, institutional stickiness, and the interlocking patterns of political and economic power that are such a ubiquitous and distinctive part of development in the region (Beeson 2009, p. 8).

It can again be argued in response that this view underestimates the rootedness of East Asian development in the post-war geopolitical conjuncture and, by extension, fails to gauge the implications of the changing international context, particularly the rise of global neoliberalism as a foreign policy goal of the United States (Nayar 2005, Veltmeyer 2005). As noted above, the double-edged success of post-war US attempts to revive the Western European and East Asian regional economies contributed to the decline in the rate of US corporate profitability from the 1970s (Brenner 1998), leading to a countermovement in the form of the rise of the hegemony of finance capital, as expressed in the 'Volcker Shock' rise in US interest rates in 1979 (Duménil and Lévy 2004b). Following the Third World debt crises of the 1980s, the United States, along with the IMF and the World Bank, took a leading role in imposing Washington Consensus policies on hitherto developing countries through stringent structural adjustment conditionality (Bello 2005, Klein 2007).

As such, the US-led modernisation project focused on national developmentalism gave way to the 'globalization project' (Berger 2004, p. 246). Strong economic growth levels along with Cold War geopolitical imperatives had initially spared the East Asian countries from excessive liberalising pressures on the part of the United States, and indeed the region benefited from the mobility of capital searching for profitable outlets (Arrighi 1996). The decline of Cold War superpower rivalry, however, served to undermine one of the key external underpinnings of the developmental state, particularly US tolerance for illiberal neomercantile capitalisms in East Asia (Stubbs 2005, pp. 184–217). The imposition of structural adjustment on Korea following the 1997 crisis thus confirmed this broader pattern of the United States and the international financial institutions (IFIs) seeking to compel developmental states to restructure along lines more closely resembling the Anglo-American model of capitalism (Cumings 1998; Gills 2000; Berger 2004, pp. 231–233).

A number of developmental state theorists have largely accepted such arguments insofar as they emphasise change over continuity in East Asian capitalisms. Yet, what has been more forthcoming from the developmental state approach has been a polemical critique of neoliberal ideology. Indeed, in this view, neoliberalism is understood largely as a set of erroneous ideas regarding the appropriate policies for development. Wade (2003), for example, sees the Uruguay Round investment measures, trade-in services, and intellectual property rights as effectively making illegal many of the industrial policy instruments deployed by East Asian developmental states to nurture their own industrial and technological capacities. Ha-Joon Chang (2002) similarly argues that the primary reason that today's poorer developing countries cannot follow the successful developmental path followed by the East Asian late developers is the harmful policy advice provided by neoliberal economists, with self-interest and a purposeful 'kicking away of the ladder' often being responsible. Many of these so-called 'Bad Samaritans' as Chang (2007, p. 17) calls them,

> are recommending free-trade, free-market policies to the poor countries in the honest but mistaken belief that those are the routes their own countries took in the past to become rich. But they are in fact making the lives of those whom they are trying to help more difficult.

As such, the neoliberal developmental paradigm is viewed as an aberration from the 'normal' or 'proper' role of the state in economic development. Yet, whilst such critiques of the ideas underpinning global neoliberalism are certainly persuasive, they stop short of providing a material analysis of *why* neoliberal ideas have become dominant, both globally and within actual and would-be developmental states over the past three decades. As Bieler and Morton (2008) argue, ideas should not be understood as simply 'falling from the sky' so to speak, but as material structures in themselves and as having their basis in social relations.

Indeed, popular accounts of the rise of global neoliberalism have tended to simply emphasise the coercive imposition of neoliberal restructuring on developing states by the United States and the IFIs. Robert Cox (1987), for example, argues that following the abandonment of the explicit norms of the Bretton Woods era, ideology had to substitute for legal orientation. The habit of policy harmonisation had been institutionalised during the two preceding decades and was reinforced. In the Third World countries, however, there has been a much more even balance of coercion and consent. The internationalisation of the Third World state has been externally determined and imposed, although it attracts internal allies and collaborators. Yet, as the case of Chile in the early 1970s, 'recalcitrant Third World governments are ultimately removed by violence if they do not conform to minimum standards of correct world-economy behaviour' (Cox 1987, p. 261).

However, this view of neoliberalism as an external force propagated through strategies of coercion and consent arguably neglects the question of how neoliberalism has been actively promoted by national political and economic elites as a response to domestic social transformations arising out of the process of national development itself. To take the example of Korea again, in countering claims made by neoclassical economists and mainstream observers that it was the 'crony capitalism' (Kang 2012) of the developmental state model that was responsible for the crisis, a number of writers have highlighted how the prior adoption by policymakers of neoliberal ideology was largely responsible. That is to say, it was precisely the excessive liberalisation of the early 1990s that was the main cause of the economic collapse. Thus, whilst the Korean financial system was basically sound, it was unsuited for a transition to a liberal Western style system (Chang *et al.* 1998, p. 754; Wade and Veneroso 1998).

Developmental state theory provides few analytical tools, however, with which to examine the domestic social transformations which arguably led to policymakers' adoption of neoliberal ideas in the first place. Though the literature is clear that the developmental state was 'autonomous' from the societal forces that otherwise might challenge the single-minded pursuit of growth at all costs, this view owes as much to the Weberian underpinnings of the theory itself as to historical reality. As such, developmental state theory has been ill-equipped to theorise the mutable underpinnings of what was after all an historically contingent relationship between state and society. On the one hand, the rise of neoliberalism as a domestic social project should be understood in terms of how catch-up industrialisation strengthened politically the capitalist class (Kim 1997a, Cho and Kim 1998). Indeed, the 'successful' experience of late development in East Asia led to a strengthening of domestic national champion corporations and their transformation into powerful multinational corporations by placing pressure on governments to liberalise specific elements of the developmental state and replace them with neoliberal arrangements. Neoliberal ideology was thus mobilised by economic and political elites as part of this broader shift in economic development strategy. Yet, it is important to note that this outward expansive impetus had its origins in broader societal shifts involving challenges to the comprehensive system of labour subordination.

The systematic repression of labour underpinning East Asia's experience of late industrialisation has not gained as much attention from developmental state theorists, though it is undeniable that the developmental state oversaw an extremely exploitative model of economic development. This was in contrast to Latin America, for example, where import substitution industrialisation (ISI) encouraged the stimulation of domestic purchasing power as a means of boosting industrial growth. This thereby served to deflect pressures from employers to lower labour costs and encouraged the government to increase welfare expenditure. As such, Latin American ISI involved a broad developmental coalition amongst the urban middle classes, industrialists, state bureaucrats, and unionised workers. In East Asia, however, there was little in the way of any linkage between domestic purchasing power and industrial growth, and instead, export competitiveness was dependent on low-cost disciplined labour (Deyo 1987, pp. 182–183). As a result, a key function of the East Asian developmental state was the enactment of repressive labour regulation that served to facilitate the exploitative mobilisation of workers. As Leftwich (1995, p. 415) has argued, developmental states were established upon 'a weak and subordinated civil society' as a central component, including '[t]he common use of internal security legislation and agencies, secret policy.'

Indeed, the implicit 'Golden Age' of the developmental state is that of the pseudo-Fascist *Yushin* era in Korea and that of the Chiang Ching-Kuo dictatorship in Taiwan, during which both countries underwent rapid heavy and chemical industrialisation. Furthermore, developmental statists have often implicitly or explicitly supported such arrangements. Alice Amsden (1990, p. 23) argues, for example, that whilst Korea was unambiguously authoritarian, the government's disciplining of business to the extent that the latter could not 'hold society to ransom' with its investment decisions meant that there was greater public accountability than that of many other early or late industrialising countries. Wade (1990, p. 71) similarly cites as a key feature of the developmental state the lack of any role for trade unions in intervening between the buyers and sellers of labour a result of government repression, but goes on to argue, '[f]or all its unsavoury aspects, Taiwan's exclusionary and authoritarian regime has allowed the country to avoid the political fate of many developing countries' (p. 267).

From a normative perspective, it is certainly questionable whether labour subordination and authoritarian dictatorship should be viewed as a necessary evil amidst the broader march toward industrialisation. Yet, the general failure to study underlying labour regimes and the use of euphemisms of 'state autonomy' ignores the history of workers' resistance in East Asia. Workers in the region actively rejected the imperatives of catch-up industrialisation, as can be seen in the Japanese 'production control' movement in the aftermath of the Second World War, in the women factory worker struggles in Korea during the 1970s, in the Taiwanese labour surge following the end of martial law in 1986, and more recently, in China's export-processing zones. Yet, despite the fact that East Asia's industrialisation was based more on 'perspiration than inspiration' (Krugman 1994) and consequently provoked workers' resistance to its underlying repressive labour regime, there has been little in the developmental state literature in the way of systematic incorporation of this history into broader analyses of national and regional development.

As Dae-oup Chang (2009, p. 4) has argued, this neglect stems from shortcomings at the theoretical level whereby the state appears to be detached from society, though in reality serves capital accumulation by exercising its force directly against the working class. To the extent that labour is incorporated into the analysis, the state–labour nexus is presented as a one-way relationship whereby labour is subordinated to the state, and the state is subsequently shown to be free from societal forces. The analysis of relations between state and society thus becomes reduced to that of government–business relations, leaving an empirical absence of the social power of labour (Chang 2009, p. 60). Labour is thereby regarded as having devoted itself to national development in spite of being oppressed in the process of capitalist development. Development is seen as a process devoid of class conflict. Any notion of class contradiction is thus absent from discussions surrounding what ultimately are capitalist social relations (Song 2011, p. 286).

As such, the developmental state literature has failed to either properly explain the historical origins of East Asian labour subordination or consider the implications of subsequent workers' resistance toward the state and capital's developmental strategies. Furthermore, it has failed to analyse how the formation of a collective subjective will on the part of labour and the emergence of subsequent labour unrest is central to understanding processes of neoliberal restructuring. As one of the few developmental state theorists to recognise this shortcoming, Peter Evans has noted how previously repressed social forces such as labour can eventually emerge to challenge the institutional underpinnings of their own subordination. With parallels to Karl Marx, the successful developmental state is seen to bring into existence the social actors that ultimately serve as the regime's 'gravediggers' (Evans 1995, p. 229). Despite this recognition of the role of class struggle in the demise of the developmental state, however, Evans' central concept of 'embedded autonomy' remains a conceptualisation of state–society relations through the exclusive prism of relations between bureaucrats and businessmen. Though relations between the two are seen as being negotiated and renegotiated, the same is not true for labour (Chang 2009, p. 168).

The developmental state approach is, therefore, characterised by a set of disjointed modes of explanation. It has largely focused on the institutional arrangements and policy initiatives of allegedly autonomous bureaucrats, with only passing reference to the underlying subordination of labour. As such, it fails to gauge the significance of either domestic processes of class formation and struggle or the significance of Cold War geopolitical contestation in shaping the emergence of developmental state–society relations in the region. The failure to adequately examine the dialectical nature of social relations underpinning late development is, therefore, combined with a conception of the international that is primarily relegated to a purely external field of causality, thereby leaving unchallenged the ontological distinction between the internal/domestic and the external/international. Through this dual neglect, developmental state theory has remained largely descriptive and consequently unable to provide an adequate explanation of either the origins of the East Asian developmental state or its subsequent transformation toward neoliberalism.

Those observers who understand neoliberalism as a form of ideology have neglected the latter's material origins in the emerging social and international contradictions of capitalism more broadly. Neoliberalism itself is largely seen as external in origin and as separate from ongoing domestic processes of social contestation. As such, in order to provide an integrative analysis of the vicissitudes of East Asian development, it is necessary to situate the latter within the context of both transformations at the levels of the social relations of production and the international order. As Chapter 1 will argue, this is precisely a problem of bringing the study of social agency, and particularly of labour, into broader understandings of international political economy.

Outline of the book

To provide a more comprehensive explanation of the constitutive role of labour in East Asian development, it is first necessary to establish a theoretical framework for elucidating the relationship between the social and the geopolitical, as well as how that relationship affects the processes of state formation. The key challenge, however, is the scarcity of approaches that examine labour beyond its domestic context. Chapter 1 of this book examines two recent bodies of literature that have sought to examine labour beyond the national comparative framework, namely the labour and globalisation literature, as well as the literature on international strike waves. Following a discussion of the shortcomings of these approaches, I propose Antonio Gramsci's understanding of state formation as a moment of 'passive revolution' as an alternative with which to understand labour's role in the broader experience of late development. I argue that this Gramscian framework can overcome problems of methodological nationalism by elucidating the role of the state in shaping social relations conducive to late development in conditions of heightened interstate geopolitical and economic rivalry. As such, it places the analysis of labour and class struggle at the centre of the late developmental experience and explores its mutually constitutive relationship with geopolitical dynamics.

Chapter 2 then applies this framework to an analysis of the formative post-war years of the Japanese political economy. Initially, the US occupation authorities sought to apply New Deal principles and nurture an independent labour movement as part of its initial aims of 'democratising' Japanese society. However, as labour's dynamism in the post-war years exceeded all expectations and the growing constraints of the Cold War led Washington to shift its support toward the recovery of Japanese industry, the occupation authorities and the Japanese government quickly adopted a more repressive approach vis-à-vis labour. The chapter also engages with the literature surrounding the famed 'Japanese employment system' and addresses the question of to what extent that system can be explained with reference to the legacies of Japan's traditional Confucian culture, as well as how those legacies may have helped Japanese employers meet the challenges and opportunities presented by late development.

In Chapter 3, this analysis is continued with reference to the Korean and Taiwanese post-war developmental experiences. With US backing, Korean and Taiwanese political elites were able to impose a system of authoritarian state corporatism based upon an ideology of anticommunism and economic development as national survival. As in Japan, the ensuing political weakness of labour laid the basis for rapid post-war industrialisation. Yet, as this process of industrialisation intensified contradictions with the United States, the latter reassessed the premises of its role in the region and began to adopt increasingly protectionist policies whilst seeking to shift the burden of restructuring onto the East Asian countries themselves. This led to a shift in industrialisation strategy in Korea and Taiwan toward the heavy and chemical industries from the 1970s.

As Chapter 4 argues, however, this was a process again in which the 'fix' to one crisis tendency laid the foundations for the next. It was the deepening of industrialisation in Korea and Taiwan during the 1970s that conferred the structural power on the working class, which would enable the latter to challenge both the political and economic underpinnings of the developmental state. Once the democratic breakthrough in the formal political sphere was achieved, workers in both countries made use of the new political opportunity structures to push for the further democratisation of labour relations. However, the transition toward democracy should be viewed as part of a broader dual transition that involved the rise of neoliberalism as the new economic orthodoxy. As such, it quickly became clear that formal democratisation was perfectly compatible with neoliberal restructuring and indeed instrumental to its formation.

In Chapter 5, I argue that East Asian political and economic elites have sought to formulate a new strategy of passive revolution in terms of seeking to secure the acquiescence of labour to the neoliberal project. This has been achieved through the institutionalisation of liberal labour relations institutions and the rhetoric of national competitiveness in conditions of heightened global competition. In contrast to the predictions made by the labour and globalisation literature, I argue that strategies of passive revolution have largely been successful in co-opting potentially militant labour movements into the institutions of liberal capitalist democracy. The increased competitive pressures that Japan, Korea, and Taiwan are faced with are also examined alongside an analysis of how increased labour costs have led to the further expansion of the East Asian regional production system into China.

The final chapter examines the implications of the preceding chapters for an analysis of the role of Chinese workers in the international political economy. I argue that the demonstrative effect of labour struggles elsewhere has meant that the CCP has been particularly conscious of the threat of increased workers' militancy, leading the state to pursue a number of reforms that in many ways resemble the institutionalisation of liberal labour relations. Nonetheless, as Chinese leaders have recognised the need to increase domestic consumption as a result of the global financial crisis, we may now be witnessing a significant departure from the post-war East Asian model that has been predicated upon the repression of labour. Given the centrality of China as the 'workshop of the world' over recent decades, this is likely to have a significant impact upon the international political economy. The main findings of the book are then summarised in the conclusion.

1

LABOUR, DEVELOPMENT, AND PASSIVE REVOLUTION

The aim of this chapter is to establish a theoretical framework for examining the nexus between labour, the international political economy, and processes of developmental state formation. It proceeds by first examining the recent literature on labour and globalisation, which has explicitly sought to elucidate the impact of globalisation on workers' wages, working conditions, and the organisational strength of labour. Furthermore, this literature has examined attempts by workers to resist global neoliberalism through new modes of organising, particularly through transnational solidarity and the building of so-called global unions. I argue, however, that this literature paradoxically accepts the flattened ontology of mainstream hyper-globalisation theory with the effect that workers are implicitly theorised as largely powerless in the face of an alleged global race to the bottom. An alternative body of literature on international strike waves provides a more promising framework with which to gauge the actual impact of workers' agency on the international political economy. However, the notion of 'the international' in this approach is limited to analysis of contemporaneous waves of labour unrest in two or more advanced industrialised countries. Beverly Silver's analysis of the spatial and temporal dynamics of labour unrest provides a potentially more useful framework for analysing the world-historical impact of the agency of labour; however, in her analysis, the agency of the state in shaping labour regimes is largely neglected (2003). Given the proactive role of the state in facilitating development based on labour repression in East Asia, Silver's approach thus fails to provide any theorisation of labour's role in late development and does not provide any analytical tools with which to examine how state-led political strategies have led to divergent national experiences across the region.

As an alternative, this chapter proposes Antonio Gramsci's understanding of state formation as a moment of passive revolution in conditions of the uneven and combined development of capitalism (Morton 2010a). Based on a historical analogy with the process of Italian state formation analysed by Gramsci, passive revolution takes the form of a state initiative to respond to geopolitical pressures by ensuring the political rule of capital as well as pre-emptively adopting certain subaltern demands. Gramsci's framework thus represents an approach that is more suitable for examining the historical emergence of the developmental state in East Asia and its proactive role in establishing labour regimes conducive to catch-up industrialisation. As such, it helps to address the issue of the role of the state in facilitating late development within broader processes of transnational accumulation and interstate rivalry. Most importantly, the framework of passive revolution can help to place the analysis of labour and of class struggle at the centre of these processes, thereby shedding light on the relationship between labour and the spatial and temporal dynamics of world capitalist industrialisation as mediated by the developmental state. By recovering the social and geopolitical moment in processes of state-led capitalist industrialisation, I argue that this approach to understanding labour in the international system can go beyond the trap of methodological nationalism inherent in mainstream approaches. This framework of passive revolution thus recognises social relations and geopolitics as being mutually constitutive.

Labour and globalisation: The race to the bottom?

The task of examining the mutually constitutive relationship between labour and the international immediately poses a challenge to the voluminous literature written on globalisation since the 1990s. A central claim of that literature was that the increased mobility of capital was in the process of bringing about a 'race to the bottom' in wages and working conditions for the majority of the world's workers. The globalisation of production, it was further argued, meant that multinational corporations (MNCs) were now able to scour the globe for the laxest regulation and lowest wages in order to cut the costs of production. It was not, however, simply the haemorrhaging of jobs from the advanced industrial countries to lower-wage production sites in the global south that constituted this race to the bottom. The ability to relocate production to lower-cost production sites led to the MNCs' increased stature as *political* actors (Sklair 1998) because they were able to pressure states to adopt capital-friendly policies by simply threatening to withdraw investment (Thomas 1997). As Susan Strange argued (1996, p. 4), this meant that 'where states were once the masters of markets, now it is the markets which, on many crucial issues, are the masters over the governments of states' (see also Ohmae 1990, Held *et al.* 1999, Cerny and Germain 2000; Giddens 2000, Scholte 2005).

These global capital flows were thereby seen as undermining the capacity of states to pursue effective social policies and as endangering those rights embedded in the state, including workers' rights (Tilly 1995, p. 5). Other writers, however, questioned this view of globalisation as a zero-sum struggle between states and markets with the latter gaining the upper hand. William Robinson, for example, argued that a key feature of globalisation was the rise of a new transnational class fraction (Robinson 2004, p. 21) accompanied by the emergence of a transnational state as the guarantor of capital accumulation at the global level. This emergent transnational state amounted to a 'a loose network comprised of inter- and supranational political and economic institutions together with national state apparatuses that have been penetrated and transformed by transnational forces' (Robinson 2008, p. 34). Along somewhat similar lines, Robert Cox (1981, p. 145) conceptualised this process as one of the 'internationalisation of the state,' understood as the progressive harmonisation of national policies, whereby the main function of domestic institutions had become one of reconciling domestic social pressures with the requirements of a world economy.

Whether the state was deemed to be merely 'retreating' or in the midst of a transformation into a new historically unprecedented transnational formation, the implications of these developments were considered to be uniformly negative for labour. Globalisation was seen as representing a transition from the Keynesian welfare state of the era of embedded liberalism (Ruggie 1982), which in the West at least constituted a relatively 'labour friendly' international regime (Zolberg 1995, p. 34) that allowed for the provision of substantive social security and labour rights. The increased mobility of capital and the heightened bargaining power of the MNCs played a key role in this reduction of returns to labour, as was manifest in the falling wages in the United States and rising unemployment in Europe, along with significant policy turnarounds such as that of the Mitterrand government's reversal of pro-labour policies in the early 1980s (Thomas 1997, p. 1).

Indeed, through the reform of labour laws so as to circumscribe the power and influence of trade unions, a key manifestation of the rise of neoliberalism was the sustained political offensive against organised labour. Workers were increasingly subjected to market discipline as governments abolished legal restrictions designed to protect job security. The status and security of workers were downgraded and restrictions against the employment of typically unprotected temporary and part-time workers were lifted. It should be noted also that the race to the bottom thesis, along with the globalisation discourse more broadly, had a performative effect (Dunn 2004, p. 5), convincing policymakers and the public alike that states did indeed have no alternative but to align social and labour policies with the dictates of global market forces. Workers fearful of losing their jobs to offshore production would thereby temper their demands whilst governments and employers would cite global competitive pressures as a rationale for job cuts and downgrading employment conditions. The message to workers was that struggles for improved wages and working conditions would only serve to accelerate this relocation of production abroad, thereby leading to further job losses.

However, this view of labour as a passive social force in the face of globalisation has been challenged by the emerging literature on labour and globalisation (Moody 1997, Waterman 1998, O'Brien 2000, Munck 2002, Webster *et al.* 2008), which itself emerged out of the new international labour studies of the 1980s (Munck 2010). Whilst this literature has accepted that globalisation is in the process of facilitating a race to the bottom in wages and working conditions, it argues that the process should be understood as a double-edged sword that not only constitutes an attack on organised labour but at the same time provides new opportunities for greater international solidarity between workers. It has been argued, for example, that whereas Cold War divisions had previously served to divide the world's workers along ideological lines, the end of the Cold War has created conditions for a genuinely *global* labour movement to emerge (Harrod and O'Brien 2002, p. 6). This has been aided by the advances in technology and communications brought by globalisation itself, which provides the technical means for greater solidarity between workers (Lee 1997). The institutions of global governance also play a contradictory role: although the establishment of the World Trade Organization seeks to extend the reach of global free trade, it also provides the possibility of incorporating labour standards into global trade regulations, thereby creating the capability to enforce such standards (O'Brien *et al.* 2000, Stevis and Boswell 2008). However, potentially the most important development brought by globalisation is the accompanying change in workers' consciousness. Whilst the intensification of international competition and concomitant neoliberal restructuring are recognised as having a damaging impact upon workers' livelihood, globalisation is also understood as undermining workers' consent for the capitalist system that had existed under Fordism, making resistance not only increasingly possible but also more likely (Moody 1997, Waterman 1998, Munck 2002).

For the most part, however, the labour and globalisation literature accepts the premises of mainstream conceptions of 'hyper-globalisation' (Held *et al.* 1999), though qualified with the additional argument that the global race to the bottom is likely to generate a Polanyian countermovement in the form of a resurgence of labour internationalism. Ronaldo Munck, for example, confirms this mainstream conception when he argues that globalisation represents a fundamental break with the past, whereby the great corporations of capitalism were once seen as 'national champions' inextricably linked with the 'national interest.' Now, it is argued, they have become global webs with no particular connection to any nation. Indeed, the very notion of a nation state is itself drawn into question (Munck 2002, pp. 3–4). Peter Waterman argues further that these transformations problematise traditional institutions of labour solidarity, such as the International Confederation of Free Trade Unions and the international trade secretariats that were appropriate to the era of national-industrial-colonial capitalism. What is needed now, Waterman (2001, pp. 313–315) argues, is a reconceptualisation of unionism and labour internationalism appropriate to a globalised/networked/informatised capitalist era.

The key problem here, however, is that for an approach that explicitly seeks to recover the study of labour, an actual *theory* of globalisation as a social process is not forthcoming. Labour is simply passively acted upon by globalisation rather than an active constituent subject in the latter's formation. As Justin Rosenberg has argued with reference to globalisation theory more broadly, globalisation itself becomes the structural cause of contemporary sociological transformations rather than the result. Thus, 'what presents itself initially as the *explanandum*—globalisation as the developing outcome of some historical process—is progressively transformed into the *explanans*: it is globalisation which now explains the changing character of the modern world' (Rosenberg 2002, p. 3). In reality, the growth of interconnectedness that is understood to define globalisation is not a causal explanation in itself but rather should be understood as a reflection of the outcome of decisions, actions, and conflicts that involve real social agents (Kiely 2005, p. 908). Indeed, it is curious in this sense that the labour and globalisation literature has neglected labour's constitutive role in the rise of globalisation because, as will be discussed below, one of the key factors in this rise was indeed the strike waves that affected the advanced capitalist world from the mid-1960s (Armstrong *et al.* 1991, pp. 192–207).

Thus, although Stevis and Boswell (2008, p. 14), for example, are surely correct to state that 'it would be surprising if unions were not affected by ... dynamics [of globalisation],' any attempt to understand the constitutive role of labour in producing globalisation surely needs to go much further. Notions of an impending Polanyian countermovement notwithstanding (Munck 2002, Webster *et al.* 2008), such mainstream conceptions of globalisation rest on rather constrained conceptions of agency. As Samuel Knafo (2010, p. 494) argues

> Agency ... tends to be wrongly conflated with resistance and thus reduced to a limited moment of analysis. When agency is discussed, it is generally associated with disadvantaged social forces that are most interested, presumably, in changing society. But, being weaker, they are often seen as struggling to garner the power needed to realize their vision of a different world. For this reason, they always seem to be 'in waiting' for the moment when they will be empowered and finally able to change things.

This is by no means to suggest that resistance by East Asian workers has been lacking or has been negligible in its concrete effects. The history of industrialisation in East Asia is interspersed with the often heroic refusal by workers to be subordinated to processes of catch-up industrialisation. Rather, the point is that, if the agency of labour is to be recovered, a much broader notion of agency must be adopted, which includes but is not limited to overt acts of resistance. It is paradoxical, therefore, that the literature which explicitly seeks to elucidate the global dimensions of labour's agency ultimately serves to obscure its constitutive role in the contemporary world order.

This narrowly conceived form of agency also leads to a constrained view of the international dimensions of labour as a social force; as such, analyses of labour and the international are largely limited to analyses of explicit transnational solidarity (Gordon and Turner 2000, Waterman and Wills 2001, Bieler *et al.* 2008) or studies of the activities of global unions (Harrod and O'Brien 2002, McIlroy and Croucher 2013). However, this focus runs the danger of relegating all other forms of workers' agency to the domestic-national realm. An alternative approach has thus been to examine the spatial and temporal dynamics of labour unrest as a means of uncovering the broader constitutive role that labour has played in the shaping of the contemporary world order. This has involved, for example, the compilation of statistical data on workers' protests over time to identify patterns of labour unrest and their relationship with broader cyclical trends in the international political economy. Whilst methods have varied, there is a strong degree of agreement amongst such analysts with regards to the timing of outbreaks of workers' militancy across the core capitalist countries of the United Kingdom, France, Italy, Germany, and the United States. Screpanti (1987, p. 107), for example, argues that there have been three big international strike waves taking place in the 1870s, 1910–20, and 1968–74. The timing of these strike waves has broadly been corroborated by other researchers working on both single-country and multi-country cases (Brecher 1972; Shorter and Tilly 1974; Cronin 1979; Gordon *et al.* 1982; Silver 1992; Mandel 1995; Kelly 1998, pp. 89–96). These strike waves have occurred at roughly 50-year intervals, and they coincide with the end of the upswings of the long waves identified by Soviet economist Nikolai Kondratieff (1979) as representing alternating phases of the higher and lower growth across the capitalist global economy.

However, the precise line of causality between labour unrest and Kondratieff waves is by no means agreed upon. Cronin (1979, p. 109) argues that the uneven character of economic development, expressed in Kondratieff waves, determines the form and expression of labour struggle. However, whilst it is certainly correct to argue that the external economic climate plays a role in influencing workers' propensity to engage in industrial action, Cronin's argument is overly deterministic and fails to address the question of how workers' struggles shape the timing of Kondratieff waves. Screpanti (1984, pp. 521–523) argues conversely that international strike waves exert an important influence on the character of capitalist development. There are strong psychological influences on long-run investment behaviour, which are shaped by political and social factors like discipline in the factories and political stability. Thus, if capitalists do not feel confidence in the political situation, they will not invest. Screpanti (1987, p. 111) argues therefore that international strike waves put an end to the prosperity phases.

This leaves unanswered the question of why these waves should be of 50-year duration. Kelly (1998) agrees that it is the class struggle that determines the timing of long waves, and that specifically, this timing owes to generational changes taking place within the labour force. Generational change means that workers tend to become aggrieved at the same time. Workers' expectations regarding employment are largely determined by the state of the labour market at the time of their entry into the labour force. Thus, generational differences account for different attitudes toward issues such as compromise with management and anticommunism. Yet, generational changes alone cannot explain the cyclical nature of capitalist development because they cannot account for the transition from a downturn to an upturn. This problem leads Ernest Mandel (1995, pp. 16–17) to dispense with the 50-year cycle aspect of long waves; he argues that although the internal logic of capitalist laws of motion can explain the cumulative nature of each long wave and the transition from an expansionist long wave to a stagnating long wave, it cannot explain the turn from the latter to the former. The transition from a downturn to an upturn can only be explained by wider factors such as wars of conquest, extensions and contractions of areas of capitalist operation, intercapitalist competition, class struggle, revolution, and counterrevolution, thereby adding a great deal of uncertainty to the rhythm of the long wave. Mandel's approach thereby suggests that a more conjunctural analysis is needed to understand the transition to upsurges in capitalist development.

This broad approach to understanding the role of labour in shaping the contemporary world order suffers from two shortcomings, however. First, it is not clear what the significance of an international strike wave is and why these alone are important for explaining the temporal dynamics of capitalist development. Waves of labour militancy that do not extend beyond national boundaries may still have profound impacts on the international system. For example, it was the high wage hike granted to striking workers in May 1968 that led Charles de Gaulle to end French advocacy of the Gold Standard (Arrighi 2003, pp. 35–36), a momentous turning point in international monetary governance initiated by a strike wave within a national society. A further problem is that it is not clear to what extent these strike waves can be regarded as 'international' in any meaningful sense. Screpanti (1987, p. 101) argues, for example, that the world engine of long cycles is constituted by the most advanced capitalist countries and that 'any macroscopic event affecting *simultaneously* the economic and social evolution of these countries will most probably be a common phenomenon of all the core capitalist countries and will be capable of reverberating at a world-wide level.' Yet, this approach is biased towards the analysis of the core advanced industrial countries and thereby neglects the manner in which the geographical unevenness is constitutive of the international capitalist system.

This notion of a single temporal dynamic to global labour unrest without any analysis of spatial unevenness fails to recognise the active role that geographical unevenness plays in the international system. As David Harvey argues, some regions of the global economy boom whilst others decline, and that these differential regional rhythms of accumulation are only loosely coordinated due to the mobilities of different forms of capital and labour. As a result, the timing of upturns and downturns in the accumulation cycle vary from one region to another. Different regional rhythms compensate for each other, and thus, the geography of uneven development helps convert the crisis tendencies of capitalism into compensating regional configurations of rapid accumulation and devaluation. This occurs through the 'spatial fix,' which involves exports of money capital, commodities, productive capacities, or imports of fresh labour powers from other regions (Harvey 1982, pp. 427–428).

Beverley Silver has drawn upon on the implications of the spatial fix for understanding how labour has shaped both the spatial and temporal dynamics of global capitalist development. Through a timeframe that extends back to the late nineteenth century, Silver argues that labour struggles have typically given rise to crises of profitability to which capital responds by adopting spatial fixes, whereby production is relocated away from labour union strongholds to regions or countries where workers are for whatever reason politically weak (Silver 2003, pp. 39–40). As such, Silver traces a pattern of labour unrest and ensuing relocation of manufacturing in the automobile industry that originated with the emergence of Fordist production in the United States in the 1930s. Faced with increasing labour militancy in the 1930s, which itself resulted from the growing structural power accruing to workers in Fordist mass production, US auto manufacturers responded by relocating production to nonunion stronghold areas of the United States and, following the Second World War, to Western Europe. In the 1950s and 1960s, this relocation in turn led to the emergence of militant labour struggles in Europe, and the response of automakers was once again to relocate production – this time to the newly industrialising countries of Brazil, South Africa, and Korea. True to the established pattern, this rise of labour again led to emergence of militant labour movements in those countries in the 1970s and 1980s (Silver 2003, pp. 47–64).

However, whilst Silver's analysis incorporates the role of geographical unevenness into understandings of labour and the international, it also has certain limitations, particularly when it is applied to regional patterns of labour unrest in East Asia. To begin with, Silver's framework is overly parsimonious in its selection of countries that fit the overall framework, particularly with regards to the newly industrialising countries, namely Brazil, South Africa, and Korea. These were by no means the only countries to benefit from the post-war relocation of production to the global south. In East Asia alone, Taiwan, Hong Kong, Singapore, Thailand, Malaysia, and Indonesia have all been integrated into global production networks, yet none of these countries have developed militant labour movements on the scale of the newly industrialising countries cited by Silver. As will be argued in subsequent chapters, Taiwan developed on the basis of many of the same geopolitical fortuities as Korea, yet its labour surge at the end of the 1980s was much weaker than the contemporaneous surge in Korea. Thus, although Silver (2003, p. 42) regards the absence of a strong labour movement in post-war Japan to be the exceptional case, from an East Asian regional perspective, it might be argued conversely that it is the relative strength of the Korean labour movement that is the exceptional case (Deyo 1989).

This inability to adequately explain differentiation between cases arises from a failure to adequately analyse the role of the state and state–society relations in general, as well as the manner in which the state mediates between world historical processes of capitalist industrialisation and workers' agency. As a result, Silver's argument that 'where capital goes, militancy goes' neglects the factors that impede the development of working class movements in the context of capitalist industrialisation. In this sense, Silver reproduces the optimism of Marx and Engels in their early view that capitalist industrialisation would necessarily bring about the revolutionary association of workers, thereby undermining the 'very foundation on which the bourgeoisie produces and appropriates products' (Marx and Engels 1967, pp. 93–94). Here, the emancipatory potential of labour was understood to be determined by the level of development of capitalist social relations. The nationalist orientation of European labour movements following the outbreak of the First World War and the incorporation of labour into Fordist modes of regulation following the Second World War are just two historical instances that serve to problematise the optimistic but rather mechanistic determinism of Marx and Engels' comments on the relationship between workers' organisations and capitalist industrialisation. Indeed, in their later work, Marx and Engels became more concerned with apparent barriers to the development of workers' revolutionary consciousness. As Richard Hyman (1971) argued, there was a transition from the optimism of the early Marx and Engels toward the pessimism of their later work, and of later Marxist thinkers such as Lenin, Trotsky, and Gramsci. Indeed, these changing views on the revolutionary potential of workers and trade unions no doubt owed much to the vicissitudes of the working class struggle itself.

The coincidence of these waves of 'optimism' and 'pessimism' with actual world-historical patterns of labour unrest points to the need for a more temporally and spatially sensitive theorisation of the relationship between the role of workers' agency and international capitalist development. There is a need to examine the historical record of how the actions of states intervene between social being and social consciousness through seeking to establish labour regimes conducive to late development. It will be argued in the next section that by understanding the formation of the developmental state as emerging from a process of passive revolution, it is possible to examine how East Asia was uniquely placed to establish labour regimes that were highly conducive towards catch-up industrialisation. By examining this regional post-war passive revolution, the aim here is not to present a single homogenous East Asian labour regime but to understand how the uneven interaction between individual social formations with broader processes of geopolitical competition served to produce a diversity of forms of labour subordination across the region.

The passive revolution of the developmental state

The world-historical relationship between labour and the international can more profitably be examined by adopting Antonio Gramsci's concept of passive revolution. Gramsci developed the concept of passive revolution precisely in order to refine and elaborate upon the primacy that Marx and Engels ascribed to social being over social consciousness, and to purge those comments of 'every residue of mechanism and fatalism' (Gramsci 1971, p. 107). More concretely, Gramsci elaborated his concept of passive revolution as part of his analysis of why, in contradistinction to the predictions of Marx and Engels, revolution had occurred in Russia and not in the West. For Gramsci, the key to understanding these differing outcomes was the hegemony of the bourgeoisie in the West, which was exercised through civil society. In such situations where civil society was developed, hegemonic rule could be achieved through a combination of force and consent by conferring a crucial role on the institutions of civil society. In contrast to liberal conceptions of civil society as a private realm of actors autonomous of the state, Gramsci viewed civil society as an extension of the state. Institutions such as schools, churches, and trade unions were the sites through which hegemony was exercised, and as such, become sites of dissemination of bourgeois hegemony, the 'common sense' in which the bourgeois worldview is deemed 'natural.' For Gramsci, this insight had important implications for revolutionary strategy. Although revolutionary forces might succeed in a 'war of manoeuvre' against the state, the state was only the 'outer ditch' behind which there stood a powerful system of fortresses and earthworks—that is, the institutions of civil society. Revolutionary strategy thus required a 'war of position,' which involved the establishment of the hegemony of the contending revolutionary forces in the realm of civil society. The situation contrasted directly with the situation in Russia, where civil society was undeveloped and revolution was consequently possible.

Sporadic revolutionary turning points aside, in situations where civil society was undeveloped or entirely subsumed by the state corporatism, instead of bourgeois hegemony, there was more typically passive revolution or 'revolution without revolution.' Gramsci's analysis of the passive revolution of the Italian *Risorgimento* is situated within the context of the spread of capitalist social relations throughout Europe and analyses the implications of this spread for processes of modern state formation. He examines specifically the historical relationship between the modern French state created by the revolution and the other modern states of continental Europe, particularly Italy. This continent-wide process of state formation is comprised of four stages: first, a revolutionary explosion in France with radical and violent transformation of social and political relations; second, European opposition to the French Revolution and any extension of it along class lines; third, war between France, under the Republic and Napoleon, and the rest of Europe, initially to avoid being stifled at birth and subsequently to establish a permanent French hegemony tending toward the creation of a universal empire; and fourth, national revolts against French hegemony and birth of the modern European states by successive small waves of reform, rather than by revolutionary explosions like the original French one (Gramsci 1971, pp. 114–115). As such, it was the spread of capitalist social relations of production and its political culmination in the French Revolution that became the driving force behind much subsequent nineteenth-century European history. Although the French Revolution had established a state on the basis of the elimination of the old feudal classes and thus achieved popular support, elsewhere in Europe, where the bourgeoisie was still too weak to establish a dominant position, successive small waves of reform occurred instead. These consisted of a combination of social struggles and, more predominantly, interventions from above of the enlightened-monarchy type (Gramsci 1971, p. 115).

Gramsci identified a key role for the state within this process of passive revolution. In a situation where new social forces are unable to achieve a position of dominance over the old order, a situation of stalemate occurs. In such situations, the state can adopt the position of the dominant social classes, as occurred in Italy whereby the potential ruling class was too weak to provide leadership over other social groups and the task was thus conferred on the Piedmont state (Gramsci 1971, pp. 104–106). In conditions of the absence or weakness of bourgeois hegemony, the modernising state thus takes a leading role in preventing the kind of revolutionary transformation that had taken place in Russia. As Sassoon argues, passive revolution involves 'the constant reorganisation of state power and its relationship to society to preserve control by the few over the many, and maintain a traditional lack of control by the mass of the population over the political and economic realms.' This is achieved through such political techniques as *caesarism,* in which a strongman steps in to resolve conflicts among opposed social forces, and *trasformismo,* where the potential leaders of subaltern groups are deliberately co-opted into ruling elites, which can be seen as common features of non-hegemonic societies (Sassoon 1982, p. 129). Within this process, passive revolution can be seen to have two distinct yet complementary aspects. First, it serves as a 'revolution from above' (see Moore 1966, pp. 433–452;

Skocpol 1979, pp. 220–224) and as a state-led initiative to ensure the political rule of capital in a situation in which the bourgeoisie is too weak to achieve such aims itself. Yet, passive revolution can only achieve this through seeking to both forestall and, at the same time, selectively adopt subaltern demands without bringing those subaltern groups into the ruling historical bloc.

Gramsci's conceptualisation of passive revolution can thus be seen as a political corrective to the more mechanistic tendencies of Marx's base/superstructure metaphor and, as originally aimed, at offering an 'interpretive criterion' to understand the forces blocking the transition from capitalism to socialism (Allinson and Anievas 2010, p. 243). Whilst Gramsci's writing is largely concerned with the specifics of Italian state formation, the framework of passive revolution is useful for a broader examination of the wider linkages between class struggle within a national social formation and the international system. As the analysis of the Italian *Risorgimento* suggests, these transformations of state-society configurations have their origins in international events, such as the spread of capitalist social relations of production and the tide of revolution. Thus, as Morton (2007a, p. 149) argues, the theory of passive revolution

> combines an appreciation of 'the international' causal dynamics shaping state formation processes as well as the relevance of 'national' class forces. What is pivotal to this theory of passive revolution is the very causal presence granted to 'the international' within a historical methodology that can account for the specific context of state formation.

As the contrast between the West and Russia shows, Gramsci's analysis of passive revolution highlights the fact that the particular political, economic, and social dynamics of individual social formations and processes of state formation must be analysed within the broader framework of a temporally and spatially differentiated global capitalist economy and the geopolitical interstates system (Morton 2010b). As such, the emergence of the developmental state in East Asia can be understood as such a moment of passive revolution whereby a specific confluence of domestic social and geopolitical pressures led to the ascendance of rapid modernising elites who viewed development as ensuring national survival. This imperative of national survival in turn led to the repression of a collective subjective will on the part of East Asia's labour and other subaltern classes.

The framework of passive revolution further enables an analysis of how specific national labour regimes emerged from historically specific intersections between domestic social contestations and international pressures. As Gramsci argues (1971, p. 182):

> International relations intertwine with these internal relations of nation-states, creating new, unique and historically concrete combinations. A particular ideology, for instance, born in a highly developed country, is disseminated in less developed countries, impinging on the local interplay of combinations.

This notion of combination in conditions of late development is one that has been addressed more directly by Gramsci's contemporary, Leon Trotsky. Indeed, Trotsky argued, with parallels to the later work of Gerschenkron (Selwyn 2011), that whilst so-called 'backward' countries were compelled to follow the advanced industrialised countries, their very backwardness allowed them to skip various intermediate stages of development through adopting the most advanced technologies available. This 'privilege of historical backwardness' even made it possible for late-developing countries to overtake the hitherto more advanced countries—the latter having already made large investments in increasingly dated and obsolete technologies. However, this very lateness of development gives the process a 'planless, complex, combined character' whereby the adaptation of advanced technologies in the context of a more 'primitive' culture gives rise to divergent and seemingly contradictory social forms. An example that Trotsky gives of this process is that of the introduction of Western military and industrial technologies under Peter I, which led to a strengthening of serfdom as the fundamental form of labour organisation (Trotsky 1997, pp. 26–27).

This conceptualisation of how geographical unevenness produces specific forms of combination has important implications for the analysis of labour regimes in late-developing societies. Indeed, national labour regimes can be viewed precisely as arising from this confluence of domestic social struggles and the intersocietal dimension of social reality. Trotsky himself had sought to elucidate how a combined form of labour, specifically that of the Russian working class in the late nineteenth and early twentieth centuries, arose from the law of unevenness. As Trotsky argues, Russia did not repeat the development of advanced countries but adapted the latter's latest achievements into their own backwardness. Separate branches of industry made a series of special leaps over technical productive stages that had been measured in the West by decades. At the same time that peasant cultivation stagnated, Russian industry in its technique and capitalist structure stood at the level of the advanced countries and, in certain respects, outstripped them. This led to the Russian working class, drawn primarily from the countryside rather than the craft guild, becoming 'hospitable to the boldest conclusions of revolutionary thought' and not carrying with it the burden of the past as in England (Trotsky 1997, pp. 30–33). As Rosenberg has argued, these comments have important implications for thinking about the interrelations between the social and the international more broadly. Trotsky's understanding of 'combined development' can be viewed as a general abstraction of the significance of intersocietal coexistence per se because no society exists in isolation, and the reproduction of society depends on intersocietal coexistence. Thus, the conditions of reproduction that define the concrete existence of any given society are not limited to the 'internal' structures of social relations, but include those external conditions that are the object of diplomatic management (Rosenberg 2006, pp. 319–320).

As such, Gramsci and Trotsky share important insights in terms of how to situate nationally specific labour regimes within a broader analysis of international relations. It is important to note where Gramsci departs from Trotsky, however. Trotsky argued that the significant use of force against labour by state and capital creates the potential for resistance and revolution—or 'permanent revolution,' to use Trotsky's terminology. Gramsci was more sceptical, however, and rejected the argument that there must never be a moment's respite in the progress of the revolution and that it would be fatal to pause before the revolution had been completely carried out (Joll 1977, p. 98). As Gramsci put it, '[t]he formula [of permanent revolution] belongs to an historical period in which the great mass political parties and the great economic trade unions did not yet exist, and society was still, so to speak, in a state of fluidity' (Gramsci 1971, p. 243). Although this difference was largely related to the question of revolutionary strategy, Gramsci's analysis of the intervening factors between social being and social consciousness, and the role of ideology in this process, means that the likelihood whereby workers will resist capitalist subordination is ultimately an empirical question. Central to that question is Gramsci's distinctive notion of 'common sense.' For Gramsci, common sense is a confused formation, in part drawn from 'official' conceptions of the world circulated by the ruling bloc, in part formed out of people's practical experiences of social life. Despite this unevenness, it offers a deeply held guide to life, directing people to act in certain ways and ruling out other modes of behaviour as unthinkable. Gramsci argues that this is not inevitable, however, because official and practical conceptions can be dismantled in order to show how they serve the interests of a ruling power (Joll 1977, p. 9). It is important to recognise, however, that different versions of common sense coexist in and across the state, and there are already a multiplicity of forms of common sense within the state as a result of earlier struggles (Bruff 2010, pp. 625–626).

Gramsci's emphasis on passive revolution under conditions of uneven and combined development thus provides the analytical tools with which to examine the emergence of nationally specific (or 'combined') forms of labour regimes. Labour regimes can be viewed conventionally as constituted by patterns of recruitment, the terms and conditions of employment that structure the articulation of workers' concerns and interests to government and to industry, and as shaped by a diverse arrangement of labour laws and social institutions, as well as by the absence of such laws and institutions. Labour regimes are also defined to the extent to which the state permits employers in the public and private sectors to evade labour laws (Candland and Sil 2001, p. 17). Yet, in addition to these more tangible characteristics, political and economic elites establish mechanisms to constrain workers' agency through the propagation of specific forms of 'common sense,' such as ideologies of nationalism, anticommunism, and labour–management cooperation and harmony in the workplace. Adam Morton, for example, cites as an example of this Gramsci's discussion of how Americanism and Fordism impacted Italian development, such as through the exultation of big cities, urban planning, and grandiose plans for development. In this discussion, Gramsci is seen as capturing 'the territorial, spatial and geographical dimensions of uneven development, as well as the combined character of its crystallisation within a social formation' (Morton 2010c, pp. 315–316).

It is also important to note, however, that labour regimes are not simply imposed from above but are the product of dynamic struggles between labour, capital, and the state. They are also based on the demonstrative examples of labour unrest in earlier industrialising countries, and the role of the capitalist state in seeking to forestall the emergence of a collective social will and to establish a subordinated labour force conducive to rapid industrialisation. This involves the deployment of strategies of coercion and consent designed to propagate a hegemonic ideology amongst workers that naturalises authoritarian developmentalism, consisting of elements associated with Fordist production (*Americanism* in Gramsci's vocabulary, including the legal framework of the advanced industrialised countries, anticommunism, etc.), as well as certain 'traditional' cultural norms reinterpreted for the purposes of labour subordination. Yet, such determinations also lead to opportunities for resistance or 'anti-passive revolution' (Buci-Glucksmann 1979), thereby necessitating a dialectical understanding of the development of labour regimes. Gramsci's situating of the ideological structures of domination within a materialist analysis of the uneven and combined nature of capitalist development thus requires a greater sensitivity to the specific forms that passive revolution takes in individual national social formations.

The approach set out above differs somewhat from that offered by what has commonly been referred to as 'neo-Gramscian' international relations, which has understood hegemony primarily as a 'global' phenomenon (Cox 1981, 1987; Augelli and Murphy 1988; Gill and Law 1988). As noted above, Robert Cox identified the 'internationalisation of the state' as a key feature of contemporary US hegemony. This was a process understood as one of the progressive harmonisation of national policies to the extent that the main function of domestic institutions had become one of reconciling domestic social pressures with the requirements of a world economy. There is now, he argued, the general recognition that measures of national economic policy affect other countries and that such consequences should be taken into account before national policies are adopted (Cox 1981, p. 145; see also Glassman 1999). Thus, whilst the state is still ascribed central importance in providing the regulatory conditions for global production, its agency is considerably reduced and determined by outside hegemonic interests (Cox 1992, p. 27). This application of Gramsci's notion of hegemony at the level of world order has been criticised on several grounds, however. As Robbie Shilliam has argued, for example, the notion of the internationalisation of the state under US hegemony paradoxically forbids a direct enquiry into the specific international dimensions of processes of social transformation. By deploying the concept of hegemony at the level of world order, neo-Gramscians implicitly universalise specific structural qualities of capitalist social relations in their analysis, obscuring the historical record of, and actual complexities involved in, the export/import of capitalist sociality across the international milieu (Shilliam 2004, pp. 62–63). The focus on the exercise of hegemony at the global level, furthermore, has paradoxically led to a neglect of an analysis of class struggle. Despite ritual references to class struggle as the source of change, these real struggles are all but invisible in the neo-Gramscian literature (Budd 2007, p. 5).

Furthermore, as Joseph Femia has argued, in Gramsci's usage, hegemony referred to the cultural or spiritual supremacy of a class or group within a particular national entity. Hegemony is achieved through 'civil society' or the ensemble of organisms commonly called 'private' and act as agents of cultural transmission. However, it is difficult to find such institutions at the global level in any meaningful sense; thus, there is an absence of global mechanisms of ideological dissemination (Femia 2005, pp. 342–343). Viewed in this light, Germain and Kenny are correct to point out the dissonance between Gramsci's concern with Italian state formation and the neo-Gramscian notion of *global* hegemony. The neo-Gramscian view of the emergent transnational managerial class as the primary agent of global capitalism within the context of a new and increasingly globalised world market runs the risk of totalising hegemony and inadequately comprehending the nature of counterhegemonic resistance. Neo-Gramscians thus see hegemony largely as a one-directional power relationship: hegemony is fashioned by this elite transnational class on its own terms and then forced or imposed on subaltern classes, which either resist such frontal assaults as best they can or capitulate (Germain and Kenny 1998, p. 17).

However, with an understanding more in line with Gramsci's own reading of processes of state formation in the context of the uneven development of international capitalism, 'the international ... should be considered in its national aspect' (Gramsci 1971, p. 240). In essence, this means that the 'national' is theorised as a point of arrival within the international condition of capitalist expansion. As Morton elaborates, Gramsci does not presuppose the 'national' as an ontologically primitive category, but instead formulates the historical argument that problems of international development become 'translated' within and through the national context as a result of the specific ways in which pre-capitalist and capitalist development occurred. As such, 'the "national" is theorised as a point of arrival within "the international" conditioning of capitalist expansion' (Morton 2007b, p. 615). There is, therefore, no need to 'scale-up' Gramsci's analysis of intersocietal relations, the conditions of unevenness within the states system, and thus how different relations of production become combined. A theorisation of the geopolitics of capitalism through the conditions of passive revolution meant that such features were already a constitutive component of Gramsci's analysis (Morton 2010a, p. 216). The national does not replace the international, but both 'levels' remain active sites of political-economic contestation (Ives and Short 2013, p. 636).

Conclusion

This chapter has proposed Gramsci's concept of passive revolution as an analytical tool with which to examine the mutual relations between labour and the international. Passive revolution enables the analysis of the social struggles underpinning state formation within conditions of uneven and combined development. It can elucidate how political and economic elites in specific national contexts are faced with the geopolitical imperative to facilitate catch-up development and, as part of that process, are compelled to take measures to prevent the emergence of labour as a social and political force. This framework thus draws on an analogy with Gramsci's analysis of Italian state formation in the shadow of the spread of capitalist social relations along with the geopolitical event of the French Revolution in spurring nineteenth-century state formation. Although important differences of course exist, developmental state formation in East Asia can nonetheless be understood as a process of the establishment of the political rule of capital in a context where the bourgeoisie was too weak to achieve such aims itself.

The application of the framework of passive revolution to explain East Asia's post-war experience of developmental state formation in turn helps to shed light on how states sought to contain the agency of labour and co-opt it into the national developmental project through strategies of *caesarism* and *trasformismo*. As the following chapters indicate, however, the balance of consent and coercion in achieving the subordination of labour differed in each national context and over time. Whilst East Asian political elites can broadly be seen as having facilitated a region-wide passive revolution in the post-war era involving the comprehensive subordination of labour, greater analytical emphasis needs to be placed on how intersocietal dynamics lead to national differentiation within the East Asian region. This is particularly important in East Asia given the pronounced hierarchical economic relations between the countries. As I will argue, as a general rule, a lower position in that regional hierarchy led to a correspondingly greater intensity in the forced march of catch-up industrialisation, and as such, led to a greater degree of labour coercion.

2

ORGANISED LABOUR AND JAPAN'S PASSIVE REVOLUTION

The US intervention following Japan's surrender in 1945 established the foundations of the labour regime that would both underpin the country's post-war economic growth and form the lynchpin of the broader regional experience of catch-up industrialisation. Initially, US occupation authorities sought to impose a set of democratising reforms from above, such as the demobilisation of the military and dissolution of the country's *zaibatsu* conglomerates. The reforms were also aimed at the strengthening of grassroots democratic tendencies by dispossessing the landlord class through land reform and encouraging the formation of trade unions through the enactment of relatively liberal labour laws based on the US New Deal model.

However, widespread economic hardship made these democratic tendencies more dynamic than the occupation authorities had expected. Workers became increasingly militant in seeking to challenge pre-war legacies of paternalism and labour subordination and sought to shape the emergent post-war order in a more egalitarian direction. However, the widening dollar gap whereby America's potential trading partners lacked the foreign exchange needed to purchase US exports alongside the advances made by communist forces in Asia and further afield facilitated a change in American strategy toward Japan from democracy promotion to economic reconstruction. This 'reverse course,' as it became to be known, can be viewed as a form of passive revolution whereby the US occupation authorities in partnership with Japanese political elites ensured the continuity of the repressive labour regime of the pre-war years. Furthermore, it was this repressive labour regime that underpinned the rapid economic growth of the post-war era. The reverse course thus represented a critical juncture in which Japan's post-war developmental path was strongly shaped by the mutually constitutive relationship between geopolitical dynamics and the vicissitudes of class struggle.

Understanding the qualitative nature of Japan's comprehensive system of labour subordination is somewhat problematised, however, by the voluminous literature emerging since the 1980s that has sought to portray Japanese labour relations as a form of 'post-Fordism' that is not only more productive than the Taylorism of the Western industrialised countries but an altogether more humane organisation of work, which has provided lifelong employment as well as a greater participatory role for labour in production. Furthermore, British sociologist Ronald Dore has argued that the basis of the Japanese employment system in the country's pre-modern Confucian culture was particularly well placed to meet the challenges of late development. Yet, as I argue in this chapter, this view of the fundamentally progressive nature of the Japanese employment system is questionable on several grounds. A re-examination of the emergent labour regime in the post-war era reveals a more repressive set of institutions and profoundly dualistic labour market that represents not a system favourable to workers but one that is characterised by the comprehensive subordination of labour as a social and political force. This argument will be elaborated through an analysis of the limitations of Japan's so-called 'three sacred treasures' – namely, lifetime employment, seniority wages, and enterprise unionism. As such, I argue that the nature of the post-surrender passive revolution in Japan should be viewed more straightforwardly as one whereby the external intervention by the United States enabled Japanese political and elites to subordinate labour to the demands of rapid reconstruction and industrialisation.

The Japanese 'New Deal'

Whilst the post-war Japanese labour regime drew on many pre-war legacies, such continuity should be understood within the context of the passive revolution facilitated by the United States in the aftermath of Japan's surrender. The broad direction of labour policies pursued by the US occupation authorities was directly linked to strategic questions surrounding America's hegemonic position after the war, thereby challenging any analytical relegation of the labour question to the 'domestic' sphere. US strategy during the war had originally been that of drawing the Soviet Union into a military campaign against Japan, but this objective became superfluous once the United States gained its atomic monopoly. US policy henceforth became one of seeking to prevent Soviet participation in the victory over Japan or any substantive role in Japan's post-war administration (Hersh 1993, p. 13). Whilst there was a façade of international control by the Allied countries under the Far Eastern Commission, the occupation of Japan was thus in reality an American undertaking. The ruling body of the US occupation was the Supreme Command for Allied Powers (SCAP), headed by its Supreme Commander, General Douglas MacArthur. As American commander-in-chief, MacArthur took orders only from the US government, through which the decisions of the Far Eastern Commission were transmitted to him, although he was left considerable discretion in carrying out those decisions (Beasley 1990, pp. 214–215).

In the early years of the occupation, SCAP proceeded to pursue a 'democratic revolution' in Japan. This revolution was aimed at the implementation of the policy enumerated in the pre-surrender Potsdam Declaration of removing 'all obstacles to the revival and strengthening of democratic tendencies among the Japanese people.'[1]

By doing so, the aim was to eradicate the roots of militarism in the country and prevent Japan's future resurgence as a militaristic power. This would include punitive measures directed against those elements of society that had supported Japanese aggression. It involved the dismantling of the Japanese military through the destruction of military supplies and installations alongside the demobilisation and repatriation of soldiers and colonial functionaries. A purge was carried out of those individuals and organisations deemed as having supported the war effort, including the execution or imprisonment of political leaders, officers, and more junior members of the armed forces. Significantly, however, these punitive measures did not extend to the emperor himself. Although Japan's imperialistic wars had been waged in his name, SCAP's decision to retain the emperor as nominal head of state reflected the Japanese public's strong attachment to him as well as the American fear that making a martyr of the emperor would make Japan more difficult to govern (Beasley 1990, pp. 215–217). SCAP also forced the Japanese government to accept a new constitution that established the principle of popular sovereignty and guaranteed a broad range of human rights, thereby turning Japan's subjects into citizens (Dower 1999, p. 82).

SCAP's democratic revolution was concerned not only with political and constitutional reform but also with the democratisation of the economic sphere. As US President Harry Truman stated in 1945, a key aim of the occupation would be to encourage the development of organisations in labour, industry, and agriculture, organized on a democratic basis. First and foremost, this promotion of democratic institutions required the reform of the *zaibatsu* conglomerates. The *zaibatsu* were the family-owned and-controlled vertically integrated businesses and financial conglomerates that typically consisted of a bank and several subsidiaries spanning numerous industries. They were widely regarded as responsible for stifling domestic competition and for playing a central role in Japan's imperialist campaigns. As a result, the Law for Elimination of Excessive Concentration of Economic Power was pushed through the Japanese Diet in December 1947, giving a Holding Company Liquidation Commission the authority to reorganise 'excessive economic concentrations' into independent companies so as to ensure a greater degree of domestic competition (Tsuru 1993, pp. 18–19).

The weakness of organised labour was similarly regarded by SCAP as constituting an impediment to the democratisation of Japanese economy and society. SCAP thus sought to reform the Japanese labour regime along the lines of America's own New Deal model (Cohen 1987). This included first and foremost the tackling of the legacies of pre-war labour repression. Following the Meiji restoration and ensuing programme of defensive modernisation, Japan had seen the emergence of a sizeable working class, particularly after the Sino-Japanese war of 1894–5 and the Russo-Japanese war of 1904–05 (Yamamura 1977). This rapid process of class formation led to strike waves at the turn of the century and in the aftermath of both the Russo-Japanese and First World Wars. They were all, however, followed by harsh state repression. The strike wave of 1900, for example, led to the enactment of the Peace and Preservation Law. Although the law did not ban unions or strikes per se, it did proscribe workers from 'instigating' or 'inciting' others to strike, join unions, or engage in collective bargaining. Union activities were thus effectively outlawed (Garon 1987, p. 30).

In this repressive climate, only the most moderate labour organisations were able to survive. The period of heightened labour unrest after the First World War, for example, led to the formation of *Sōdōmei* (Japan Federation of Labour), whose origins were in the Friendly Society (*Yuaikai*), a moderate organisation with links to the American Federation of Labor. By 1926, however, *Sōdōmei* had split into left, right, and centrist federations. In 1937, following the outbreak of war with China, the left-wing federation was declared illegal, and the government succeeded in co-opting both the rightist (still known as *Sōdōmei*) and the centrist federations. Indeed, the rightist *Sōdōmei* had adopted a strategy of union–management cooperation and renounced strikes altogether. Furthermore, in 1940, with the full cooperation of *Sōdōmei*, the government established its own 'labour front' organisation as the Patriotic Industrial Association (*Sangyo Hokokuka)* or *Sampō*. This government-mandated form of class collaboration thus signalled the disappearance of the independent trade union movement altogether (Baker 1965).

SCAP saw this repressive pre-war labour regime as a central underpinning of Japan's militarism and, as such, sought to eradicate its influence. On 30th September 1945, SCAP abolished the *Sampō* and demanded that the Japanese government release political prisoners and end restrictions to civil liberties. It also instructed the government to establish a new, more liberal, legal framework governing labour relations. The Trade Unions Act was subsequently passed in 1945, followed by the Labour Relations Act in 1946 and the Labour Standards Act in 1947. As MacArthur's directive to then–Prime Minister Kijūrō Shidehara stated, the unionisation of labour was required so 'that it may be clothed with such dignity as will permit it an initial voice in safeguarding the working man from exploitation and abuse and raising his living standard to a higher level; with the institution of such measures as may be necessary to correct the evils which now exist in child labour practices' (quoted in Ayusawa 1966, p. 247). Given the more repressive direction that labour relations would subsequently take in Japan and in the wider East Asia region, this liberal component to SCAP's early labour reforms is particularly noteworthy. The lifting of restrictions on political parties provided a newfound space for the Japanese Communist Party (JCP). In drawing up the new labour laws, SCAP even worked together with Kyūichi Tokuda, secretary-general of the JCP. Furthermore, prominent communists participated in various governmental bodies, such as the central and local labour relations commissions (Ayusawa 1966, p. 251).

In addition to these labour reforms, the land reform carried out by SCAP had a further significant impact on post-war social relations in Japan. Indeed, land reform was arguably the most successful and enduring of SCAP's 'democratising' reforms. It was carried out in the belief that agrarian unrest had been a key contributor to the extreme forms of nationalism and military aggression in Japan. Strongly supported by Washington, land reform served to dispossess the rural landlord class and destroy the widespread system of exploitative tenancy, creating in its place a huge constituency of small owner-farmers (Dower 1999, p. 82). It also played a key role in tempering any potential revolutionary impulses in the countryside and established the basis there for conservative hegemony. As William Beasley (1990, p. 223) has argued, the reforms to Japan's land ownership structure turned the country into one of peasant proprietors. It not only improved their economic status but also established a wider domestic market and basis for industrial growth. Furthermore, it created a largely conservative peasantry that went on to form a key pillar of support for Japan's successive right-wing governments. As such, the reform significantly reduced the ground on which the Japanese left might have been expected to gain popularity on. As one official of SCAP's Natural Resources Section argued, almost the entire history of the JCP had revolved around the issue of rural reform. A successful Japanese land reform respecting individual rights and private property could 'embarrass the Communist position throughout the world' (Hewes 1955, cited in Burkett and Hart-Landsberg 2000, p. 95).

Despite the notable success of land reform, SCAP's broader attempts to restructure Japan into a democratic society was an undertaking that was plagued from the outset by contradictions (Dower 1999, pp. 80–81). The reforms were carried out on the basis of the overly confident assumption by SCAP that a stable democratic society could be imposed from above. Whilst this strategy may have been successful with regards to Japan's peasantry, it failed to pacify workers in a context of increased economic hardship and, at the same time, a more permissive legal framework for workers to organise and vent their grievances. With the lifting of restrictions on union organising, there followed an unprecedented surge in unionisation. Between January 1946 and June 1948, the number of unions in Japan rose from 1,179 to 33,900, with membership rising from 900,000 to 6,655,483 over the same period (Halliday 1975, p. 206). It is true that many of these unions represented a continuation of the class collaboration ethos of the *Sampō* and were effectively 'self-preservation communities' in the context of ongoing economic hardship. Nonetheless, a significant number of these new unions were driven by strong grassroots dynamics and, as such, they mobilised a diverse array of demands and tactics that often failed to conform to the liberal democratic ideals envisaged by the Trade Union Act (Price 1997, p. 41). This surge in union organisation should, however, be understood in the context of the harsh economic conditions faced by Japanese workers in the immediate post-war era. Mass dismissals resulting from factory closures were compounded by the return of millions of military personnel from overseas. During the first winter of the occupation, unemployment rose to a level of 10 to 12 million out of a total non-agricultural workforce of 18 million. Widespread starvation in the urban areas was averted only by US food aid (Moore 1997, pp. 11–12).

Much of this economic hardship was the result of an investment strike by capital. Even though the government had, against the orders of the United States, facilitated a massive transfer of wealth to business, the latter nonetheless refused to invest in production. Military supplies were transferred to the *zaibatsu,* and the Bank of Japan extended massive loans to war contractors, ostensibly to facilitate their transition to peacetime production. However, Japanese capital either hoarded any goods received or made vast profits by selling them on the black market (Dower 1999, pp. 113–114).

This rush by the government to distribute assets and the refusal of the *zaibatsu* to invest was spurred by the occupation's early deconcentration and reparations policies. However, Japan's political and business leaders also believed that economic stagnation could both discipline the working class and win US support for the renewal of Japan's political economy in its pre-war form. In light of the hardship that such policies created, however, workers felt they had little choice but to take production into their own hands. 'Production control' (*seisan kanri*) was a movement whereby workers seized the control of factories, took over management, and organised the production and delivery of goods or services themselves (Burkett and Hart-Landsberg 2003, p. 33).

A key instance of production control took place at the Tokyo-based *Yoimuri* newspaper. The newspaper and its president, Matsutarō Shōriki, had played a key role in the wartime government's propaganda effort, and after Japan's surrender, Shōriki remained deeply suspicious of labour organising. It was his intransigence that led workers to take over production of the newspaper directly. Placed under worker control, the *Yoimuri* adopted a progressive editorial stance and quickly became the most left-leaning and outspoken of Japan's major newspapers. Furthermore, the new direction of the newspaper gained widespread public approval, with circulation rising to nearly 1,700,000 copies (Moore 1997, p. 18). Therefore, in contrast to strikes, which ran the risk of aggravating the economic situation and incurring public hostility, production control struggles were in essence congruent with SCAP's democratising objectives. Production control achieved a degree of public legitimacy because it was the employers themselves that were refusing to engage in production; as such, production control was a strategy whereby workers could address Japan's shortage of goods and directly contribute to the country's industrial recovery (Ayusawa 1966, p. 260). Furthermore, as Jon Halliday (1975, pp. 208–209) has argued, production control served to challenge traditional notions of industrial relations as well as the institution of private property. As such, it transcended the usual negativity of industrial action under capitalism. Yet, on 1st February 1946, a number of Japanese ministries issued a joint declaration labelling production control as an 'illegal act in violation of property rights' that should be dealt with by the police. However, given the overriding objective of the democratisation of the economy, SCAP was still reluctant to take measures against the production control movement, arguing that the issue should be dealt with through the courts rather than the police (Moore 1997, p. 24).

The labour movement reached an organisational peak in April and May 1946, when the national-level Democratisation People's League was established. In addition to calls for incumbent Prime Minister Shidehara's resignation due to his conservative economic policies and close connections with the Mitsubishi *zaibatsu*, the programme of the Democratisation People's League made numerous demands, such as the adoption of a new constitution through democratic means, the dismantling of the bureaucracy, the establishment of a democratically planned economy and industrial democracy, the democratisation of villages, relief measures for small businessmen, the democratisation of food distribution, the liberation of women, educational reform, and an international system based on peace and justice (Moore 1983, p. 173). These organisational advances took place alongside workers' mass actions. On May Day 1946, for example, an unprecedented mass protest took place against the regime to prevent Shigeru Yoshida, a conservative politician who had supported the Japanese imperial project but opposed the war with the United States, from forming a cabinet following the April general elections that year. This protest was followed by the so-called Food May Day on 19th May, when approximately one quarter of a million people staged a rally in Tokyo demanding an end to the food crisis by placing the distribution of food under popular control (Moore 1997, p. 36). As such, Japan experienced a genuine workers' uprising in the immediate post-war years. One might say therefore that the SCAP's democratising reforms has been a little too successful. Indeed, as working-class organisations and protests grew in strength, SCAP began to respond with increasingly more forceful countermeasures. Following Food May Day, MacArthur warned that '[i]f minor elements of Japanese society are unable to exercise … self restraint … I shall be forced to take the necessary steps to control and remedy such a deplorable situation' (quoted in Halliday 1975, p. 210). This intervention had the effect of boosting the position of conservatives within the Japanese government and strengthening their resolve to mobilise their own counterattack. Production control thus saw a decline in June following SCAP's sanctioning of a government crackdown on its use (Moore 1997, pp. 36–38).

After the production control struggles died down, the focus of the labour movement shifted toward the more conventional use of strikes as the primary expression of workers' militancy. At the same time, trade unions were increasingly seen as the principal vehicle for securing workers' rights and livelihood within the emergent capitalist order (Moore 1997, p. 7). Part of this shift involved increased emphasis on the building of national-level federations. In August 1946, following the failure of talks to form a joint federation, two separate labour federations emerged: *Sanbetsu* on the left and a resurrection of the pre-war *Sōdōmei* on the right, which were allied with the JCP and the Japanese Socialist Party (JSP), respectively. *Sōdōmei* represented the collaborationist enterprise-level unions that had emerged from the *Sampō*. The more powerful *Sanbetsu*, on the other hand, was organised by the leftist majority to counter efforts by business to reconstruct the pre-war capitalist system and re-establish enterprise-level collective bargaining (Halliday 1975, p. 209; Moore 1997, p. 8). *Sanbetsu,* which stressed the importance of organising unions at the industry level, elicited greater support from workers than *Sōdōmei,* which stressed regional federations across industrial lines. Furthermore, the evidence suggests that Japan's wage-bargaining structure in these years did see a relative shift from the enterprise to the industrial level. In the first quarter of 1947, for example, 64 contracts covering 1.9 million workers were negotiated through centralised bargaining, as opposed to 881 contracts covering 244,000 workers negotiated at the enterprise level. Thus, this wage-bargaining structure and the strength of the *Sanbetsu* movement more broadly raises into doubt common assumptions of a 'natural' predisposition on the part of Japanese workers toward enterprise unionism (Price 1997, pp. 52–53).

Japanese labour and the reverse course

The tide soon began to turn against the *Sanbetsu*-centred labour movement, however. On 20th September 1946, the Japanese government under Prime Minister Yoshida established a legal framework for conciliation, mediation, or arbitration between labour and capital. However, this framework placed stringent restrictions on strikes by the government workers who formed the stronghold of *Sanbetsu*'s membership base. Whilst government workers were allowed to organise unions under this legal framework, they could not strike for thirty days after making an appeal for mediation from one of the newly established Labour Relations Committees. Furthermore, workers in organisations designated as public utilities such as transport, post, telephone, water, gas, electricity, and health, were all excluded from the right to strike. The law also gave the government the power to designate further industries as public utilities at will (Tsuru 1993, p. 24). As such, these legal measures represented a significant curtailment of the scope for action by the Japanese labour movement. Furthermore, SCAP's banning of a planned general strike for 1st February 1947 demanding food, job security, wage increases, and the resignation of the Yoshida government signified a broader reversal in SCAP's policies toward labour in Japan. This intervention by SCAP thus marked a watershed in the history of Japan's post-war labour movement, leading to the eventual decline of *Sanbetsu* and a reversal of the early programme of substantive democratisation through encouragement of the formation of unions.

Yet, SCAP's reversal was also shaped by changing US strategic priorities. The United States had emerged from the Second World War in a position of unprecedented economic and military strength and, as a consequence, in the context of a highly uneven international political economy. With the destruction of Japan and the other major industrial powers at the end of the war, the United States emerged by a large margin as the world's dominant power. US gross national product had grown from $209.4 billion in 1939 to $355.2 billion in 1945 (in constant 1958 prices), amounting to approximately half of the world's goods and services. Steel production had increased from 53 million tons in 1939 to 80 million in 1945. Whilst the United States accounted for only 6 per cent of the world's population, it possessed 46 per cent of the world's electric power and 54 per cent of its telephones, and US corporations owned or controlled 59 per cent of world oil reserves. US car production was eight times that of France, Britain, and Germany combined (Lundestad 1986, p. 264). The global unevenness inherent in this supremacy was at the same time one of the greatest strategic challenges faced by the United States in the post-war era. A shortfall in foreign dollar accounts occurred as a result of an annual $10 billion surplus of US exports over imports. This 'dollar gap' meant that a key challenge for the United States, or at least for those policymakers located in the State Department who understood the economics of the problem, was that of reducing the domination of the world economy by American producers. Any failure to do so would mean that foreign states would become insolvent vis-à-vis the United States and thereby be unable to purchase American goods (Borden 1984, p. 6). By 1947, this dollar gap had reached the level of $8 billion. As then Under Secretary of State Dean Acheson recognised, the inability of the rest of the world to buy US goods would remain a 'grim fact of life' if the European and Asian economies were not revived (quoted in Hersh 1993, p. 18).

What ultimately prevented the dollar gap from developing into a full-blown collapse of world trade were the massive amounts of US aid provided to Europe, Japan, and elsewhere to fund reconstruction and economic revival. Yet, this aid could not in itself serve as a permanent solution to the problem of global disequilibrium as it was dependent on periodic congressional approval. US Congress operated on orthodox principles of balanced budgets, low taxes, and primacy over foreign industrial rivals; as such, it was not inclined to lower tariffs and encourage imports in order to tackle the dollar gap. Ultimately, the State Department was only able to overcome congressional resistance through the invocation of the 'communist threat' as a means of justifying the incorporation of economic aid into rapidly growing foreign military aid programmes (Borden 1984, pp. 24–25). Indeed, the Marshall Plan was promoted primarily as enabling European recovery in order to combat the spread of communism. Congress was, therefore, misled from the outset about the aims of foreign aid. It was told that the war had damaged European production and that a potential turn to communism there would imperil American security, rather than framing the problem in terms of fundamental disequilibrium in the global economy. To convince Congress, the pledge was made that aid would decrease each year and would not continue beyond 1952 (Borden 1984, pp. 30–31).

This is not to suggest that the communist threat was simply an invention designed to justify massive amounts of US foreign aid. Changing US strategy in East Asia also reflected the intense social upheaval in the region following the end of the Second World War. This upheaval was manifest in the significant advances made by the Chinese Communist Party (CCP) against America's problematic ally, the nationalist Kuomintang (KMT), thereby dampening hitherto strong support in the US State Department for China as the US ally of choice in the region. Korea also had a vibrant communist movement and the Taiwanese population was in the process of mobilising a strong resistance against the retreating mainlander KMT army. Furthermore, the rise of national liberation movements in Western Europe's Southeast Asian colonial hinterland threatened the former's own precarious economic reconstruction. Finally, as the previous discussion has shown, within Japan itself, the occupation and increasing economic hardship had led to increasing social unrest and communist influence. As such, the reversal of the aims of the US occupation in Japan can be seen as an inevitable outcome of the contradictory rationale of the democratic 'revolution from above,' whereby the considerable economic hardship faced by workers made the vision of a Japanese 'New Deal' highly unrealistic. In such conditions, liberal labour laws were unlikely to give rise to a compliant and passive workforce. Furthermore, the emphasis on democracy promotion came under heavy criticism from a particularly influential group of American businessmen with direct interests in Japan, who were outraged by the implications of SCAP's *zaibatsu* dissolution programme and labour reforms (Kolko and Kolko 1972, pp. 510–512).

Thus, amidst the continued massive outflow of aid to Japan, Washington became increasingly cognisant of the tensions between the thrust of SCAP's democratising reforms and the broader aims of establishing Japanese self-sufficiency.

From early 1947, therefore, Washington began to openly express its disquiet at those reforms considered to be a direct impediment to economic revival. One key area of reversal was the policy of economic deconcentration and the purge of economic leaders. Whilst the deconcentration bill was passed through the Japanese Diet in 1947, actual decisions on which of the corporations were to be dissolved were made by a board of American businessmen with interests in the Japanese economy. As a result, the number of corporations scheduled for dissolution dropped from the original 1,200 to a final figure of 9. Similarly, in a visit to Tokyo in 1948, George Kennan personally pressured MacArthur to halt the purges of Japanese businessmen (Kolko and Kolko 1972, pp. 512–517). At the same time, Washington believed that it would be too costly to yield to any of the demands of the labour movement, and that before the United States could promote policies aimed at economic revival, it would have to break this potential threat (Kolko and Kolko 1972, p. 521). Thus, as the Japanese right consolidated its power following a short-lived and ineffectual JSP government, a full-scale anti-communist and anti-working-class campaign was launched.

Following the banning of the 1st February general strike, the Japanese government passed an amendment of the National Public Service Law. As noted earlier, the government had in 1946 already placed stringent restrictions on industrial action by government employees. Arguing that the government could not have its power usurped by any private group, the Japanese government made it illegal for government employees to engage in any form of dispute, including collective bargaining (Ayusawa 1966, pp. 290–294). This gave the government considerable powers over public-sector employees who had hitherto formed the vanguard of the labour movement in post-surrender Japan. The reappointment of conservative President Shigeru Yoshida in October 1948 led employers to seek further legal changes that would enable the re-establishment of managerial prerogative within the private sector. The rationale for these revisions was that many of the collective agreements reached during the high tide of the labour struggle were deemed by business to be overly favourable to workers. They had included such provisions as the prohibition of layoffs unless agreed to by the union and the automatic renewal of workers' contracts until new collective agreements were reached. Thus, in May 1949, the Yoshida government revised the Trade Union Act and prohibited perpetual duration clauses in collective agreements. It also weakened the protection of unions under the civil codes and forced unions to abide by stringent rules of secrecy in strike votes and internal elections (Price 1997, pp. 77–81).

Beyond these legal changes, SCAP launched a more direct offensive against the militant labour movement through the promotion and support of anticommunist labour groups known as 'democratisation leagues.' These anticommunist cells claimed to be expressions of rank-and-file discontent with the policies of left-wing union leaders and were specifically designed to weaken *Sanbetsu*. Furthermore, they adopted a strategy of promoting anticommunism by claiming that the JCP was manipulating the unions and that the JSP was subservient to Moscow (Halliday 1975, p. 217). With the support of business, these democratisation leagues played a key role in fostering splits between rightists and leftists within the unions, which in many cases led to the establishment of breakaway unions. Union federations also began to disaffiliate from *Sanbetsu,* leading to the rapid decline of the national union centre by 1950 (Price 1997, p. 86). Indeed, the membership of *Sanbetsu* declined from 290,000 in 1950 to 47,000 by 1951 (Harari 1973, pp. 72–73), The Japanese government, with the support of SCAP, also launched the so-called 'Red Purge' against the JCP, whereby roughly 13,000 alleged JCP members were fired from their public- or private-sector jobs on the grounds that their political activities were impeding the goals of the occupation (Gordon 2003, p. 239). This offensive against the JCP took place in the context of the growing success of the CCP in China, the entrenchment of the Cold War in Europe, as well as Senator Joseph McCarthy's anticommunist witch hunt in Washington. As a result, these events marked the decline of the JCP and the public sector labour movement (Allinson 2004, pp. 54–55).

The reversal of the post-war wave of labour militancy was both a prerequisite to, and indeed an immediate outcome of, attempts at reviving the ailing Japanese economy. In early 1949, former Chairman of the Detroit Bank Joseph Dodge was sent by Washington to Japan to impose an anti-inflationary programme aimed at stabilising prices and balancing the budget as a means of restoring Japan's economic competitiveness and reducing the country's dependence on US aid. To achieve a balanced budget, the so-called Dodge Plan involved a substantial reduction in the number of government employees, the elimination of subsidies to industry and the resulting creation of further unemployment, the raising of the prices of its services, and greater efforts by the government to collect taxes. Washington also expected Japan to increase its export capacity and thereby decrease its reliance on aid. To increase exports, Japanese workers were thus expected to work hard, consume little, and be disciplined and quiescent (Kolko and Kolko 1972, p. 519). The austerity policies underpinning the Dodge Plan did succeed in bringing inflation under control, but this came at the expense of shattering the little economic recovery Japan had achieved. The abrupt cut-off of government price subsidies and loans to industry served to eliminate the main source of capital into the system, and there were few alternative sources of capital in either the savings of enterprises or in the new capital market that SCAP was attempting to foster (Johnson 1982, pp. 199–200). The mass layoffs were successful, however, in further weakening and subordinating the labour movement. Large sections of the militant left leadership were targeted, thus leading the way for the anticommunist democratisation leagues to take over leadership of the unions. In 1949 alone, 435,465 workers were dismissed from their jobs, and the figure for the whole 1949–50 retrenchment was approximately 700,000. The devastating effect that this had on the union movement as a whole is apparent in the drop in the number of unions by over 5,000 and in union membership by 880,000 (Halliday 1975, p. 218). Thus, whilst union membership had reached 56 per cent of the entire labour force in 1949, by the mid-1950s, unionisation had seen a sharp decline to below 30 per cent (Whittaker 2003, p. 281).

Whilst the austerity brought by the Dodge Plan served to undermine labour militancy in Japan, it did little in itself to revive the economy. Rather, it was the external factor of the outbreak of the Korean War that set Japan on the path to recovery and sustainable economic growth. The war not only freed American policymakers from fiscal and military constraints, but it had a positive effect on the reconstruction of a multilateral world economy. It spurred a flood of US aid to rearm Europe, and it financed the French re-conquest of Indochina. Moreover, it set off a massive speculative buying boom by business, transforming the world buyer's market into a seller's market. It created strong US demand for primary materials from European dependencies, thereby bringing windfall profits to raw materials producers and reviving triangular trade (Borden 1984, p. 50). It also had a dramatic impact on Japan's economic revival. Japan became the predominant source of special procurements for the United Nations' military effort on the Korean peninsula. Dollar payments for special procurements amounted to $2.5 billion over the course of the war. This was in addition to the $1.7 billion of US aid that continued to be channelled to Japan. As such, the war effort led to a rapid increase in Japanese production. The influx of technology and strong external demand were crucial foundations for Japan's later economic growth and helped to revive heavy industries in particular. Many of Japan's major exporting companies, such as Nissan, Toyota, Bridgestone, and Kawasaki, incorporated new technologies into their production processes as a result of Korean War special procurement contracts (Stubbs 2005, pp. 68–70).

Despite the decline of *Sanbetsu,* Japan's trade unions still remained important social actors. In 1950, SCAP, the Japanese government, and the business federation *Nikkeiren* encouraged the formation of a new national centre based on the anticommunist democratisation leagues known as *Sōhyō*. Barely a year after its formation, however, the organisation's leadership was taken over by a left-wing faction. One of the key innovations of this new left-oriented leadership was the *Shuntō,* or 'spring offensive,' which was designed to form a united front amongst unions through the articulation of joint demands and coordinated tactics (Weathers 2008). Furthermore, given that the organisation represented the majority of the public sector unions, one of the key demands of *Sōhyō* was the restoration of the right of government employees to strike. However, the contrast with the labour activism of the immediate postwar years was clear. Through its strategy of pursuing the interests of its most immediate membership base, *Sōhyō* was unable to overcome the growing dualism in Japanese labour relations; indeed, it was itself an expression of that dualism (Allinson 2004, p. 71). The organisation did, however, maintain a progressive international policy in that it was strongly opposed to the resurgence of militarism in Japan and adopted a position of neutrality toward the increasingly fractious international labour movement. *Sōhyō* refused to align itself with either the International Confederation of Free Trade Unions or the World Federation of Trade Unions (Nakakita 2008).

It was this neutrality in the climate of the Cold War that led the American Federation of Labor (AFL) to view *Sōhyō* as fundamentally communist in orientation. Instead, the AFL supported a smaller organisation called *Zenrō*, which had broken away from *Sōhyō* in 1954 and eventually became *Dōmei* in 1964. In line with the orientation of its predecessor, *Dōmei* was a conservative and pro-Western union that sought to undermine the brand of independent unionism represented by *Sōhyō*, arguing that poor wages and working conditions were a result of Japan's lack of competitiveness in international markets, and as such, labour needed to adopt a more 'constructive' approach based on cooperation with management and wage restraint (Carlile 1994b, p. 152). *Sōhyō* did receive international support, however, from the Democratic Kennedy administration, the Congress of Industrial Organizations, the International Confederation of Free Trade Unions, and the British Trade Union Congress—all of whom understood *Sōhyō* as neutral rather than communist in orientation and thereby saw potential for drawing *Sōhyō* into the 'free world.' This relative shift from the anti-communism of the Eisenhower administration to the Kennedy administration should, however, also be understood in relation to Japan's changing position within the international system. The greater strength and representation of *Sōhyō* meant that it was regarded as the organisation most capable of winning gains in wages and working conditions for Japanese workers and thereby for reducing Japan's competitive threat to workers in the West (Nakakita 2008, p. 213).

Despite these developments at the national level, the labour movement at the grassroots enterprise level was in the 1950s faced with repeated setbacks. Although a number of labour struggles sought to contest managerial control in the workplace, they frequently resulted in the formation of breakaway unions. The Nissan strike in 1953, for example, led to successful efforts by the company management, with support from *Nikkeiren*, in encouraging the formation of a breakaway union. More broadly, enterprise unionism became widespread in the strategic industries and in automobile production in particular (Price 1997, p. 125). By the late 1950s, therefore, enterprise unionism had become the dominant trend within Japanese labour relations. Furthermore, there was a close association between this increasing subordination of labour through enterprise unionism and Japan's broader industrialisation strategy in the post-war era. Japanese government policy in the 1950s was oriented toward the development of heavy industry, and the centrality of the latter in the Japanese economy lent weight to employers' claims that it was necessary to repress wages in order to ensure international competitiveness. This meant that wages saw only a minimal rise during this period despite the lengthening of the working week between 1952 and 1957. In the steel sector, management adopted a particularly uncompromising attitude toward strikes through the mobilisation of 'ability to pay' arguments. As a result of the conservative unions' moderation in terms of wage demands, labour costs per ton of steel in Japan actually dropped between 1957 and 1964 when labour costs in Germany rose by over 40 per cent in the same period, making Japan the world's most efficient steel producer (Price 1997, pp. 129–134).

Late development, culture, and paternalism

As argued previously, the passive revolution of the post-war years laid the foundations for a comprehensive system of labour subordination in Japan. Against the sustained surge of labour militancy in the immediate post-war era, SCAP, along with Japanese state and capital, sought to reverse the gains made by the workers' movement by repressing efforts to build industrial-level unions and by re-establishing the more authoritarian elements of the pre-war labour regime. However, this analysis runs counter to a significant body of literature that has sought to present Japanese labour relations and work practices in an altogether more positive light. In this view, the so-called Japanese employment system represents a qualitatively more productive and worker-friendly post-Fordist organisation of production and serves as a viable alternative to the Taylorist production methods found more typically in the West. Kenny and Florida (1988, p. 123) argue, for example, that Japanese post-Fordism is characterised by work teams, job rotation, flexible production, learning by doing (whereby the shop floor becomes a centre of working interaction and information sharing), and just-in-time production (whereby Japanese manufacturing firms organise supply transactions through multilayered supplier complexes rather than internalising them through vertical integration). In turn, the Japanese employment system plays a key role in facilitating workers' participation in production and eliciting their wider consent to the post-Fordist accumulation regime. Central to this employment system is what has commonly been referred to as the 'three sacred treasures' of lifetime employment, seniority wages, and enterprise unionism. The security provided by these institutions, along with the post-Fordist organisation of production, is understood to produce a work atmosphere in which workers are pleased 'to acknowledge that they get some satisfaction out of their work and some feeling of pride from the exercise of their skills' (Dore 1973, p. 277). Thus, not only is the Japanese employment system held to be more productive, but this is in large part due to the fact that it is more appealing to workers.

For some, these 'sacred treasures' have their origins in traditional Japanese culture and a culturally determined predilection for harmony and cooperation within the workplace (Abegglen 1959; Yoshino 1968, p. 66; see also Dore 1973, pp. 401–402). For example, Ronald Dore, in his influential comparative study of British and Japanese industrial relations, argued that the confluence of Japan's traditional Confucian culture and the lateness of its development in world-historical time served to create a distinctive 'combined' labour regime that was particularly conducive to rapid industrialisation. As Dore argues, at the onset of Britain's industrialisation, the ideology of market individualism was more firmly entrenched and labour was correspondingly widely viewed as a commodity. In Japan, however, the onset of industrialisation occurred at a time when agriculture and handicrafts were still organised along family lines and Confucian ideology remained pervasive, thereby exerting a strong influence on the emergent employment system. The importance of these legacies of Confucian paternalism was amplified by the specific challenges and opportunities of late development. For example, there were differences in the role of the state in solving problems associated with capitalist development. As demonstrated by such political movements as the Corn Law League and the Chartists, and innovations such as the Poor Laws, the Factory Acts, the hospitals, and the state pension schemes, the state was the dominant political entity in Britain. Such national collectivist solutions were, however, less visible in Japan's more cellular society, where charity was expected to begin at home from one's employers and subordinates (Dore 1973, pp. 408–409). The timing of the industrialisation effort was also significant in that Japanese labour relations were influenced by the demonstrative effect of labour struggles in earlier industrialising countries. Thus, during their respective periods of industrialisation, Japanese employers were, Dore argues, more aware than their British counterparts of the inevitability of strikes and class conflict; consequently, they realised at an earlier stage that they had to accept and accommodate labour unions. As such, they were able to adjust to the reality of labour's social power through institutional innovations *before* unions became so strong that management's options were foreclosed (Dore 1973, p. 410).

The imperatives of late development also, Dore argues, led to differences in the education system. The greater tendency of Japanese industry to employ school leavers stemmed from the fact that universal primary schooling did not occur until late in the history of British industrialisation. In Japan, however, approximately 90 per cent of boys attended primary schools at the beginning of the twentieth century, and Japanese employers preferred to recruit youngsters because they were more likely to have to do their own training as a result of the challenges associated with importing existing technologies in a context in which traditional artisan skills were dominant. Apprenticeships, whereby techniques were passed from worker to worker, were less appropriate in a situation in which industry was expanding rapidly (Dore 1973, pp. 411–412). Furthermore, given the more advanced capital-intensive technology underpinning late-industrialisation, labour costs represented a smaller proportion of total costs for the average manufacturer; thus, as Dore argues, there was less need for labour repression. The other side of the coin, however, was that leaving plants idle was more expensive; thus, absenteeism and high labour turnover posed a more serious drain on profits. Together, it is argued, these factors contributed toward the development of lifetime employment. In a situation where employees were consequently less concerned with wage levels in other companies and sectors, the enterprise union was considered to be the more appropriate medium of worker representation (Dore 1973, pp. 413–414). As such, Japan's extraordinary economic growth can be seen to have resulted from a fortuitous coincidence of the legacies of Japan's Confucian paternalistic traditions and the specific demands associated with late development. These traditions were not, in this view, simply manifested in workers' deference to their employers but shaped the way that employers treated their workers. Dore argues that the Confucian worldview which prevailed at the onset of industrialisation in nineteenth-century Japan assumed original virtue rather than original sin, and as a result, those in positions of authority were, in comparison to their Western counterparts, more inclined to see workers as human beings and as responsive to moral appeals (Dore 1973, pp. 401–402).

In reality, however, the pervading ideology of familialism and consensus in Japanese corporations is more a reflection of the fact that Japanese leaders were adept in using traditional symbols to secure the legitimation of the new institutional arrangements associated with lifetime employment (Cole 1978, p. 262). As such, the apparent prevalence of Confucian ideals in post-war Japanese labour relations should be explained more as emerging out of the dynamics of class struggle rather than simply assumed in any deterministic fashion. Indeed, cultural explanations in themselves fail to explain why it is that management has had the monopoly over the mobilisation of traditional cultural values. As E.P. Thompson's (1963) work on English working-class formation lucidly demonstrates, traditional cultural values were as much a weapon in the hands of the working class against employers as they were the preserve of management. In the East Asian case, cultural deterministic explanations fail to explain variations across countries that are broadly considered to be 'Confucian.' For example, it fails to answer the question of how Confucianism allegedly became the basis for harmony and cooperation between labour and capital in Japan, but how attempts to mobilise a form of Confucian paternalism in Korea became one of the key grievances of striking workers in the 1980s (see Koo 2001). Thus, as Chalmers Johnson (1982, p. 8) has said of cultural essentialist modes of explanation, '[p]ositing some "special capacity to cooperate" as an irreducible Japanese cultural trait leads inquiry away from the question of *why* Japanese cooperate when they do … and away from the probability that this cooperation can be, and on occasion has been, quite deliberately engineered by the government and others.'

During the era of Meiji industrialisation, there were strong efforts by employers to promote the key features of the Japanese employment system as a means of creating a stable proletariat, and such attempts often made reference to harmonious labour relations as being ingrained in Japanese culture. For example, Shōda Heigorō, director of the Mitsubishi Nagasaki Shipyard, argued in 1910 (quoted in Gordon 1985, p. 67):

> Since ancient times, Japan has possessed the beautiful custom of master-servant relations based firmly on a spirit of sacrifice and compassion, a custom not seen in many other countries of the world. Even with the recent progress in transportation, the development of ideas about rights, the expansion of markets, and the growing scale of industrial society, this master-servant relationship persists securely. This relationship is not weak like that of the Western nations, but has its roots in our family system and will persist as long as that system exists. Because of this relationship, the employer loves the employee and the employee respects his master. Interdependent and helping each other, the two preserve industrial peace.

These pronouncements should be viewed, however, not as statement of historical reality but as part of a wider attempt to formulate and propagate a hegemonic ideology of paternalism and harmonious labour relations against the formation of a working-class consciousness. They were first directed at workers in the context of the militant labour struggles in the years following the Sino-Japanese (1894–5) and the Russo-Japanese wars (1904–05), both of which had led to a rapid rise in heavy industry and working-class formation (Yamamura 1977, pp. 113–114). The latter half of 1897, for example, saw 302 labour disputes involving 3,517 workers, which was followed in 1898 by 413 disputes involving 6,292 workers (Totten 1960, p. 189). A strike wave in 1907 involved more workers than in any year previously, further demonstrating the militancy of workers in heavy industry.

Whilst these strikes were partly a response to post-war inflation, they were also a result of workers' dissatisfaction with efforts to impose direct forms of management in the workplace (Garon 1987, p. 31). As such, Japanese labour relations were evolving in a way that was rather at odds with the 'beautiful customs' promoted by employers. Yet, these pretensions of Japanese traditions of loyalty were not only an attempt to establish ideological hegemony over workers but were also a means of dissuading the government from enacting stricter labour standards (Gordon 1985, p. 55). Whilst discussions amongst politicians and bureaucrats over the need for a Factory Law had been taking place since the 1880s, these waves of intense workers' militancy served to completely undermine management's argument that the alleged 'beautiful customs' alone were enough to guarantee 'healthy' industrial development (Gordon 1985, p. 67). It should be noted also that in addition to the threat posed by increased labour militancy, the Factory Law was also a response to the deepening contradiction between the Meiji aims of rich country (*fukuko*) and strong army (*kyōhei*). The exploitation of workers that underpinned Meiji industrialisation was in the process of endangering the supply of healthy and intelligent soldiers to Japan's military. The government was thus compelled to ignore the short-term interests of capital and introduce legislation that outlawed the overwork of youths in their early years (Taira 1997, p. 272).

Other features of Japan's emerging labour paternalism had their origins in broader management strategies to tackle the specific challenges posed by Japan's late and rapid transition to capitalism. A key challenge for employers during the Meiji era was the high mobility of skilled workers, who were unfamiliar with and resistant to strict discipline. Workers had little inclination to remain at particular enterprises and would move from company to company in search of the highest wages. This mobility was very much a legacy of the artisan origins of skilled workers. Without guilds to limit their numbers, traditional craft artisans travelled from workshop to workshop, competing with one another as they sought to accumulate the skill, capital, and backing needed to become masters of their craft. Thus, during the Meiji era, this unregulated lifestyle was reproduced by workers trained in the new heavy industries. They frequently desired independence through changing jobs and moved from small workshops to large factories and back, thereby disregarding ineffective craft restrictions (Gordon 1985, pp. 24–25, 47). This problem of worker mobility was exacerbated by the fact that instead of recruiting, training, and supervising workers directly, companies in heavy industry during the early Meiji era relied on the *oyakata-kokata* (master-apprentice) relationship of pre-modern feudal artisan society. Managers subcontracted *oyakata* to act as labour bosses who would recruit, train, and supervise workers on behalf of the company. Whilst such a system was effective in overcoming labour problems in the early stages of industrialisation, the *oyakata* were themselves highly mobile. Thus, when the *oyakata* moved out of a factory to take up work elsewhere, they generally took their apprentices with them, thereby posing a significant barrier to the creation of a skilled and committed labour force

(Large 1979, p. 21). The attempt by Meiji-era employers to institute a more direct form of management and a more loyal and committed labour force was thus also a key factor encouraging the development of paternalism in Japanese labour relations. The task of exerting direct authority over workers and instilling loyal to the company began with turning the *oyakata* into foremen employed directly by the company. Some of the largest companies, such as the Mitsubishi Nagasaki Shipyard and the Yahata Ironworks, circumvented the *oyakata* networks entirely by creating training programmes and vocational schools designed to cultivate a core group of committed workers, potential foremen, and shop-floor leaders (Gordon 1985, p. 54).

Companies also sought to nurture worker loyalty by guaranteeing lifetime employment and providing other incentives to remain at the firm, such as company housing at low rates, the use of company baths, barbershops, refectories, baseball fields, marriage arrangements, and personal counselling services, as well as improved working conditions. Workers were also encouraged to identify with the firm by joining enterprise unions rather than the industrial unions established by the labour movement. Workers were also allowed to nominate representatives to sit on labour–management work councils to discuss company-related problems (Large 1979, p. 23). The seniority wage system also arose out of these developments. Management recognised that lack of opportunity for advancement was an important cause of turnover and loss of skilled workers. The introduction of wage ladders was thereby an attempt to encourage workers to stay with the company and advance in rank and pay (Gordon 1985, pp. 44–46).

These new paternalistic management strategies emerged first in the government-run arsenals and shipyards, such as in the huge industrial complex at Yokosuka, and were replicated at other industrial centres, such as the Yawata Steelworks. In these enterprises, management was able to establish firm control over the recruitment and training of a stable and skilled workforce and thereby was able to reduce the fluidity of labour markets. However, until the First World War, paternalism coexisted with rather than replaced the *oyakata* system. After the war, however, Japan experienced a severe recession, forcing Japanese state and capital to further rationalise production to facilitate economic recovery. This provided the opportunity to promote paternalistic management practices throughout Japanese industry. The independent 'wanderer' or 'man of moods' of the past was thus replaced by the loyal skilled worker, and the labour movement began to find itself squeezed out of the large, modern enterprises into the smaller firms where wage-competitive labour markets were still dominant (Large 1979, pp. 21–24).

Aside from tendencies toward cultural determinism, one of the key shortcomings of the mainstream literature on the Japanese employment system is that it rests upon an overly positive assessment of the nature of class relations in the immediate post-1945 era; thereby, sharply contrasting with the picture presented above. It has been argued, for example, that during the counteroffensive of the late 1940s, capital was unable to entirely impose its will on labour and was forced to accommodate a number of labour's key demands, which in turn were integrated into the emergent labour regime (see also Dore 1973, pp. 115–119; Kenny and Florida 1988, pp. 126–129).

As the analysis here has shown, however, the struggles of the late 1940s in fact had a devastating impact on the working-class movement in Japan. The job insecurity that arose as a result of the Dodge Plan's anti-labour offensive made it increasingly difficult for workers and their organisations to challenge management and thereby allowed the latter to impose enterprise unionism on the Japanese labour movement. This had important implications in terms of the degree to which workers were able to achieve representation throughout the post-war era. In the late 1940s, when labour had been on the offensive, enterprise unions had included all employees working in the enterprise. However, in the context of the increasingly precarious employment situation brought by the Dodge austerity, employers were able to push for union membership to only include those 'permanent workers' who constituted the minimum workforce that the company would retain in times of retrenchment (Halliday 1975, p. 218).

Thus, in the post-war era, the enterprise union became more indicative of Japan's dualistic employment structure than the 'enterprise as community' ideal with which they are often associated. Enterprise unions thus typically exclude temporary, part-time, and day labourers and are more likely to settle for moderate wage gains out of fear of the impact that higher wages would have on the competitiveness of the firm and that business and jobs would consequently be lost to competing firms. When profits have come under pressure, such as during the oil shocks of the 1970s and the recession of the 1990s, enterprise unions have for the most part adopted an accommodating position (Tsuru and Rebitzer 1995, p. 482). To be sure, enterprise unionism itself represents only one structural fetter to the development of working-class solidarity. Japanese, Taiwanese, and Korean labour regimes are all characterised by enterprise unionism, yet workers in all three countries have exhibited different degrees of militancy. Nonetheless, there is a clear pattern in which enterprise unionism on the whole tends to be associated with low union density, strong identity with the company rather than class consciousness, decentralised collective bargaining, inequalities within the working class, and the political ineffectiveness of labour. It is thus no accident that government and employers across East Asia have sought to impose enterprise unionism (Lee 2011, p. 33).

The dualism of the Japanese employment system is also apparent with regards to the famed 'lifetime employment' system. As with the enterprise unions, lifetime employment only covers permanent workers, who constitute around 20–30 per cent of the entire workforce. The vast majority of these are male workers in the government or large private firms. Employment continuity is provided to this core group by shifting the risks associated with economic change onto smaller subcontractor firms. However, even within the larger firms, temporary and part-time workers who often work alongside the permanent staff have no protection and are subject to layoffs. Furthermore, 'lifetime employment' itself is something of a misnomer as permanent workers are often forced to take early retirement before the official age of 60, meaning that many older workers are forced to re-enter the labour market on more precarious terms (Takahashi 1997, pp. 58–61). As such, 'lifetime employment' does not mean that dismissals are impossible, but rather that management first takes other steps during times of retrenchment before resorting to layoffs, such as the reduction of overtime, the cutting of part-time workers, freezes in recruitment, the reduction of board members' remuneration, and calls for voluntary retirement (Thelen and Kume 1999, p. 483). The counterpart to this largely male permanent workforce is the predominantly female force of peripheral workers, namely temporary, day, and part-time workers. In 1988, for example, 20 per cent of female manufacturing workers were either temporary workers or day labourers, compared to only 3 per cent of male manufacturing workers. Women in turn accounted for 79 per cent of all temporary workers and 75 per cent of day labourers (Houseman and Abraham 1993).

Furthermore, in further contrast to the myth of the more 'humane' organisation of production, Dohse *et al.* (1985, pp. 126–133), in their study of the Japanese car industry, have argued that the superlative efficiency of Japanese industry is not the result of a more enlightened participatory system of production control. Instead, Japanese labour relations are characterised by the more exploitative application of Taylorist forms of job control. In companies such as Toyota, workers' knowledge of the production process is, as the more celebratory accounts of Japanese industry suggest, extensively used as part of the rationalisation of the production process. Yet, the primary purpose of worker participation is the setting of time and production standards in a manner which leads to the heightened intensification of work itself. Thus, in comparison to car manufacturers in Europe and North America, Japanese workers spend a much smaller proportion of their time idle. Furthermore, this allegedly more 'humane' form of labour relations does not seem congruent with Japan's famously long working hours. In 1995, for example, Japanese workers still worked an average of 1,910 hours per year, compared to 1,849 in the United States and 1,542 in France (Organisation for Economic Co-operation and Development, 2014). As Price (1997, p. 6) has argued, 'Why, one might ask, should workers have to work harder if the system is more efficient?'

The wage system does not quite live up to its reputation either. Indeed, it is again a misnomer to refer to Japan's wages as 'seniority wages.' A significant proportion of Japanese wages is calculated according to the work effort of the individual by the worker's supervisor. At Toyota, for example, this evaluated component amounts to approximately 40 per cent of the monthly wage. Given the lack of mobility between Japanese companies and the importance of the internal labour markets, supervisors have considerable influence over the material reward and career advancement of individual workers. The individualism inherent in the wage system discourages solidarity between workers and reflects the broader weakness of labour vis-à-vis capital as well as the failure of Japanese unions to effectively regulate employment relations within the corporation. Enterprise unions are less able to display indifference toward the individual company's commercial success and, in turn, toward the company's productivity and cost structure. Conflicting goals with respect to the utilisation of labour are thereby avoided, and the enterprise unions concentrate more on compensation and job security rather than job control (Dohse *et al.* 1985, pp. 135–137).

It is, however, this pliant attitude on the part of enterprise unions and their receptiveness to changes in work practices that, in part, explains Japan's extraordinary ability to adapt new technologies (Itoh 1994, p. 31). In a similar vein, the just-in-time production system presents a very different picture to that depicted in the mainstream Japanese labour relations literature. As Delbridge *et al.* (1992) have argued, just-in-time production implies an intensification of work as a result of increased surveillance and monitoring of workers' activities, heightened responsibility and accountability, and the harnessing of peer pressure within work teams. Thus, in marked contrast to the rhetoric of increased autonomy and discretion, just-in-time production is designed as a process of continued improvements in the production process and increased control over workers to eliminate workers' idle time. It is not surprising, therefore, that when such production techniques were copied by Western corporations in the 1980s and 1990s, their primary impact was the intensification of work. Indeed, as Laurie Graham's (1994, p. 137) participant observation found, in the Subaru-Isuzu Automotive plant in the United States, the goal was 'for workers to be working every second of every minute.'

Conclusion

In this chapter, I have argued that the US intervention following the Japanese surrender of 1945 led to an outburst of labour militancy that serves to challenge widespread notions that the roots of the country's harmonious labour relations can be explained with reference to Japan's traditional Confucian culture. Whilst US strategy was initially directed at the promotion of democracy and the development of a bona fide trade union movement along New Deal lines, as the broader challenges of global economic restructuring became more apparent to US policymakers, this strategy quickly shifted toward one of the repression of labour and the encouragement of economic reconstruction. The passive revolution of the late 1940s can thus be understood as ensuring, through the intervention of US and Japanese elites, the continuity of the more repressive elements of Japan's pre-war labour regime. It was the legacies of this labour repression and their continuity in the post-war era, rather than any underlying culture of labour–management cooperation, that explains how it was that Japan was particularly well placed to meet the challenges of late development. As such, there was nothing preordained about the re-imposition of paternalistic labour relations in Japan; it was contingent upon the dynamics of class struggle and their intersection with the changing global strategy of the United States. As a result, the post-war labour regime represents the comprehensive defeat of the working-class movement in Japan. In this sense, the imperatives of late development can be viewed as favouring not harmonious labour relations but comprehensive labour subordination. Indeed, as we move on to examine the cases of Korea, Taiwan, and China, this fundamental characteristic of late development becomes all the more apparent.

This subordination of Japanese labour went on to form a key underpinning of the Japanese state's extraordinary capacity for industrial upgrading and, by extension, of the broader East Asian regional experience of catch-up industrialisation. However, despite the central role of the United States in establishing the conditions for the country's post-war development, Japan's resulting export competitiveness increasingly began to challenge the US manufacturing sector. Indeed, these pressures on Japan over its trading practices had already begun by the late 1950s (Hersh 1993, p. 26). This led to pressures from the US government on Japan to restrict certain exports and liberalise features of the country's neomercantile political economy. The Japanese government thereby responded through facilitating a process of national and regional industrial upgrading involving the relocation of domestic industries to offshore locations throughout East Asia. Through a process of what Rob Steven (1990, pp. 12–16) has referred to as one of 'scrap and build,' the Japanese government mobilised the extraordinary directive capacity of the developmental state to facilitate the restructuring and, by extension, the regionalisation of the Japanese political economy. Indeed, this process of industrial upgrading encouraged Japanese capital to shift production to lower-wage locations in Korea and Taiwan, and later to Southeast Asia (Hart-Landsberg and Burkett 1998, pp. 92–97). This domestic and regional process of restructuring relied not only on the compliance of Japanese unions and weakness of labour in general, but also on the pre-existing subordination of labour in the other East Asian countries. Thus, as I will argue in Chapter 3, this meant that the post-war passive revolution was from the outset regional in scope and was aimed at suppression of the working-class movement throughout East Asia as part of the broader integration of the region into the US-centred world order. However, the subordination of labour in Korea and Taiwan in particular occurred in an altogether more brutal fashion.

Note

1 "Potsdam Declaration," *National Diet Library*. Available online at http://www.ndl.go.jp/constitution/e/etc/c06.html (accessed 4 July 2014).

3

LABOUR ON THE FRONT LINE IN KOREA AND TAIWAN

As noted in Chapter 2, the economic and military predominance of the United States vis-à-vis the rest of the world in the immediate post-war era constituted a global imbalance whereby the underlying dollar gap threatened continued US prosperity. If the United States wished to maintain its economic and political world supremacy, it needed to construct an open multilateral global trading system and revive the productive capacities of the key capitalist economies (Hersh 1993, pp. 4–5). As could be seen with the US intervention in Japan, this process involved the active restructuring of state–society relations so as to facilitate the subordination of the labour movement along with other social forces potentially opposed to catch-up industrialisation. The upheaval in Japan following the country's surrender in 1945 was, however, part of a broader regional upsurge of social unrest. The rise of communism on the Asian mainland in particular posed a geopolitical threat to Japan and threatened Japan's access to its former colonial hinterlands, which would be essential for the country's economic revival. In this sense, the post-war passive revolution needed to be regional in scope. The United States would have to establish alliances with the pre-war anticommunist political elites across the region in order to counter the threat posed by labour and other social forces seeking a more egalitarian post-war social order. As such, the repression of these forces and the establishment of authoritarian developmental states on the front line of an increasingly militarised Cold War laid the foundations for the region's broader experience of catch-up industrialisation.

Korea and Taiwan—as divided nations on the front line of the emerging US-centred world order and as East Asia's two most prominent newly industrialising countries—bear a remarkably parallel modern history. Korea's nominally more liberal labour laws notwithstanding, neither Korea nor Taiwan was subject to any initial New Deal-type 'democratic experiment' as seen in Japan, and post-war labour policy was of an immediately more repressive nature in both countries. Thus, with

US backing, Korean and Taiwanese political elites imposed a system of authoritarian state corporatism—an arrangement that remained in place until at least the late 1980s. This comprehensive system of labour subordination was central to the integration of the two countries into the broader Japan-centred regional production system. Yet, from the outset, a set of contradictions was inherent within this regional industrialisation effort. As the East Asian countries became increasingly competitive vis-à-vis the United States, the latter reassessed the premises of its role in facilitating upward mobility in the region and began to adopt increasingly protectionist policies alongside attempts at shifting the burden of policing the geopolitical borders of the regional Cold War order onto the Asian countries themselves. From the early 1970s, the Korean and Taiwanese developmental states responded to this challenge by facilitating industrial deepening. However, this was a shift in strategy that would ultimately confer greater structural power on the working class, enabling the latter to challenge the authoritarian developmental state. Although broad similarities exist between the cases of Korea and Taiwan, the working-class movement has been stronger in Korea—a comparative fact that owes much to the differential integration of the two countries into the Japanese imperial project in the pre-war era. This fact of divergent colonial legacies led to passive revolution taking a rather different form in each country.

Korea and Taiwan's post-war passive revolutions

In the immediate aftermath of the Japanese surrender, there were few indications in either Korea or Taiwan of the developmental dynamism that would manifest itself over the coming decades. Both ex-colonies found themselves in dire economic straits. The division of the Korean peninsula in 1945 lead to the South's loss of the country's heavy industrial base and major coal deposits, and almost all of the country's power-generating capacity was located in the northern part of the peninsular. The abrupt departure of Japanese managers and technicians exerted a negative impact on industrial production. Furthermore, high inflation meant that by 1946 food prices had risen a hundredfold compared to their pre-war level (Cole and Lyman 1971, p. 18). Korea also experienced widespread destruction as a result of the fratricidal civil war of 1950–53, which devastated the economy and physically spared only a small segment of the southeast. The state was unable to feed its people or provide them with basic necessities; the standard of living dropped to below Second World War levels and was not to equal them again until 1957. Urban degradation and the 'spring hunger' of the countryside became the pattern rather than the exception (Steinberg 1985, p. 18). Following the Kuomintang (KMT)'s retreat in the late 1940s, conditions in Taiwan were similarly bleak. The sudden influx of between one and two million refugees from the mainland to an existing population of six million exacerbated shortages of food, shelter, and the basic necessities of living (Gold 1986, pp. 54–55). Heavy military spending created huge deficits in the KMT's budget and price inflation appeared to be on the verge of causing a repeat of the events that had contributed to the KMT's defeat in the civil war on the mainland. Despite efforts to isolate Taiwan from the deteriorating conditions on mainland China, the Taipei wholesale price index rose by 260 per cent in 1946, 360 per cent in 1947, 520 per cent in 1948, and 3,500 per cent in 1949. The KMT also lost around $90 million in gold and convertible currencies, thus reducing its foreign exchange to below a minimum operating level (Jacoby 1966, p. 30; Ho 1978, p. 104).

As in Japan, these economic difficulties challenged attempts by the United States to establish politically friendly regimes in both countries. Following their arrival on the southern half of the Korean peninsula in September 1945, US forces were confronted with newly established structures of governance that had emerged in the days and weeks following the Japanese surrender. The national-level Committee for the Preparation of Korean Independence was underpinned by a network of regional and local committees that sought to ensure peace, organise punishment of Japanese collaborators, and maintain continuity in factory production and food distribution. However, the fact that these emergent institutions were often headed by communists and other leftists was enough to provoke US hostility (Hart-Landsberg 1993, p. 119), and the occupying US forces instead sought to revive the basic structures of the colonial state more or less intact. The bureaucracy, the military, and the police of the postcolonial South Korean state were all thus essentially colonial creations and continued to function as key sources of repressive stability (Cumings 1981, pp. 151–169). The nucleus of the future Republic of Korea Army, over which the United States would retain operative command, was staffed with Japanese-trained officers. These repressive forces, overseen by previously exiled independence activist Syngman Rhee, were immediately unleashed against a rebellion that spread across the South in 1948 sparked by protests against police terror on Cheju Island. Just as under the Japanese, tens of thousands of protestors were jailed and many more were sent to 'guidance camps' for anticommunist re-education. This period of re-imposition of state power also saw the repression of independent unions.

The strength of labour resistance in the immediate post-war era owes much to the stronger process of working class formation under colonialism. Whilst the role of colonial Korea in the broader Japanese empire was primarily that of an agricultural producer, from the 1930s it had undergone an increasing degree of industrialisation. This nascent process of industrialisation, it should be stressed, was not for the benefit of the Korean people. Industries that were established remained largely in Japanese hands and agricultural surpluses were shipped to Japan. Nonetheless, as a result of its proximity to the frontline of the Sino-Japanese war, Korea became a key site for wartime production, leading to the emergence of a sizeable indigenous working class. The expansion of largely Japanese-owned industrial enterprises, particularly in the field of mining, chemicals, railways, and hydroelectric plants, led to an increase in the number of factory workers: 49,000 in 1921 to 80,000 in 1925 to 102,000 in 1930 (Koo 2001, p. 25). The outbreak of the Sino-Japanese war in 1937 led to further industrial growth and demand for labour. Rural outmigration took the form of migration from the poorer southern provinces toward the urban and industrial centres of the northern provinces. At the same time, Japan's attempts to construct an East Asian 'co-prosperity sphere' led to the establishment of a regional labour market in which large numbers of Korean workers migrated to Manchuria and Japan. Between

1930 and 1940, approximately 1.3 million Koreans voluntarily migrated to Japan and Manchuria in search of industrial employment and higher wages. A further one million Koreans underwent forced mobilisation after 1939 (Park 1999, pp. 14–19).

This process of colonial industrialisation in Korea had also led to the emergence of a distinctive workers' identity. Aside from the fact of national subjugation itself, this identity had its origins in the colonial labour system Whilst Koreans formed the majority of day labourers and dominated the agricultural, forestry, and fishery sectors, the Japanese dominated professional jobs and formal-sector employment in the bureaucracy, commerce, transport, factories, and mines (Park 1999, p. 22). These racialised labour relations gave labour disputes a particularly nationalistic character, with anti-Japanese consciousness forming an important part of early working-class conciousness in Korea. The majority of strikes during the colonial era were therefore linked to national issues. For example, during a 1903 dispute against Japanese merchants, striking dockworkers' demands for the expulsion of the Japanese took precedence over more material demands for better wages and working conditions. Korean workers also played a key role alongside students, regular citizens, and farmers during the March 1st movement of 1919 against Japanese rule. Striking factory workers led demonstrations and threatened Korean workers who did not participate, and they sought to disrupt factory work by throwing stones and cutting wires. The formation of a national identity amongst workers based on resistance to imperialism thereby occurred prior to the formation of a specifically working-class identity. Labour disputes were linked to national issues, and there was a close relationship between the nationalist and the working-class movement (Kim 2000b, pp. 66–68). In the 1930s, the colonial government by its own actions also served to increase working-class support for Korea's indigenous communist movement. The authorities sought to bind Koreans to the colonial system by creating a fear of communism. However, attempts to designate all instances of labour unrest as part of a communist plot only served to increase the prestige of the communists and helped to produce a highly politicised labour movement that would go on to play an important role in the immediate post-war year (Park 1999, p. 42).

Thus, following the Japanese surrender, widespread economic hardship led to the spontaneous re-emergence of labour unrest. Workers made demands for the redistribution of wealth, the creation of a more equal society, and the confiscation of property from Korean 'traitors' who had collaborated with the Japanese. Workers also took over factories owned by the Japanese and their Korean collaborators, and they set up their own factory self-governing committees (Kim 2000b, pp. 74–77). Furthermore, a national-level workers' organization, *Chŏnp'yŏng,* was formed on 5th November 1945. *Chŏnp'yŏng* supported the northern Korean People's Republic following the division of the country, although many of its demands were in reality reformist in nature (Cumings 1981, pp. 197–201). However, suspicious of independent union activity, Rhee and the right-wing political establishment saw *Chŏnp'yŏng* as a threat. *Chŏnp'yŏng* for its part refused to register with the US military authorities because to do so would be tantamount to recognition of the latter's legitimacy. That refusal, however, meant that *Chŏnp'yŏng* was denied the right to collective bargaining (Ogle 1990, p. 9).

As part of a campaign to undermine *Chŏnp'yŏng* further, the right-wing political camp established the anticommunist Federation of Korean Trade Unions (*Daehannoch'ong,* FKTU) on 3rd October 1946. In a climate of heightened repression, the left-wing leaders of *Chŏnp'yŏng* were either arrested or killed; in general, leftists were forced to submit to the emergent South Korean state. Conversion to the right became a matter of survival and *Chŏnp'yŏng* itself was forcibly disbanded in 1947 (Kim 2000b, p. 80). The transition from *Chŏnp'yŏng* to the FKTU also led to a broader transition in the structure of unionism in the South. *Chŏnp'yŏng* had integrated the existing and newly organised enterprise unions into several industrial unions. Following the demise of *Chŏnp'yŏng,* however, the FKTU dissolved the industrial unions and facilitated a return to enterprise unionism (Lee and Yi 2012, p. 480). State and labour relations were thus subsequently conducted though the FKTU, with the corporatist system acting to moderate union demands, implement government policy, discipline recalcitrant workers, and act as a messenger for the government (Deyo 1989, pp. 120–121).

On the face of it, the labour laws passed by the military authorities were, as in Japan, relatively liberal. However, there was much space between the letter of the law and the actual strictures placed on labour. For example, the 1948 constitution guaranteed core labour rights and even included a provision on the sharing of corporate profits between employer and employee. These rights were again confirmed in the labour laws passed by the Rhee government in 1953. The Labour Standard Law, for example, stipulated labour conditions, guaranteed workers a minimum standard of living, and promoted the development of a balanced national economy. The Trade Union Law provided for the three basic labour rights guaranteed by the constitution, whereas the Labour Dispute Regulation Law guaranteed the freedom of workers' collective action and regulated labour disputes (Chang 2008, pp. 97–98). In reality, however, the 1950s saw the imposition of a highly authoritarian system of control over labour, which drew on the legacies of the colonial era. For example, following the outbreak of the Sino-Japanese war in 1937, the Japanese colonial government had sought to elicit the consent of the rapidly expanding and frequently restive working class through spiritual 'Japanisation' and the *Sampō* movement of government-sponsored workers' organisations. This involved an ideological campaign aimed at encouraging emperor worship amongst workers alongside greater sacrifice and increased productivity. Whilst the campaign did little to create any genuine pro-Japanese sentiment, this wartime industrial relations system, and particularly the *Sampō* movement, left a deep impact on Korean labour practices by introducing the tradition of enterprise unionism and labour–management councils to Korea (Park 1999, p. 46). The Japanese colonial era had thus firmly established the tradition of state intervention in labour relations, with almost no incidents of labour unrest that did not lead to the intervention of the colonial state through deployment of the police or the military (Chang 2009, p. 78). Thus, following the Japanese surrender, the US military authorities and the right-wing government of Rhee ensured that these features would continue to underpin the political economy of the post-colonial Korean state.

As argued in Chapter 2, enterprise unionism was by its very nature easily manipulated to serve the status quo. Whilst the 1953 labour law did not proscribe multiple unions in a single workplace, pressure from employers and the authorities made it particularly difficult. Union finances received no state subsidies and were limited by law to members' dues, meaning that union activities were minimal and, as a result, workers had little motivation to become members (Shim-Han 1987, pp. 102–103). At the national level, the FKTU was subordinated to Rhee's Liberal Party. As Choi (1989, p. 29) has argued, '[i]n the 1950s, labor unions were an auxiliary organization of the ruling party, used in its pure form as a political instrument to buttress Rhee's rule, and totally lacking any meaningful rank and file organizational base.' As such, the Rhee government had deployed a classic strategy of *trasformismo* toward the FKTU leadership and, in doing so, was able to confine labour struggles to the level of the individual or, failing that, of the single workplace. In exchange, the FKTU leadership was offered economic and political privileges. Thus, whilst a number of conflicts at the shop floor level did take place during the 1950s, few of these were organised by trade unions (Chang 2009, p. 88). The Korean labour regime in the immediate post-war era was thereby a specific combination of colonial and American influences. Internally, labour continued to be effectively organised under the legacies of the *Sampō* system. However, it was also underpinned by American-style labour laws reissued by Rhee in 1953 in such a manner that labour grievances would be bottled up in endless legal manipulations. When this arrangement failed to contain independent labour action, the state never hesitated to deploy harsh repression (Ogle 1990, p. 13).

In addition to this thoroughgoing subordination of labour, the US military government carried out a number of reforms in the post-war years that were aimed at achieving a degree of rule by consensus as part of a broader aim of reducing the appeal of communism amongst the larger South Korean population. As in Japan, land reform played a key role in this process. The first stage of land reform in Korea was carried out by the US military authorities immediately following the Japanese surrender. The Japanese had been significant landowners in Korea, and former Japanese-owned lands were distributed to tenants, amounting to around 14 per cent of total farmland. A further 'land to the tiller' reform act was passed in 1949, but the continued landlord influence in the Rhee government led to resistance to further reform. It was only the Korean War and the manifest popularity of land reform both in the North and occupied areas of the South that further weakened the hold of the landowner class and led Rhee to relent to US pressure. The land reform was highly significant for Korea's subsequent development (Kay 2002, Grinberg and Starosta 2009). In addition to significantly removing the threat of socialist revolution in the countryside, it helped keep down food costs and thereby wages for workers, which in turned aided industrialisation (Wiegersma and Medley 2000, pp. 43–45). Thus, with thoroughgoing land reform and the elimination of the traditionally powerful landowner classes, alongside the repression of workers' and left-wing organisations, these crucial US interventions were instrumental in creating 'passive consent' (Cho 2008) toward the postcolonial state and in establishing a degree of autonomy between state and society that would underpin developmentalism in the coming decades. Furthermore, whereas the dominance of colonial Korean industry by Japanese capital had hindered the development of an indigenous bourgeoisie, the Rhee government's privatisation of colonial government property under US pressure led to the emergence of a nascent capitalist class. The transfer of these assets largely occurred on the basis of political acquaintances, resulting in a close but highly corrupt relationship between state and businesses whereby political contributions were given in response to the provision of foreign exchange and import licenses (Cheng 1990, pp. 146–151).

Significant friction existed between US aid officials and President Rhee as a result of the latter's aversion to economic liberalisation and the re-establishment of Korea's dependency vis-à-vis Japan. Rhee was able to exploit the contradiction in US policymakers' preference for both strengthening South Korea as an anticommunist forward defence state and liberalisation of the country's domestic economy through deploying threats of a renewed northern invasion and re-ignition of the Korean War (Woo 1991, pp. 47–48). As such, Rhee prioritised state-building over stable economic development and insisted on the building of factories through import substitution industrialisation (ISI) policies aimed at turning Korea into an overnight Japan rather than accepting the position of neocolonial hinterland. The ISI era thus witnessed rapid growth in the manufacturing sector. Exports contributed 5.1 per cent to manufacturing, whereas ISI accounted for 24.5 per cent. The annual average growth rate for industry in the 1950s was 10 per cent compared to 2.5 per cent for the primary sector and 3.9 per cent for the service sector. Rhee had therefore succeeded in channelling US project aid predominantly into manufacturing, transportation, and electric power (Woo 1991, pp. 49–59). However, his ISI programme also led to severe economic difficulties. Inflation remained high throughout the 1950s and the currency was overvalued. The need for large quantities of chemical fertilisers in particular exacerbated the shortage of foreign exchange (Stubbs 2005, pp. 106–107). It was these endemic economic problems combined with the increasing political weakness of the incumbent government that led to the student revolution of April 1960 and to the downfall of the Rhee regime.

As in Korea, the KMT in Taiwan sought to facilitate a general crackdown on labour and the left in the late 1940s. This anti-labour stance was something quite different than that expressed in the founding platform of the KMT. In the immediate aftermath of the 1911 Xinhai revolution, the KMT's founder Sun Yat-sen had in fact given strong support to the formation of labour unions in foreign-invested companies and sought to promote the participation of workers via their unions in the economic affairs of the country (Kleingartner and Peng 1991, p. 430; Pan 2006). However, during the course of the civil war, the Chinese Communist Party (CCP) had gained the upper hand vis-à-vis the KMT under Chiang Kai-Shek by organising workers and rallying them around the struggle against foreign exploitation, capitalism, and militarism. The KMT, following a brief alliance with the CCP, had turned on labour through a massacre of communist labour leaders and workers in 1927. As such, the KMT's experience on the mainland had already led it to view labour as something to be controlled rather than allied with, and thus, it sought to impose a form of state corporatism to constrain labour and other social groups. As an alternative to the communist All-China Federation of Trade Unions, the KMT established the Chinese Federation of Labour (CFL) in 1935, under which all labour and union activities were to be placed. All workers were required to join unions and all unions had to be members of the CFL (Ho 1990, p. 11). This form of labour subordination was underpinned by a set of authoritarian labour laws aimed at demobilising workers, such as the Labour Union Law passed in 1929, the Labour–Management Dispute Settlement Law passed in 1928, and the Collective Agreement Law passed in 1930. Although these laws had little influence during the KMT's rule on the mainland, they provided a comprehensive legal framework for constraining labour activities following the retreat to Taiwan (Hsu 1989, pp. 3–4).

In comparison to Korea, there was little in the way of a workers' uprising following the departure of the Japanese. Taiwan's role in the regional political economy had been more that of agricultural producer. Although the island did undergo a degree of dependent capitalist industrialisation and a concomitant process of proletarianisation and semi-proletarianisation, in contrast with Korea, Taiwan's integration into the Japanese formal empire had led to a weaker process of working-class formation. Indeed, by 1930, there were still only around 87,000 factory workers (Lai 199 pp. 52–53). In comparative terms, Taiwan did not play any significant role in Japan's imperialist expansion until 1941, when an economic and industrial policy was established to enable Taiwan to facilitate Japan's expansion in Southeast Asia. However, in 1941, the number of industrial workers was still only 137,000, though double that of 1931 (Nakano 1998, p. 4). As a result, the colonial experience was overall considerably less disruptive for Taiwan. Whereas Korea experienced frequent rebellions and guerrilla movements as well as large population shifts from the land, Taiwanese agriculture was more productive and experienced less social turmoil. The result was also that Taiwan's nationalist impulse was weaker than that of Korea's (Cumings 1984, pp. 11–12).

These weaker processes of working-class formation did not mean that a workers' movement was completely absent in colonial Taiwan. The regional prevalence of socialist ideas and movements meant that left-wing activists took a leading role in the mobilisation of collective campaigns against Japanese capitalists. Between 1925 and 1933, the number of labour organisations in Taiwan rose from 10 to 127, with a rise in membership from 1,608 to 21,957. The number of participants in labour confrontations increased sharply between 1926 and 1931, with workers' collectivism reaching a high point in 1930 (Lai 1993, p. 53). This rise in labour unrest and other social movements enabled leftists in April 1928 to establish the Taiwanese Communist Party (TCP). The TCP was established in Shanghai as a 'Nationality Branch of the Japanese Communist Party,' emphasising class struggle and the overthrow of Japanese imperial rule. However, the party experienced intense internal struggles over political strategy between those allied with the Japanese Communist Party, which was experiencing its own factional tensions in the 1920s, and those more closely aligned to the Chinese Communist Party and its pro-peasant strategy. The Comintern also exerted a strong influence on the TCP and the shifts in the

Third International's line following the Sixth Comintern Congress also acted as a constraint on the party (Hsiao and Sullivan 1983). The year of the establishment of the TCP had also seen the establishment of the Federation of Taiwanese Workers, which was established with the aim of mobilising workers to engage in strikes and other forms of industrial action. However, this workers' movement was heavily repressed by the Japanese authorities. As in Korea and Japan itself, the outbreak of the Sino-Japanese war led to a crackdown on labour movement activists and their organisations. In 1931, large numbers of left-wing activists were imprisoned, with many of them receiving long sentences. The repression of the TCP in 1933 furthermore marked the final demise of the colonial labour movement in Taiwan. Those activists who were not imprisoned by and large escaped to mainland China to participate in the revolution there (Lai 1993, p. 55). Thus, as the KMT established its control over the island in 1945, it found it relatively easy to eliminate any remnants of the left, and was not faced with any significant worker unrest.

KMT repression was not limited to the left, however. It is widely acknowledged that a key factor in the KMT's defeat in the civil war on the mainland was the regime's endemic corruption and incompetence. Following the surrender of Japan and the end of the Second World War, furthermore, the KMT did little better in Taiwan. As Denny Roy has argued, the arrival of KMT troops in Taiwan was followed by widespread confiscation of both Japanese and Taiwanese property in order to fund the continuing war effort on the mainland. Governor-General Chen Yi sought to impose an economic model of state socialism which involved government-controlled monopolies of more than 90 per cent of the economy, leaving the local Taiwanese community largely excluded (Roy 2003, pp. 60–67). Furthermore, in line with its experience on the mainland, the KMT government quickly became known in Taiwan for its nepotism and arrogance. This animosity culminated on 28th February 1947, when protests against KMT rule led to the massacre of tens of thousands of local Taiwanese. The killing was not indiscriminate, however, and was directed toward the social bases of potential resistance to mainlander rule on Taiwan, including Taiwanese intellectuals and the middle and upper classes (Gold 1986, p. 51). Whilst the heavy-handed nature by which the KMT established its authority on Taiwan shaped the intense ethnic rivalry between the local Taiwanese and the mainlander KMT that would shape Taiwanese politics and society from the 1980s, it did for a time eliminate the possibility of further resistance to KMT rule during the immediate post-war decades. Nonetheless, the retreat of the KMT to Taiwan and its capacity for repression provided for a level of state autonomy that had simply been unattainable on the mainland. Yet, as in Korea, a specifically *developmental* orientation did not materialise immediately. The immediate concern of Chiang Kai-shek upon his retreat to Taiwan was the retaking of the mainland, and this overriding military objective led to the neglect of Taiwan as a going economic concern.

The experience of Taiwan serves as further evidence that rapid catch-up development must be explained with reference to the role of the United States in facilitating a region-wide passive revolution. The relationship between the United States and the KMT was by no means smooth, however. Following the entry of the United States into the Pacific War in 1941, the KMT became a key American ally and recipient of massive amounts of US military aid. Even after the end of the war, the United States continued to provide generous funding for the KMT's civil war with the CCP. However, the KMT's loss of the mainland led the United States to distance itself from the KMT, announcing in early 1950 that it would no longer provide military aid and advice and, as such, appeared to be ready to abandon both the KMT and Taiwan to the advancing CCP forces (Roy 2003, pp. 108–110). It was only the attempt of Kim Il-Sung's Korean People's Army to reunify the Korean peninsula in June 1950 that led the United States to reverse this policy of distancing itself from the KMT. Literally overnight, KMT-ruled Taiwan was transformed from 'lost cause' into strategically vital forward defence state. The US Seventh Fleet was immediately dispatched to the Taiwan Straits, and channels of economic and military aid were reopened.

In addition to securing the existence of Taiwan as a *de facto* political entity through military defence of the island, the United States also played a key role in shoring up the relative autonomy of the KMT state. Whilst the KMT had initially established this autonomy through brute force, the United States helped the KMT to secure its rule on a more consensual basis through widespread land reform. Overseen by the Sino-American Joint Commission on Rural Reconstruction, the land reform took place in three stages. The first involved the 'confiscation of enemy property' whereby Japanese properties were seized, amounting to a total of 20 per cent of all arable land. The second stage involved the imposition of rent reductions, whereby rents were limited to 37.5 per cent of the value of the major crop. The third and final stage of the reform was the 'land to the tiller' stage, in which an additional 16 per cent of all arable lands were expropriated and subject to compulsory sale (Wiegersma and Medley 2000, pp. 39–40). The lack of resistance on the part of the KMT to land reform stemmed from the realisation that on the mainland the KMT's social basis in the landlord class and resultant failure to carry out land reform was a key factor in the widespread peasant discontent and phenomenal success of the CCP. Land reform in Taiwan was facilitated by the fact that the majority of landowners were local Taiwanese with no political influence (McBeath 1997, p. 1147).

In comparison to the CCP's reform on the mainland, the Taiwanese land reform was relatively bloodless, though this should be understood in the context of the harsh repression of the preceding years. Very few families were unaffected by the violence of 1946–7, so the lack of resistance to the ensueing land reform was hardly surprising (Gold 1986, p. 66). As in Korea, the reform played a key role in establishing a basis for subsequent industrialisation, as rising agricultural productivity provided a source of rapid labour transfers into industry as well as a significant source of domestic savings. Furthermore, agricultural exports provided a key source of foreign exchange during the 1950s and helped to finance the initial capital and raw material imports required by the growing industrial sector (Ho 1978, p. 106). The KMT also provided generous compensation to dispossessed landowners, which itself facilitated a transfer of wealth to the private industrial sector, thereby stimulating development (Jacoby 1966, pp. 109–110). Furthermore, as in Japan and Korea, the Taiwanese land reform secured a degree of legitimacy insofar as the basis for social discontent and mobilisation in the countryside was greatly reduced. The reform also meant that Taiwan's economic development was relatively equitable as a result. Nonetheless, with the landlord class swept from power, the state took over the role of squeezing agriculture for the purposes of fuelling the industrialisation drive. The government's 'fertiliser exchange policy' was significant in this respect. Farmers had to pay for their fertiliser with rice from a government-controlled monopoly, the Taiwan Fertilizer Corporation, on terms that were very unfavourable to the farmers. Political control over the countryside also remained strong as farmers were organised into associations and incorporated into the KMT's corporatist structure. As a consequence, the retreat of the KMT to Taiwan and the land reform and repression of the late 1940s laid the basis for the autonomy of the post-war developmental state. As Thomas Gold (1986, p. 64) has argued:

> Between 1947 and 1949, Taiwan's old intellectual and political elites had been liquidated. There was no indigenous capitalist or financial class to challenge the regime economically. Taiwan had no warlords. Peasants were not mobilized or agitating for land reform. There was no organized political movement nor armed force to threaten KMT-mainlander hegemony. Because on the one hand, the regime faced no internal opposition and, on the other, as an external occupying force it had no base with Taiwanese society, it had free rein for activity.

In this respect, the KMT's domination of society was more thorough and complete than that of Korea's authoritarian governments. The KMT resurrected its highly restrictive labour laws established on the mainland, which served to severely constrain any scope for resistance by workers. It stipulated, for example, a mandatory death sentence for those striking or inciting strikes and restricted freedom of speech, publishing, assembly, association, and movement in and out of the country. Definitions of conspiracy, disturbing public peace, sedition, spreading rumours, and 'crimes against the safety of the Republic' criminalised a host of activities which would normally be considered the exercise of labour rights (Lai 1993). Whilst the KMT inherited many of the colonial mechanisms of social and political control in Taiwan (Gold 1988, pp. 116–117), state autonomy was also institutionalised through the organisational structure of the KMT itself. Whilst KMT ideology was one of virulent anticommunism, the KMT was rather unusual in that this was combined with a Leninist party structure that existed alongside and was often indistinguishable from the state. Through this structure, key social groups, including labour, were integrated into the party in corporatist fashion (Ho 2007). In this corporatist structure, which remained largely intact until the 1980s, there were few areas of social life that were not brought into the political system. A vast array of local-level organisations and special-interest groups were integrated into the sprawling state apparatus. Furthermore, the KMT did not simply confine itself to repression or co-optation, but deployed a range of mechanisms of control and co-optation throughout a wide variety of institutional spheres to prevent conflict getting out of hand. As such, the state only intervened directly when these mechanisms fail to operate effectively (Hsu 1989, p. 5).

In comparison to the intransigence of the Rhee government in Korea, which was able to exploit the contradictions in US objectives for its own goals, the KMT was more open to the influence of US advisers. Dependence on US aid gave American policymakers *de facto* veto over the KMT's economic policies. Indeed, the KMT was more compliant with US strategy compared to its own experience on the mainland, where it had been notorious for the manner in which it was able to bend US will to provide aid with few strings attached through threatening to abandon the war effort and make a separate peace with Japan. As suggested above with the issue of land reform, this closer alignment between US aid bureaucrats and the KMT on Taiwan can be explained with reference to the KMT's 'turning over a new leaf' upon its arrival on the island. It should be recognised, however, that there was little commitment within the US State Department or US military for continued support for the KMT regime. The US aid administration was the only entity willing to provide resources to the KMT; whilst aid bureaucrats demanded a high price in terms of reform, the KMT had little choice but to comply (Barrett 1988, pp. 130–133). US aid bureaucrats were thus from the outset able to exert stronger influence on the KMT's policymaking in the early years of its rule on Taiwan. For example, US aid pressured the KMT to encourage the growth of the private sector, and indeed, without the influence and active intervention by US aid bureaucrats, it is unlikely that the private sector would have become the primary source of economic growth (Ho 1978, p. 117). US aid thus provided much of the capital with which the KMT was able to nurture the growth of a private capitalist class. The state promoted capitalists in key sectors, such as cotton textiles and flour milling, and supplied venture capital through the Small Industry Loan Fund and Model Factory Program. In short, this supply of capital unleashed a productive boom on the island. Infant industries were protected through multiple exchange rates, tariffs, and import restrictions, making Taiwan's ISI programme extraordinarily successful (Gold 1986, p. 72).

Labour and export-led industrialisation

As noted, Syngman Rhee had resisted the reincorporation of Korea into the Japan-centred political economy and instead pursued a policy of ISI, which by the late 1950s was becoming increasingly less viable. Failing to produce significant economic growth, Korea's continued dependency on US military and economic aid led to a reorientation of US policy. Whereas George Kennan's policy of containment had viewed Korea as little more than a neocolonial adjunct to the Japanese economy, the incoming Kennedy administration sought to facilitate a shift from big military budgets and ISI to a new era of export-oriented growth and the adoption of Rostovian ideas on economic development (Woo 1991, pp. 73–78).

Following the intransigence of the Rhee government, the opportunity to engineer such a transition came in the form of the political turmoil at the turn of the decade, out of which emerged General Park Chung-Hee's *coup d'état* of 1961. In April 1960, student-led protests erupted in the southern city of Masan against electoral corruption and a high school student was killed by a tear gas canister. After the student's body was found washed up on the beach, the authorities sought to cover up his death by claiming that the student had drowned. As protests extended to Seoul, students marched on the presidential Blue House, whereupon approximately 200 were shot dead with many more wounded. On 19th April, Syngman Rhee finally stepped down as president. The demise of the Rhee regime led to a resurgence of labour demonstrations and disputes, this time joined by white-collar workers and public-sector workers. As Deyo (1989, p. 120) has argued, during this ensuing short political liberal interlude, unions flourished, particularly amongst white-collar and public-sector workers. The number of registered unions increased from 621 to 821, union membership grew by 25,000, and disputes and stoppages escalated sharply. Especially prominent in this outburst of labour unrest was the Korean Teachers' League, along with railroad and other state enterprise workers, as well as textile workers. This expansion of labour unionism demonstrated that the violent destruction of *Chŏnp'yŏng* in the late 1940s had not eradicated the roots of the radical labour movement.

The failure of the subsequent Chang Myŏn government to tackle this increased social disorder thus provoked Park's military *coup d'état* in May 1961. This increased prominence of the military can be seen as a longer-term consequence of the US intervention following the country's incorporation into the US-centred regional order. As Cumings (1984, p. 26) has argued, America's nurturing of the military gave disciplined training and basic literacy to a mass of young people whilst rearing officers and managers who later populated state bureaucracies and big corporations. Furthermore, the military played a decisive role in the reintegration of Korea into the Japan-centred regional political economy. Indeed, Park's military junta immediately sought to restructure state–society relations in a direction more conducive to rapid catch-up industrialisation. As noted above, state–business relations under the Rhee government had been highly corrupt. Following a populist anti-corruption campaign aimed at 'illicit profiteers,' the junta reached a deal with ten major business leaders whereby criminal prosecutions were dropped in exchange for promises to establish specific industrial firms and donate shares to the government. As the developmental state literature has widely documented, this led to a model of political economy in which business lacked its own access to capital outside government provision of credit. Capital was thus strategically directed toward those industrial sectors deemed by the bureaucracy to have the greatest potential on export markets.

Following the coup, the junta also sought to re-establish control in labour relations. During the latter years of the Rhee regime, the Federation of Korean Trade Unions (*Daehan Noch'ong*) was increasingly challenged by a dissident minority group known as the National Council of Trade Unions (*Nohyŏp*). Following the downfall of Rhee, *Nohyŏp* had taken an increasingly militant posture and established an alliance with the Korean Teachers' League, the most organised and radical union during this brief interlude. Park's junta thus moved to re-establish control over the labour movement through the newly established Korean Central Intelligence Agency (KCIA), headed by Park's ally Kim Jong-Pil. The KCIA was an elaborate and effective security apparatus whose authority extended into all fields of government and politics. After arresting the radical labour leaders at the forefront of labour unrest under the Chang Myŏn government, the KCIA selected a group of moderate labour representatives to be trained in labour union organising. However, this organising was to be achieved in a purely top-down corporatist manner, beginning with the establishment of a new national centre, *Han'guk No'chong* (also known in English as the Federation of Korean Trade Unions, FKTU) (Choi 1984, p. 30). Although enterprise-level collective bargaining was retained, the FKTU was headed by a leadership whose selection and subsequent behaviour were strongly influenced by the government; as such, the organisation became an important watchdog over local labour affairs. No craft or occupational unions were permitted. At the same time, new legislation empowered the earlier established Labour Committees with increased government representation so as to dismiss 'illegal' union demands at the outset of mediation efforts, as well as to unilaterally deregister unions and dictate the terms of settlement (Deyo 1989, p. 121). The military junta also required enterprise unions to register with one of seventeen industrial federations. Unions in the textile, metal, chemical, and transport sectors were all organised into their industrial federations, and each industrial federation was required join the FKTU (Ogle 1990, p. 15). As such, a thoroughly repressive labour regime had been re-imposed on Korea's workers by the time of the country's transition to export-oriented industrialisation (EOI) in the mid-1960s.

Indeed, whereas Rhee had stubbornly resisted re-establishing Korea's subordinate position vis-à-vis the Japanese economy and had pursued a policy of ISI whilst seeking the maximisation of US aid, Park's coup provided an opportunity for the United States to push for a change in economic strategy. Initially, Park's economic policies had been directed toward the construction of a 'self-reliant economy.' His first five-year plan had spoken of mobilising a 'guided capitalism' to build a heavy-industrial base, funded by primary commodity exports (Hart-Landsberg 1993, p. 140). The failure of this self-reliance strategy led Park to submit to US pressures to re-establish trading relations with Japan, at the same time continuing to pursue an illiberal developmental state model of catch-up industrialisation though directed toward exports. In reality, Park was the perfect figure to carry out this shift toward EOI. As a former officer in the Japanese army, Park was strongly influenced by Japanese ideas concerning the active role of the state in bringing about industrialisation (Moon and Jun 2011) and, despite a number of 'liberalisation measures' imposed by the United States was able to maintain protection of the domestic economy and a strong interventionist role for the state. Whilst the re-establishment of diplomatic relations with Japan took place amidst widespread public opposition, it opened up a new source of capital in the context of declining US aid. Although the Japanese had intended the capital to be used for investment in light industry, it quickly found its way into other industries, notably steel: a project that had previously been shunned by all foreign countries as well as the World Bank as unrealistic (Woo 1991, pp. 87–88).

The defeat of the radical labour leaders at the outset of the decade and the imposition of a restrictive legal framework governing labour relations meant that Korea was well positioned for a transition toward EOI. However, this development strategy was also based on Korea's surplus of labour, which meant low wages and an extraordinary degree of competitiveness on international markets. It also meant that, in the 1960s at least, the Korean government's labour policy for the most part hardly required much in the way of continued state repression because the large reserve army of labour meant that repression could mostly take place through market mechanisms. The Korean economy suffered from severe unemployment and underemployment; thus, workers were more concerned with gaining any employment opportunity than with achieving wage gains or more favourable working conditions (Park 1992, pp. 326–327). This is not to say that no labour protests took place in the 1960s, however. Intolerable working conditions, delayed payments, and extremely long working hours (usually more than twelve hours a day) inevitably led to some degree of resistance by workers. However, these were rarely if at all organised by trade unions. Instead, they tended to take the form of spontaneous responses to hyper-exploitation and were almost invariably suppressed through employer and police repression (Chang 2009, p. 97).

Taiwan did not experience an equivalent to the recalcitrant Rhee government in Korea, and as noted, from the first decade of the KMT's rule on Taiwan, there was relative agreement between KMT and US policymakers on what the appropriate economic strategy should be for Taiwan. Thus, not only was the United States able to deploy the carrot and stick of aid to influence the KMT's economic policy, but the United States played a central role in Taiwan's industrialisation through the provision of its own market as the key source of demand. The KMT's first four-year development plan (1953–6) entailed an ISI programme that sought to promote amongst other industries the domestic production of cement, glass, fertilizer, and textiles. Only the export of agricultural products was encouraged (Hsueh *et al.* 2001, p. 14). This strategy was supported by the United States because it was recognised that Taiwan did not have either a dynamic private sector or sufficient infrastructure that could uphold a recovery programme such as the Marshall Plan (Tsai 2001, p. 104).

By the late 1950s, however, this ISI programme ran into difficulties, thus prompting a change in economic strategy. The domestic market was already saturated for many kinds of consumer goods and an increasing number of firms were facing bankruptcy (Wade 1990, p. 109). However, as in Korea, the KMT's dependence on US aid provided the latter with a crucial lever over which it was able to influence Taiwan's overall industrialisation strategy. The KMT was thus compelled to devise a new strategy that could form the basis of a more self-sufficient capitalist forward defence state free of dependence on US aid. The United States demanded the introduction of a uniform and realistic exchange rate, a reduction of military expenditures, noninflationary fiscal and monetary policies, tax reforms, liberalisation of foreign exchange controls, and privatisation of state enterprises. Subsequently, a nineteen-point proposal drawn up by the Council for US Aid emphasised the need for investment promotion, restriction of consumption, and the encouragement of exports. Significantly, however, the proposal did not end the protection of selective industries and state monopolies; rather, it provided incentives for the emergence of new export industries alongside the domestic market. Thus, the ISI strategy continued to exist alongside EOI (Ngo 2005, pp. 104–105). Compared to Korea, Taiwan saw less in the way of the formal provision of aid from the Japanese government, but the shift in economic strategy nonetheless led to the emergence of Taiwan as a key site of investment for Japanese as well as American firms. US aid officials took an active role in promoting Taiwan as an attractive investment site, and from the mid-1960s, Taiwan also became a key part in both Japanese and American production networks (Gold 1986, p. 79).

In contrast to Korea, however, there was more continuity in the form of labour regime underpinning EOI. As noted above, the KMT sought to impose the state-corporatist model of industrial relations that it had developed earlier in mainland China. This state corporatism was facilitated by the KMT's own Leninist party structure, in which party cadres at the grassroots level were able to exert a high level of control. According to the principles of democratic centralism, all party branches were required to adhere to the policy made by the Central Standing Committee of the KMT (Lee 2007a, p. 7). The CFL formed the peak labour body within this state-corporatist system. As with the KMT itself, the CFL was transferred from mainland China and imposed on Taiwanese workers whilst maintaining its claim to represent the whole of China. Representatives elected in the mainland became life members of the CFL congress on Taiwan, ostensibly until such time as national elections could be held again on the mainland. In the 1970s, the rules were changed to allow supplementary members to be appointed to the CFL National Council, though this was only to replace those senior members who had died or had failed to accompany the KMT in its retreat to Taiwan in 1949 (Ho 1990, p. 12). As such, there was little chance of the CFL taking an independent line from the government. As the sole national 'representative' of labour, the CFL received funding from the KMT, and the CFL directorship was reserved for those with close political and personal ties with the KMT leadership. Whilst it was compulsory for unions to be members of the CFL, such membership did not confer any union influence on the CFL's policy-making. Needless to say, the CFL did not use this privileged access to government policymaking to champion the rights of workers (Ho 2006a, p. 111). Furthermore, the KMT used the CFL as an organisational network to establish 'clientele' relations with workers, particularly to mobilise their votes during local elections. It is important to point out in this regard that, even under the martial law, the KMT did not prohibit electoral contestation altogether. It permitted local elections from the 1950s onwards as a strategy of *trasformismo* to incorporate the local Taiwanese and to stabilise the government's rule over the island. As such, the KMT candidates running in these local elections often drew CFL cadres into their election campaigns and assigned them to encourage the votes of union members (Lee 2011, p. 59). The CFL also played an important role in Taiwan's foreign relations after Taiwan was expelled from the United Nations in 1971 and became an key conduit for Taiwan's foreign policy (Rice 2006, p. 165).

Below the level of the CFL, there existed two kinds of unions in Taiwan: 'industrial unions' (*chanye gonghui*) and 'occupational unions' (*zhiye gonghui*). Both terms are somewhat misleading, however. Industrial unions do not, in fact, refer to unions organised to represent workers in an entire industry but are effectively enterprise unions established in workplaces with more than 30 employees. Thus, even if a single company had multiple workplaces, each workplace was required to have its own individual union and to join the appropriate regional federation. This structure was enforced by the KMT as a means of weakening the strength and unity of unions and impeding the development of horizontal solidarity between workers (Huang 2002, p. 312; Zhu 2008, p. 70). The exception to this rule was the state-owned enterprises, which were allowed to form a single union for all workers within the company and, as such, were able to exert their influence beyond a single locality. Occupational unions, on the other hand, could be organised by groups of more than 30 workers (including the self-employed) in the same city or county. They were as a consequence easier to organise than industrial unions but were even less likely to engage in collective action on behalf of their members as a result of their more diverse socioeconomic constituency and fractious interests. Indeed, the primary motivation for workers to join occupational unions was that membership was a prerequisite for access to government-supported labour insurance. It is questionable, therefore, whether they can properly be regarded as labour unions, and as such, their role in inflating the relatively high unionisation rate in Taiwan should be taken into account. Indeed, it was not the occupational unions but the industrial unions, particularly those in state-owned enterprises, that played the central role in the emerging independent labour movement of the 1980s (Ho 2006a, pp. 112–113).

Thus, as in Korea during the Park Chung-Hee era, trade unions in Taiwan ultimately served as institutions of control rather than organisations representing workers' interests. The KMT supported and subsidised union activities, and workers were required to join unions where they existed. Newly organised unions and their officials required approval by local KMT committees, and because unions included within their ranks all enterprise employees, managers and supervisors were able to become union officials. Local KMT cadres could also assume important leadership roles (Deyo 1989, pp. 117–118). Under this system, the role of unions was therefore one of mediation rather than interest representation. Local government agencies regulated unions and made it illegal for strikes to be called prior to mediation and arbitration, making strikes all but impossible to carry out. Furthermore, unions were unable to demand an increase in wages that exceeded the 'standard wage' – a vague category determined by the government, which enabled them to declare any wage demand illegal (Deyo 1989, pp. 115–116). Thus, the KMT's controls were as secure at the grassroots level as they were at the national level. Being a KMT member was a precondition for nomination as an official candidate in union elections, and opportunities for higher union posts or political status were held out only to the most compliant unionists (Lee 2007a, pp. 6–7). As such, prior to the mid-1980s, Taiwanese trade unions should be understood as administrative arms of the government for the implementation of the national industrialisation effort (Chen *et al.* 2003, p. 319). This overarching system of social control, which extended right down to the local level, made actual government involvement in the day-to-day resolution of labour disputes largely unnecessary. Most disputes were resolved through *ad hoc* mediating committees organised at the enterprise level; thus, there was little need for a nationally integrated administrative structure to deal with labour disputes (Deyo 1989, p. 117).

An example of the proactive role of the KMT in establishing unions can be seen in the case of the Taiwan Railway Labour Union (TRLU), one of the earliest and most important unions in Taiwan. The TRLU was established in 1947 with the full support of the party-state. The KMT provided guidance during the establishment of the TRLU, as well as full financial support. The union can thus be seen not as providing any indication of labour consciousness but as a mechanism of party control (Lee 2007a, p. 7). The TRLU's founding mission statement, as presented at the TRLU's inaugural meeting in 1947, gave a clear indication of the union's relationship with the government (quoted in Lee 2007a, p. 8):

> We will never hesitate to sacrifice ourselves in support of the government to eliminate rebellion in order to preserve our national independence and territory intact. We will fight against those who attempt to ruin our nation's unity and to obstruct social progress to the end.

Emerging contradictions of East Asian capitalism

As has been argued, the regional post-war passive revolution involved a top-down reorganisation of social relations in a manner commensurate with successful capitalist industrialisation. A combination of geopolitical contingency and historical legacies conducive to successful catch-up industrialisation meant that, in contrast to Latin America, for example, labour subordination in East Asia was achieved prior to the transition toward export-led industrialisation (Deyo 1989, p. 133), facilitating the integration of Korea and Taiwan into what Arrighi *et al.* (1993) have termed the Japanese 'multilayered subcontracting system.' This regional dimension of East Asian development is crucial to understanding the extraordinary dynamism of the region. Actual advances in the value-added hierarchy of the capitalist world economy did not begin until Korea and Taiwan were re-integrated into the hierarchically organised East Asian regional political economy, centred on Japan and extending outwards toward the immediate East Asian periphery as well as to Southeast Asia (Arrighi 1996). Ultimately, this regional system depended on the US market as an outlet for its manufactured goods, although the core of this regional system, particularly after the decline of US aid in the 1960s, was Japanese capital and technology (Gills 2000, pp. 389–390). However, this regional passive revolution itself contained within it the seeds of its own demise because it contributed to deepening the contradictions between America's global hegemonic role and its more immediate 'national interests.' That the East Asian passive revolution took the form of a specifically *developmental* form of state also meant that the concomitant form of state–society relations could not remain frozen in time since industrialisation itself provoked molecular changes in the social relations of production that would undermine the comprehensive subordination of labour. It was the dynamic interaction between these two sets of contradictions – the one at the geopolitical level and the other at the level of the social relations of production – that led to the subsequent transformation of the region. As Bruce Cumings has argued (1984, p. 20),

> [t]he strategic lines of the new Northeast Asian political economy … brought the peculiar nature of American hegemony to the fore. There is a paradox at the heart of it: nonterritorial in contrast to Old World imperialism, organising great spaces and knocking down the barriers to trade, it has outer limits sufficient to keep countries *in* the system but not sufficient to maintain effective dependency relations or a frozen hierarchy. The system permits upward mobility.

Indeed, it was precisely this upward mobility that served to challenge the willingness of the United States to maintain this arrangement. In addition, the failure of the United States to divide the Vietnamese nation along Cold War lines forced the United States to readmit China to normal commercial and diplomatic intercourse with the rest of Asia (Arrighi *et al.* 2003, p. 310). In the short term, these geopolitical events did not immediately have an adverse impact upon Korea or Taiwan but actually acted as a spur to development. South Vietnam's own developmental quagmire and the massive US-led war effort there provided a significant boost to the Korean and Taiwanese economies. As Richard Stubbs has argued, from the mid-1960s, there was a rapid increase in spending in Taiwanese exports to South Vietnam. Importantly, these were exports in Taiwan's nascent heavy industries, such as cement, iron and steel, aluminium products, machinery, and transportation equipment. There was also an explosion of demand within the US market, which Taiwan was well placed to take advantage of, establishing a rapid surplus by the early 1970s. For Korea too, just as the Korean War had provided the impetus for the revival of the Japanese economy through military procurement, the Vietnam War served as an opportunity for further growth and industrial upgrading through contracts for Korea's nascent conglomerates and dollar earnings as a result of the Korean military's participation in the war (Stubbs 2005, pp. 131–133). For the United States, however, the outflow of dollars associated with the war effort was, conversely, an increasing burden and had a long-term impact upon the nature of the US hegemony in East Asia. President Nixon sought to tackle the growing US balance of payments deficit by attacking its root causes, including the dollar outflows that were part of the costs of maintaining its wider US empire in Asia (Woo 1991, p. 121). This involved a reassessment of America's role in the provision of direct military assistance in policing the international system. Indeed, the Nixon Doctrine held that 'Asian hands must shape the Asian future,' meaning that immediate self-defence responsibilities should be transferred to military forces.

Although this shift in US strategy also reflected the growing industrial strength and defensive capabilities of late developers such as Korea and Taiwan, it was interpreted by the latter countries' leaderships as portending an existential crisis. In Korea, this change in US policy occurred in the midst of a deteriorating relationship with North Korea. Park Chung-Hee saw the Nixon Doctrine and, in particular, the withdrawal of the Seventh Division of the US Eighth Army from Korea as a weakening of the US commitment to defend the country against its northern neighbour. This perception was reinforced when Nixon announced that he was opening diplomatic relations with the People's Republic of China in 1972 (Shorrock 1986, p. 1197). Park Chung-Hee's heavy and chemical industrialisation (HCI) programme, launched in January 1973, was a direct response to these challenges. Owing to the legacies of Japanese colonialism, North Korea had a strong heavy industrial manufacturing base and was a successful producer of steel, which in turn formed the backbone of its armaments industry. Thus, Park's promotion of a massive state-owned steel works (POSCO) in the southeastern city of P'ohang was clearly motivated by the perceived necessity to catch up with or even surpass the North. This security and self-sufficiency motivation of the HCI programme was also evident in the Ch'angwŏn Machine-Building Industrial Complex, which was established to both build machines for other industries and to form a vital part of an autonomous defence industry, was located on the southeastern coast, as far from the border with the North as possible (Woo 1991, pp. 133–144).

The political counterpart to the HCI drive was the *Yushin* regime. Martial law was declared, and what remained of the façade of liberal democracy was abandoned with the dissolution of the National Assembly. Park thereby enjoyed unlimited decree powers and strengthened the role of the police, KCIA, and military intelligence. In 1970, the Park regime had already passed new laws restricting the rights of unions to engage in collective bargaining and strikes in order to attract foreign investment in the heavy and chemical sector. This was followed by a further legal reform in 1971, which restricted the collective actions of workers further if they were deemed to risk 'undermining national security.' Unions were henceforth required to request arbitration from the government before engaging in collective bargaining or industrial action. Finally, in 1973, all work stoppages became illegal, thereby abandoning any pretence of democracy in Korean labour relations (Chang 2009, p. 101). Ideological indoctrination was intensified in the form of the Factory *Saemaŭl* movement as a means of enhancing labour productivity and workers' compliance in the workplace (Lee 2011, p. 54). This did not mean that the government banned unions altogether. In line with the principles of state corporatism, union membership was permitted and even encouraged. The aim was to have unions serve as a mechanism of control over labour, and indeed some companies had 'union shop' clauses in which employees were required to join the union. What was strictly proscribed was any form of collective bargaining, let alone industrial action (Park 1992, p. 328).

These changes in US policy toward the East Asian region arguably had even more profound implications for the fate of Taiwan as both an economic and political entity. In reality, the guarantee by the United States of Taiwan's existence as a distinct state was always secondary to the wider dynamics of US–China relations. The Truman administration had, prior to the outbreak of the Korean War, appeared ready to abandon Taiwan when it appeared that it might be possible to break China away from the Soviet Union. That possibility arose again following the Sino–Soviet split of the 1960s. As relations between China and the United States warmed, the

KMT regime on Taiwan appeared increasingly expendable. Whilst the Taiwan Relations Act of 1979 did stress a continued US commitment to Taiwan's security, Taipei continued to suffer numerous diplomatic setbacks, including the expulsion of Taiwan from the United Nations. Taiwan's response to these challenges showed some significant similarities with that of Korea's, however. The KMT government sought to stimulate the economy through a large-scale industrial programme called the 'Ten Major Construction Projects,' announced by Chiang Ching-Kuo in 1974. These projects included a national highway linking Keelung to Kaohsiung city, the electrification of the Western Line railway, a North-Link Line railway, the Chiang Kai-Shek airport, Taichung and Su-ao Ports, the China Shipbuilding Corporation Shipyard in Kaohsiung, an oil refinery and industrial park, and a nuclear power plant. The Ten Major Construction Projects formed part of a broader aggressive strategy of compensating for Taiwan's growing diplomatic isolation and overcoming its vulnerability to global economic instability by building up heavy and chemical industries and modernising Taiwan's infrastructure. These aims underpinned the Six-Year Plan (1976–1981), which replaced the Sixth Four-Year Plan that had been scrapped in 1975 due to the adverse impact of the world economic recession. The Six-Year Plan focused in particular on steel and petrochemicals. Whilst projects such as the integrated steel mill were originally intended as a joint state-private enterprise, the state was forced to take a 100 per cent ownership after private investors pulled out. In 1977, the newly formed pilot agency, the Council for Economic Planning and Development (CEPD), devised a new inventive package to channel capital into strategic industries such as computers, telecommunications, and robotics. As part of this broader industrial upgrading strategy, the CEPD planned to let labour-intensive industries, such as textiles and footwear, decline and placed pressure on five unstable synthetic-textile manufacturers to merge to create economies of scale, upgrade technology, and improve their global competitive position (Gold 1986, pp. 100–102).

Despite these significant changes in Taiwan's industrialisation strategy, there was little accompanying change in labour legislation, although there were, as in Korea, attempts to strengthen the state-corporatist labour regime. The KMT's top-down control over labour was intensified so as to address labour disputes more quickly. This involved founding new unions, recruiting union activists into the party, reserving leadership positions for party members, and planting party cells inside workplaces to monitor labour activities. Unions continued to be limited to workplaces with thirty employees or more, and for the unorganised small and medium enterprises, labour disputes were handled through compulsory arbitration. This would involve the establishment by the city or county governments of a Labour Dispute Arbitration Board, which effectively prohibited any lockout, strike, or work slowdown without first going through compulsory arbitration, thereby making industrial action all but impossible (Liu 2011, pp. 28–29). As such, these state-led measures were designed to increase the scope for the resolution of disputes at the grassroots level and to encourage paternalistic personnel practices. Factory councils came to play a bigger role in the resolution of disputes, and there was an expansion of the role of the employee welfare fund. This 'state-mandated enterprise paternalism' was further strengthened by encouraging employer support for company unions. The government increased pressure on employers to establish unions and for unions to assume key welfare functions in organising health and education programmes for workers. As such, these measures actually obviated the need for a direct state role in the management of employment relations. Furthermore, they served to tie workers ever more tightly to their employers by bonds of obligation and self-interest. The strength of these managerial controls is evident in the absence of state involvement in wage setting and the reliance on informal settlement procedures and nongovernment arbitration of disputes (Deyo 1989, pp. 133–135).

However, the Korean and Taiwanese heavy industrialisation programmes of the 1970s led to some important structural changes in their respective labour forces. Taiwan reached its Lewisian turning point in the late 1960s and Korea in the mid-1970s (Fei and Ranis 1975, Bai 2007), whereby the transition from the 'unlimited labour supply' to limited labour supply led to increased structural power (Wright 2000) on the part of workers. These transitions ultimately underpinned the rise of labour movements in the 1980s and led to wage increases that ultimately undermined the authoritarian labour regime. In Korea, in 1963 there were around 2.4 million workers in industry, rising to 4.8 million in 1975 and to 8 million by 1985. This amounted to an increase of 235 per cent in the space of just twenty-two years (Koo 2001, p. 35). Whilst the 1970s had already seen an increasing number of militant strikes at labour-intensive workplaces, they were often unsuccessful in gaining concessions from employers and were met with high levels of employer repression. This began to change in the 1980s as a response to the shift toward HCI and the emergence of large workplaces (Deyo 1989, pp. 75–77). The industrial workforce in Taiwan increased about seven times between 1956 and 1990, from 554,000 to 3.8 million. In the decade and a half between 1966 and 1980, the percentage of the labour force employed as wage workers increased from 47.5 per cent to 61.9 per cent, a direct result of the expansion of the export-oriented industries (Sen and Koo 1992, p. 47). Throughout most of the 1970s, however, industrial relations in Taiwan remained relatively quiescent, although wages continued to rise as a result of the longer-run demographic changes outlined above. It was the resulting increased costs of production in these countries that, along with aggressive US exchange rate policies, led to the growing relocation of manufacturing to China (and Southeast Asia) from the 1990s.

Conclusion

As in Japan, US intervention in the immediate post-war era laid the basis for Korean and Taiwanese catch-up industrialisation by facilitating a process of passive revolution. This revolution from above was aimed at ensuring state autonomy through the repression of labour and other potential oppositional social forces. However, the divergent nature of Korea and Taiwan's geopolitical contexts and resultant state–society relations have meant that the nature of the passive revolution and ensuing labour regime have diverged to some extent. In the aftermath of the Japanese surrender, Korean workers proceeded to engage in widespread strikes and organisation building and were strongly opposed to the re-imposition of rule by right-wing political forces under US auspices. Indeed, Korean workers played a more central role in the intermittent episodes of unrest that marked the country's post-war history, to the extent that by the 1970s, a genuine workers' movement could be said to have emerged in the country's labour-intensive export sectors. The Taiwanese labour movement, on the other hand, has been comparatively more subdued. The differential nature of labour militancy in the post-war years owed much to the countries' respective colonial experiences. By the time of the Japanese surrender, the remnants of the left in Taiwan had largely been destroyed and resistance to the KMT took the form of a broader societal uprising, whose grievances were largely expressed in sub-ethnic terms.

Whilst late industrialisation was predicated upon the political weakness of labour, the very 'success' of the post-war passive revolution served to challenge that political weakness. This is because industrialisation expanded the working class and strengthened its structural power within the social relations of production. This created increased challenges for the East Asian developmental state from the 1970s, which were amplified by the increased pressure that East Asian manufacturers placed on US manufacturers and the response that provoked from American policymakers. The latter sought to tackle these pressures through protectionism and an attempt to shift the burden of military defence onto the East Asian countries themselves. The resulting increased perception of geopolitical insecurity by Taiwanese and Korean elites led to the HCI drives, which further strengthened the structural power of the working class, and led to increased labour resistance to authoritarian developmentalism. As Chapter 5 will argue, however, the ensuing decompression of the developmental state model occurred within the context of the growing role of the capitalist logic of power in shaping US grand strategy. The double-edged success of post-war US attempts to revive the Western European and East Asian regions contributed toward the decline in the rate of US corporate profitability from the 1970s, which in turn led to the rise of global neoliberalism. It is first necessary, however, to examine the impact that the rise of labour and of social forces more broadly had on the politics of the post-war developmental regimes in Korea and Taiwan.

4

LABOUR AND DEMOCRATISATION IN EAST ASIA

The changes in US geopolitical strategy toward the East Asian region in the 1970s spurred the Korean and Taiwanese developmental state elites to reorient their national economies toward the heavy and chemical sectors. The world economic crisis of that decade also meant that Korea and Taiwan were able to tap into increasingly mobile global flows of capital in search of more productive outlets, not the least of which was Japanese capital, as Japan itself was faced with a considerably less buoyant domestic economy following the global oil shock in 1973. This shift in Korea and Taiwan's developmental strategy was, however, a process whereby the 'fix' to one crisis tendency laid the foundations for the broader crisis of the developmental state itself. The heavy and chemical industrialisation (HCI) programme of the 1970s, whilst highly successful on its own terms, also served to confer structural power on the working class, thereby allowing it to challenge the political and economic underpinnings of authoritarian developmentalism.

The rise of labour as a collective social actor occurred in tandem with the emergence of broader movements for political democracy. Furthermore, once the democratic breakthrough in the formal political sphere was achieved, workers in both countries made use of the new political space to push for the democratisation of labour relations. This included in the first instance a full-scale assault against labour subordination in the workplace as workers challenged management prerogative, democratised existing 'yellow' unions, and established new unions in previously non-unionised companies. Though the democratic aperture brought a degree of liberalisation to the legal frameworks governing labour, the workers' movements in both Korea and Taiwan remained fettered by the legacies of state corporatism. As we shall see, therefore, the democratisation of labour relations was a drawn-out process as state and capital sought to maintain international competitiveness by attacking wages and working conditions, as well as carrying out legal reforms, allowing for the greater flexibilisation of labour.

The process of democratisation cannot be explained with sole reference to social processes within Korea and Taiwan, however. As the two cases suggest, for most of the post-war era, the United States had no qualms with regards to the support for dictatorships in the Third World. Furthermore, as General Pinochet's *coup d'état* in Chile had signified, there was initially no necessary contradiction between neoliberalism and authoritarian repression. By the 1980s, however, the United States had shifted its strategy toward the overt promotion of formal democracy. This was at least in part due to recognition of the fact that authoritarian repression of labour had underpinned the rapid catch-up industrialisation of America's key economic competitors and, as a result, had been a central factor in the challenge to US economic supremacy. Thus, it was a result of both internal and external pressures that Korea and Taiwan experienced a dual transition from authoritarian developmentalism to formal democracy combined with economic liberalisation. This was in line with the US strategy of the promotion of polyarchy under the broader *zeitgeist* of global neoliberalism. As such, formal political democracy was far from an impediment to the spread of global neoliberalism, but was in fact conducive to it. Liberal democracy's separation of politics and economics became a new means whereby political and economic elites could achieve the repression of organised labour.

Late industrialisation and the rise of labour

As noted in Chapter 3, the 1960s labour regime in Korea required minimal government repression because the unlimited supply of labour meant that discipline could largely be carried out via market mechanisms (Lee 1998, pp. 348–349). By the early 1970s, however, the country's state-corporatist labour regime proved to be increasingly inept at restraining labour militancy, and the government's approach to labour relations became one of increased surveillance and repression. The growing concentration of workers in sweatshop factories and the emergence of working-class communities led to a growing collective workers' identity based on a shared sense of injustice regarding their low social status and the systematic infringement of their rights. Thus, whilst the labour struggles of the 1970s have sometimes pejoratively been labelled as 'defensive' in character, they nonetheless were an expression of a broad class-conscious struggle against the 'growth first' ideology of Park Chung-Hee's catch-up industrialisation drive. This rejection of the subordination of labour perhaps received its most tragic expression in the protest suicide of the young male factory worker Chŏn T'aeil, who in 1970 burned himself to death in protest of the labour conditions endured by around 25,000 predominantly female workers in the sweatshops located around Seoul's P'yŏnghwa Market. As employers and the police sought to repress attempts by workers at establishing independent unions, Chŏn's self-immolation drew attention to the wide disparity between the letter of the labour law and the reality of hyper-exploitation.

The emergence of a working-class consciousness in the 1970s was not spontaneous, however; it was aided by progressive religious organisations, such as the Catholic *Jeunnesse Ouvrière Chrétienne* and the protestant Urban Industrial Mission (UIM).

These organisations were motivated by indigenous forms of Korean liberation theology that were strongly aligned against authoritarian developmentalism and its underlying system of labour exploitation. They ran educational programmes designed to develop workers' class consciousness and knowledge of their rights, including leadership training for democratic union activities and night schools aimed at educating workers on labour ethics and the labour legal code. They also frequently facilitated the arbitration of labour disputes. Although the number of activist clergy was not large (numbering around 25 in total for the UIM), they were nonetheless responsible for producing a considerable number of labour activists (Chang 1998b, pp. 450–451). It was no coincidence, therefore, that many of the most important union democratisation struggles of the 1970s, such as those that took place at Wonpoong, Tongil, and YH Trading, took place within the Seoul-Inch'ŏn-Kyŏnggi area where the industrial missions were located rather than in the industrialising southeast, for example (Koo 2001, pp. 74–85).

The long, drawn-out struggle at Tongil Textile Company in Inch'ŏn was indicative of this nurturing role played by the industrial missionaries. George Ogle, himself a UIM activist until his arrest and deportation by the Korean Central Intelligence Agency (KCIA) in 1974, describes how the pro-management union at Tongil had traditionally been dominated by male workers, despite the fact that 1,100 of the company's 1,300 workers were the women who endured poor and hazardous working conditions at the factory. However, in 1972, a female UIM Methodist minister, Rev. Cho Wha Soon, began to organise workers at the factory, and the female employees were encouraged to launch a campaign to wrest control of the union leadership. Despite physical threats and assaults by the company's male workers and the police, the female workers successfully democratised the union through leadership elections in 1972, and again in 1976. This short-lived era of union democracy came to an end, however, during a further contestation for the union's leadership in February 1978. When the female workers arrived at a scheduled election in a company hall, male workers began to throw buckets of excrement at them. Ballot boxes in the hall were also broken. Following the incident, 124 of the female workers were accused by the company management of 'damaging company property' and were subsequently dismissed and placed on government and employer blacklists. Furthermore, the government-sanctioned Federation of Korean Trade Unions (FKTU) stayed true to its anti-worker orientation, withdrawing the union's licence and dismissing its officials (Ogle 1990, pp. 84–87).

One the one hand, the struggle for union democracy at Tongil underlines the fact that the labour force that underpinned Korea's export-oriented industrialisation (EOI) did not fit the stereotypical depiction of the docile female East Asian worker (Chun 2003). Yet, the experience also shows that the struggles of the 1970s were rarely successful in gaining significant concessions from employers and were often met with violent company repression with the backing of the police. However, the sweatshop struggles of the 1970s formed an important precedent for the further development of the movement in the 1980s. As Ogle (1990, p. 86) notes, '[w]hen in the mid-eighties the male workers began to take action of their own, they found that they were standing on the shoulders of women who had been struggling for justice for more than ten years.'

The struggles of the 1970s also had political consequences that extended far beyond the factory walls. In August 1979, the government sent approximately 400 riot police to attack a group of 200 striking women at YH Trading who were engaged in a sit-in at the opposition New Democratic Party's headquarters. This sit-in was in protest of the closing of their factory by management and the subsequent loss of approximately 4,000 jobs. The ensuing death of one of the female strikers led to the denunciation of this disproportionate mobilisation of the police force by a broad coalition of social organisations, including the Human Rights Committee of the Korean National Council of Churches and the Association of Families of Prisoners of Conscience. Furthermore, the expulsion of opposition leader Kim Young-Sam from his seat in the National Assembly provoked mass protests in Kim's home district of Pusan. On 26th October 1979, as the political situation was becoming increasingly unstable, President Park Chung-Hee was assassinated by his own head of the KCIA.

The brief democratic aperture that followed saw an intense period of activism by workers and students. Between January and May 1980, a total of 900 strikes took place, involving miners, textile workers, machinists, and pharmaceutical workers. This outburst of labour unrest involved more strikes than had taken place under the preceding seven years of the *Yushin* regime (Katsiaficas 2012a, p. 156). It was testament to how workers' grievances had accumulated under Park's industrialisation programme and were waiting for an opportunity for expression. Strikes were aimed at better pay and working conditions, the democratisation of existing unions, and the establishment of new ones. Miners in Sabuk (Kangwŏn province) struck for higher wages and even went on a rampage in the town after learning that three miners had been hit by a police car. They destroyed a police station and the mining company office and kidnapped the company manager's wife before turning themselves in to police three days later. A similarly violent strike took place at the Tongkook Chekang steel mill in Pusan. As Hagen Koo (2001, pp. 101–102) argues, these highly emotional, violent, unorganised, and short-lived strikes were typical of the era. As a rule, workers failed to extend these struggles to build industry- or regional-level solidarity organisations. Indeed, this is something that would not occur until the labour struggles of the late 1980s.

In a fragile political situation resembling that of the Chang Myŏn government at the outset of the 1960s, General Chun Doo-Hwan and his allies in the secret military club *Hanahoe* moved to establish their control over the state apparatus. This unfolding *coup d'etat* was, however, met with strong resistance by Korea's students. On 17th May 1980, a mass student rally directed against the military's renewed interference in politics took place in front of Seoul Station, drawing more than 100,000 participants. Further demonstrations took place in other cities across the country. With subsequent mass arrests of student leaders and threats of the mobilisation of troops against the students, the remaining student leaders in Seoul backed down and called off the protests. However, this retreat served to isolate students and citizens in Kwangju, the capital of the southwestern Chŏlla province, who refused to heed the military's threats and abandon their protests. Paratroopers sent in to suppress the demonstrations subsequently went on a killing rampage in the city. Kwangju's students and citizens fought back, however, seizing weapons and driving the troops back, and in the process, they gained control of the city. The people of Kwangju were thus, for a time at least, able to establish what George Katsiaficas has described as a system of 'direct democracy,' which bore similarities to, but in some respects surpassed that of, the 1871 Paris Commune (Katsiaficas 2012a, p. 187).

It did not take long, however, for Chun Doo-Hwan to respond with the full weight of military power. On 27th May 1980, special forces launched a full-scale assault on Kwangju and managed to retake the city, though not without a death toll estimated to be between 200 and 2,000. Much debate has surrounded the question of the degree of US complicity in the Kwangju massacre, specifically on the question of whether the US military gave the green light for special forces to be deployed against Kwangju's students and citizens. On the one hand, special forces were outside the structure of the Combined Forces Command, so technically permission was not required from the United States for their redeployment to Kwangju. However, Chalmers Johnson (2002) has argued that cable communications between the US embassy and Washington suggest US complicity in the Korean military's operations in Kwangju. On 7th May 1980, Ambassador William Gleysteen, who was largely given a free hand in managing the Korean crisis due to the Carter administration's embroilment in other foreign policy crises, commented on Chun's request for troop movements, 'There has been no request for such approval yet, but [Commander in Chief of the United Nations Command] would agree if asked.' Again, on 22nd May, Gleysteen told the Korean foreign minister, 'We had not and did not intend to publicize our actions because we feared we would be charged with colluding with the martial law authorities and risk fanning anti-American sentiment in the Kwangju area' (Johnson 2002, pp. 117–118). Furthermore, the incoming US president Ronald Reagan also quickly sought to confer legitimacy on the new military regime by making Chun Doo-Hwan the first head of state to be invited to the White House under his administration. The events of Kwangju thus suggest that the United States still had few qualms at the outset of the 1980s about supporting authoritarian regimes.

The suppression of the democratic aspirations of workers, students, and the wider public was of course by no means limited to Korea, though the repression of the Kwangju uprising was perhaps over-determined by the specific conjuncture of the late 1970s. The Iranian revolution, the Sandinista revolution in Nicaragua, and the growing strength of revolutionary movements in the Philippines and El Salvador meant that the United States was extremely sensitive to the threat of unrest in Korea (Shorrock 1986, p. 1200). These concerns regarding unrest were combined with those relating to Korea's serious external debt crisis following the second oil shock and sharp rises in US interest rates (Park 2005, p. 3), as well as the possibility of capital flight by US investors. Much as in Chile in 1973 and Turkey in the 1980s,

Chun's rise to power was therefore an opportunity for the United States to push for neoliberal reform as a means of both maintaining investor confidence and extending the reach of US capital in the country (Katsiaficas 2012a, p. 226).

Following the coup, Chun proceeded to adopt a number of liberalisation policies designed to deal with the economic crisis, including the stabilisation of inflation through a tightening of the money supply and strict regulation of fiscal policy. There were policies aimed at the restructuring of the heavy and chemical industrial sector and the scaling back of the large incentives given to the *chaebŏl*, such as preferential interest rates, prohibitive tariffs, and tax exemptions. Furthermore, elements of free market competition were introduced in order to enhance the efficiency of business, and there were attempts to facilitate a transition in the economy toward high-tech and consumer goods (Lee 1988, p. 111). Despite these measures, however, the state's control over capital remained largely unimpaired. It was not until the 1990s and the reforms of the Kim Young-Sam government that the dismantling of the developmental state and the liberalisation of finance properly got under way.

The severe authoritarian repression of the early 1980s did not end with the Kwangju massacre. With clear parallels to the state-orchestrated violence following Pinochet's rise-to-power coup seven years earlier in Chile, the Chun Doo-Hwan government proceeded to incarcerate large numbers of people in the months and years after the coup. The Roh Mu-Hyun government's 2006 report into the activities of the military junta in the early 1980s found that nearly 40,000 people were detained in the so-called *Samch'ŏng* Education Camps. Though the military claimed that the 're-education' was for gangsters and criminals, the report found that those numbers included 980 students, including 17 middle-school students, and 319 women (The Hankyoreh 2006). In response to the heightened labour unrest, the military took measures to weaken the labour movement through harsh repression combined with a series of reforms to the legal code governing labour relations. In August 1980, for example, Chun's government promulgated the 'Guidelines for the Purification of Labour Unions,' which led to the resignation of eleven of the seventeen national industrial union presidents as well as the dismissal of 106 regional leaders and nearly 200 local officers from their unions. Shortly afterwards, a new set of labour laws were passed that sought to isolate local bargaining from industrial unions and the FKTU as well as prohibit any 'third-party interventions' from church groups such as the UIM or the *Jeunnesse Ouvrière Chrétienne* (Ogle 1990, p. 102). These reforms thus amounted to a strong reinforcement of enterprise unionism. They also included the prohibition of multiple unions in a single workplace, so that once a pro-management union had already been established, there was no alternative route by which workers could achieve genuine representation at the factory level (Lee 2011, p. 54). These legal changes thus imposed further weaknesses on labour, and, indeed, much of the labour movement's efforts following the democratic aperture in 1987 revolved around trying to reverse these authoritarian labour laws.

Furthermore, the unions that had been at the forefront of the struggles of the 1970s were systematically crushed through state and company repression. By late

1983, however, the Chun regime had begun to adopt a number of measures aimed at political liberalisation, reflecting the regime's confidence about its legitimacy rather than any decline in the widespread antipathy held toward Chun's government (Kim 1997c, p. 1135). In reality, these liberalisation measures provided not legitimacy but space from which a broad pro-democracy movement encompassing workers, students, farmers, and other marginalised social groups would emerge.

For this oppositional movement, the brutality of the military's *coup d'état* and its violent suppression of the student and citizen protests in Kwangju had been defining events, and there was much reflection on what had led to the failure to prevent Chun from taking power in 1980. One of the key effects of the coup and the ensuing repression was therefore to radicalise the student movement and leave little space for reformism (Park 2008). The students came to view labour as the central actor not only in the pro-democracy movement but in the broader struggle for revolution. Thus, whereas in the 1970s it was church groups that sought to facilitate the growth of the labour movement, from the 1980s, it was the student movement. Students adopted a strategy whereby they would disguise their identities and take ordinary factory jobs with the primary purpose of raising the revolutionary consciousness of workers and organising independent unions. The movement of 'students turned workers' primarily took place around the metropolitan area of Seoul, Inch'ŏn and Kyŏnggi province, and it has been estimated that as many as 10,000 students took part.

It was not long before this strategy began to reap concrete results. In May 1985, disguised student organisers played a key role at a strike in the Kuro industrial complex on the outskirts of Seoul. A strike at one company in the complex, Daewoo Apparel, had originally been centred on demands for wage increases. However, the legal charges brought against the union by management and the arrest and imprisonment of its leadership led to a wider solidarity strike across the Kuro complex. The scale of the strike thus marked an important turning point in the qualitative development of the labour movement. In comparison to the more defensive struggles of the past, the Kuro strike took on an explicitly political character through calling for the release of the union leadership, the guarantee of workers' rights to engage in collective action, and the resignation of the labour minister. Whilst it ultimately ended in failure, the strike served as a watershed moment in terms of the level of solidarity achieved across multiple workplaces. Prior to the Kuro strike, labour activists could be seen as more interested in protecting their own organisations than building solidarity. The fact that solidarity in this instance had extended beyond the factory wall was seen as a major step toward the development of a higher working-class consciousness (Lee 2007b, p. 252).

By the 1980s, however, emerging labour shortages and increasing wage demands by workers meant that the days were numbered for the kind of labour-intensive light manufacturing to be found in the Kuro industrial complex. The HCI drive had meant that the locus of the economy was shifting rapidly. An important dispute in this regard took place in 1985 at the Daewoo Motors plant in Pup'yŏng, Inch'ŏn, which demonstrated the extent to which the labour movement was shifting toward the male-skilled workers in large enterprises and also how the emergence of labour shortages gave workers greater bargaining power (Lee 1998, p. 350). The strike was first and foremost centred on demands for higher wages and the democratisation of the pro-management union. The union leadership had hitherto taken the lead in collective bargaining and the signing of contracts, with little input from rank-and-file workers. Workers at the company had not received wage increases since the early 1980s due to the company's alleged poor financial position. Thus, in April 1985, when an improvement in the company's financial position was reported, workers rejected a proposal for modest wage increases and expressed their distrust of the incumbent union leadership by selecting a new wage negotiating team. After several days of negotiations, the workers went on strike. The strike soon became a sensitive political issue nationally and the company came under heavy pressure from the government to settle the matter quickly so as to prevent unrest spreading to other companies. After the personal intervention of Daewoo CEO Kim Woo Chong, a wage package was offered which was close to the workers' original demands, including a 10 per cent increase in basic wage rates, a new allowance of 4 per cent, and the expansion of company welfare facilities, including the construction of new company apartments (Koo 2001, pp. 110–111). Furthermore, as state and capital had feared, the achievement of substantial wage increases at Daewoo Motors encouraged workers elsewhere. In the same year, workers at Hyosung Mulsan achieved wage increases of 26.5 per cent, Daewoo Apparel of 18.5 per cent, Yungchang Piano of 16 per cent, Sejin Electronics of 15.5 per cent, Karibong of 17.5 per cent, and Rom Korea of 17.5 per cent (Lee 1987, p. 159).

Taiwan also witnessed a steady increase in labour unrest as EOI progressed and the structural power of the workforce grew. Whilst the total employed population more than doubled between the 1960s and 1970s, the number of disputes increased tenfold. This heightened working-class activism was for the most part aimed not at the establishment of independent unions but was related to more defensive issues, such as wage arrears and injury compensation. One exception to this general tendency, however, was the struggle to form an independent union at the Far Eastern Textile Company in 1977 (Ho 1990, p. 16). When workers at the company sought help from the county government in establishing a union, management quickly took the initiative by pre-emptively establishing its own pro-company 'yellow' union. As a result of the prohibition under Taiwanese trade union law of multiple unions at a single workplace, workers had few choices but to try and gain control of the company-backed union through leadership elections. The success of this approach meant that the Far Eastern Textile Company Union became the first union in Taiwan to be controlled by the workers themselves. Despite subsequent pressure from management on the union leadership, workers managed to maintain the union's independence, succeeded in inducing management to engage in collective bargaining, and achieved significant improvements in wages and working conditions (Ho 1990, pp. 17–19).

The qualitative growth of the Taiwanese labour movement continued throughout the 1980s. Between 1981 and 1988, a total of 10,441 labour disputes were registered with the authorities, and there was a significant increase in disputes over labour rights and demands for allowances (Hsiao 1992a, pp. 157–158), though these workplace collective actions were for the most part unconnected to formal labour organisations. Labour activists also campaigned for new legislation guaranteeing minimum wage rates and working conditions. Whilst the Kuomintang (KMT) had resisted such pressures in the past, by the mid-1980s, strong economic growth, rising real wages, low unemployment, and severe labour shortages, along with heightened industrial unrest, led the KMT to re-examine its labour policies (Minns and Tierney 2003, p. 114). In contrast to the Chun Doo-Hwan regime in Korea, therefore, the KMT's strategy was one of pre-emptive legal reform vis-à-vis the rise of the independent labour movement. This involved the passing of the Labour Standards Law (LSL) in 1984, which set out minimum working conditions in primary and secondary industries, and covered termination of employment, wages, working hours, leave, retirement benefits, compensation for occupational accidents, and special provisions for women and child workers as well as apprentices (Cooney 1996, p. 8).

On the one hand, this strategy of pre-emptive labour legislation owed much to the potential threat to the KMT of an alliance between labour and the rising *dangwai* political opposition movement. The *dangwai* was comprised of native Taiwanese politicians who were independent of or excluded from the KMT. They protested against the monolithic nature of KMT rule and the basis of that monopoly in martial law. Furthermore, they opposed the KMT's professed 'sacred mission' of the re-conquest of the mainland and unification of the country; in particular, they were opposed to the manner in which that overriding objective had shaped Taiwan's political institutions. Even partial national elections, for example, were not held until 1969. Even then, political institutions continued to be monopolised by the mainlander elites. The *dangwai* were also opposed to the KMT's education policy which promoted Chinese identity at the expense of Taiwanese cultural and historical identity (Ferhat-Dana 1998, p. 30). Following a degree of political liberalisation after Chiang Kai-Shek's death and succession by his son Chiang Ching-Kuo, *dangwai* politicians were able to make significant gains in the local elections that were permitted under Taiwan's martial law system. Whilst making these electoral gains, the *dangwai* also organised and built linkages with other social actors opposed to minority rule by the KMT mainlander elite, establishing linkages with workers, students, women, and environmentalists around a nativist Taiwanese identity (Lee 2011, pp. 61–62).

However, it is also important to note that the KMT was under increased pressure from the United States, particularly from the US Congress, to enact humanitarian labour legislation as a result of the widening US–Taiwan trade imbalance. Indeed, the timing of the legislation coincides with the revision of the US Generalized System of Preferences (GSP), a system whereby developing countries could gain exemption from the requirement under most favoured nation rules to match the tariff reductions of rich countries. As a result of the worsening trade balance, the rules of the GSP were amended so that no country could be designated a beneficiary developing country if it had not taken or was not taking steps to guarantee internationally-recognised workers' rights domestically (Organisation for Economic Co-operation and Development [OECD] 2000, p. 67). Taiwan at that point was the largest beneficiary of the GSP, and the increasing trade imbalance with the United States led to an alliance between US corporations and trade unions aimed at the removal of Taiwan's import barriers as well as the imposition of restrictions on Taiwanese goods entering the US market.

From the perspective of Taiwanese labour, however, the LSL suffered from some serious limitations. With regards to the provisions designed to strengthen labour standards, a key problem was that of the law's poor enforcement and evasion of its provisions by employers. The law both failed to achieve its stated objectives of providing substantive conditions of employment and a participatory role for employees and failed to provide any mechanism whereby unions could negotiate matters covered within the law (Kleingartner and Peng 1991, p. 430). The power to set minimum wages and conditions remained heavily concentrated in the state bureaucracy, specifically in the newly established Basic Wage Commission, which provided minimal representation for organised labour. The legislation also did not allow for improvements in wages and working conditions in the service sector, which employed approximately 2 million workers (Minns and Tierney 2003, p. 114). As such, US pressure on Taiwan to improve its labour practices continued throughout the 1980s. A delegation of the US Labor Department and American Federation of Labor and Congress of Industrial Organizations (AFL-CIO) trade unionists in April 1986, for example, recognised the continued role of labour subordination in Taiwan's export success and criticised the country's repressive union system, which continued to outlaw unionisation for large sections of the workforce, prohibit strikes, and allow government interference in the union election system (Ho 1990, pp. 37–39).

These limitations meant, however, that the LSL became a strategic tool for the emerging independent labour movement. Labour actions throughout the 1980s were often centred around demands for the full implementation of the LSL, a strategy known within the movement as 'fight for what the law offers' (順法鬥爭) (Chen and Wong 2002, p. 36). The Taiwan Labor Front (TLF) was a key organisation in this regard. Originally known as Taiwan Labor Legal Assistance Organization, the TLF was established in 1984 by social activists associated with the New Tide faction of the *dangwai* movement, many of whom had been imprisoned in the aftermath of the Kaohsiung Incident, a mass demonstration in December 1979 that is often regarded as marking the rise of the pro-democracy movement. The main aim of the TLF was to raise consciousness of socialist ideology and labour rights, as well as to provide free legal consultation to workers (Yiu 2004), although it was not until later that the organisation began to play a key role in collective actions. Since the 1990s, it has been affiliated with eleven large independent unions, including the National Postal Union, the Taipei Bus Union, the Fertilizer Union, and the Tatung Appliance Union. From 1992, however, the TLF also became increasingly involved in political campaigns, such as that of extending the LSL to workers in the service sector, along with efforts to minimise the offshore relocation of Taiwan's manufacturing capital (Minns and Tierney 2005, p. 101).

In many respects, the broad contours of how Taiwan's catch-up industrialisation engendered the independent labour movement of the 1980s bears remarkable similarities with the case of Korea. Whilst most comparative studies of the Korean and Taiwanese labour movements have sought to highlight their differences, as Hwa-Jen Liu (2012, p. 214) has argued, paying attention exclusively to differences runs the risk of sidestepping similarities, exaggerating divergence, and conflating difference in kind and difference in degree. With that caveat in mind, it is nonetheless the case that the divergences are also significant in terms of how the uneven development of capitalism in East Asia has led to divergent experiences of passive revolution and emergent labour regimes underpinning development. In this respect, a key feature of the Taiwanese case is the *relative* weakness of the workers' movement. Accurately gauging the organisational strength of the Taiwanese labour movement is not a straightforward task, however. Taiwan's comparatively high union density serves more as a measure of the effectiveness of the subordination of labour through state-corporatist institutions than evidence of a strong working-class movement *per se*. As Joseph Lee points out, 59.8 per cent of workers who joined unions in 1987 did so at the request of their own employers, whereas only 25.1 per cent did so out of their own conviction. Indeed, the Taiwanese government's pressure on employers to expand union membership was often cited by foreign governments as evidence of the unfair competitive advantage conferred by the authoritarian labour regime. However, following democratisation and the decline of state-corporatist labour relations, only 29.2 per cent of workers in 1991 joined unions at the request of their employers, whereas 66.0 per cent did so out of their own conviction (Lee 1994, pp. 2–3). Unionisation rates aside, the data on industrial unrest unequivocally demonstrate a more quiescent labour movement in Taiwan as compared to that of Korea. Between 1980 and 1986, an average of 28,000 workers per year were involved in labour disputes in Korea compared to 8,500 in Taiwan. Furthermore, in Korea, each dispute involved an average of 135 workers, compared to just 10 workers per dispute in Taiwan (Kong 2005, pp. 163–164). Although comparative data on workdays lost is unavailable for the 1980s, the annual average workdays lost per 1,000 workers between 1989 to 2007 was 191.6 in Korea, compared to just 0.8 in Taiwan (Lee 2011, p. 15).

Several explanations can be given for the relative weakness of the Taiwanese workers' movement. The first has already been alluded to in Chapter 3. The position of Taiwan in the Japanese colonial empire led to weaker processes of working-class formation and associated class consciousness, as evidenced in the relative absence of any sustained surge in labour militancy in the aftermath of the Japanese surrender. However, the extent to which this explanation can account for Taiwanese labour's relative docility throughout the entire post-war era is doubtful. A further explanation in the literature on Taiwan has thus been the more constraining role of Taiwan's labour regulations. It has been argued, for example, that under Taiwan's more comprehensive system of state-corporatist labour relations, industrial action by workers was strongly proscribed; even after the lifting of martial law in 1987, strikes, slowdowns, picket lines, and boycotts were not allowed to take place until mediation had failed, and only then after a majority of members had voted in favour by means of secret ballot (Chen *et al.* 2003, p. 332). Given the comparative context of Korea, however, such an explanation is unconvincing. The Korean labour movement was faced with similarly restrictive labour laws, yet workers resisted the often vicious repression of government and business through militant struggles to establish independent unions despite the existence of stringent labour laws.

A more convincing explanation is that of the distinctive nature of Taiwan's industrial structure. Korean industrialisation has been more conducive to unionisation due to the prevalence of large-scale plants and heavy industry concentrated in the form of the *chaebŏl*. Korea's political economy was also more centrally directed; thus labour disputes easily became politicised. In Taiwan, on the other hand, industries characterised by large enterprises were for the most part under mainlander KMT control, whereas the majority of the local Taiwanese were confined to the small and medium enterprise (SME) sector. This pattern was by no means an accident of history but was again a product of the specificities of Taiwan's post-war passive revolution. In the 1950s, the KMT was reluctant to promote large private enterprises because it did not wish to empower the local Taiwanese businessmen who at the time outnumbered mainlander capitalists. Furthermore, though Taiwan carried out a programme of HCI in the 1970s, this phase was not as prolonged as that of Korea's, so the heavy industrial sector was smaller. As a result, Taiwanese workers were far more likely to work in smaller workplaces (Kong 2005, p. 183). More generally, 42 per cent of all employees in Taiwan worked in factories of at least 100 employees in 1961. This number rose to 64 per cent in 1971, but then declined to 33 per cent by 1980. In Korea, however, the corresponding figures were 33 per cent in 1960, 56 per cent in 1968, and 74 per cent in 1974 (Deyo 1987, p. 195). Even in the 1980s, almost a third of all wage workers in Taiwan were employed in small establishments hiring fewer than ten workers. Furthermore, the wider geographic dispersion of industrial activities in Taiwan as compared to Korea acted as a deterrence to the development of worker identity and working-class community (Sen and Koo 1992, pp. 57–58). It should be noted, however, that there is no automatic correlation between an economy based upon SMEs and labour acquiescence. Indeed, Northern Italy, which is dominated by SMEs, has been one of the most strike-prone regions in the world (Huang 2000a, p. 15). However, workers in small workshops in Taiwan are often literally family members of the owners, the latter of whom have been able to exploit familial ideology and enforce close scrutiny over their employees. In turn, many workers harbour hopes of becoming small factory owners themselves one day, further reducing their commitment to collective action (Chu 1996, pp. 496–497).

It is the case that since the 1990s, economic restructuring in both countries has led to growing convergence in their industrial structure, with SMEs comprising around 95 per cent of all enterprises and around 80 per cent of employment opportunities

(Lee 2011, p. 20). However, over the broader course of post-war history in Taiwan, it is undeniable that Taiwan's industrial structure played a significant role in impeding the formation of working-class identity, not least because it was interpreted by Taiwanese workers as constituting a fundamentally sub-ethnic form of domination. As the KMT's post-war developmental policies were kept the native Taiwanese economically and politically excluded and the mainlanders took over the better positions in state-owned enterprises (SOEs), the imposition of Leninist control served to further aggravate these sub-ethnic differences. This allowed the KMT to place party cadres throughout Taiwan's factories and establish a vast redistributive network amongst KMT loyalists. This discrimination in the workplace would therefore become a key grievance in workers' protests from the 1980s onwards (Ho 2007, pp. 164–165). However, as noted above, and in further contrast to the Korean case, the KMT compensated for this exclusion through the provision of an electoral space at the grassroots level. Whilst this was designed to elicit a certain degree of consent from the Taiwanese population, it ultimately provided the space for the formation in 1986 of the Democratic Progressive Party (DPP), which also defined its pursuit of democracy largely in sub-ethnic terms, thereby greatly influencing how unions subsequently interpreted their political environments and the choices that they made (Lee 2011, pp. 60–63).

As such, a key feature of the Taiwanese passive revolution was that this ethnically oriented mode of state corporatism became a key grievance for both Taiwanese labour and the emerging mainstream political opposition, laying the groundwork for a close relationship between the two. In the December 1986 legislative elections, the DPP did well out of labour dissatisfaction with the KMT, with two relatively obscure DPP candidates elected as workers' functional representatives. Though now defunct, the functional representative seats were a feature of Taiwan's state-corporatist system, whereby 23 of the 101 seats in the Legislative Yuan were reserved for representatives of functional constituencies, such as occupational groups (including labour, farmers, and educational personnel) as well as aborigines. Originally these seats, and the Fujian provincial seat, were tightly controlled by the KMT. The ability of the DPP to get labour representatives elected was thus a significant development in the ongoing democratisation process (Anon 1990, p. 4). It also demonstrated that the DPP was becoming an increasingly attractive outlet for workers' grievances. The DPP in turn recognised the advantage of aiding efforts to establish an alternative independent federation of labour due to the KMT's continued use of the Chinese Federation of Labour (CFL) to mobilise votes. The CFL, with its dense network of constituent unions and historical role in securing working-class support for the KMT, was largely considered to be at best irrelevant by the emerging independent labour movement. Indeed, from the mid-1990s, the KMT even reserved a seat on its Central Standing Committee for the CFL president (Ho 2006a, pp. 116–117). As will be argued in Chapter 5, however, this alliance between the DPP and the independent labour movement has continued to have mixed implications for organised labour's ability to play an significant role in Taiwanese society.

Explaining the democratic transition in Korea and Taiwan

The more dramatic changes to labour relations in the Korean and Taiwanese labour regimes came in the late 1980s following the democratic aperture. In the most immediate sense, formal democratisation was a result of a push from a wide coalition of social forces that were strongly opposed to the authoritarianism that had underpinned the developmental state model. In Korea, the rallies staged in June 1987 were amongst the largest in the country's history, with over 1 million people demonstrating on 26th June across 34 Korean cities (Adesnik and Kim 2008). This democracy movement was a coalition of students, religious leaders, workers, and the public more broadly, which was generally conducted in a manner that transcended class and regional divisions. Following weeks of sustained protests, the Chun Doo-Hwan government finally relented on 29th June. Chun's appointed successor, Roh Tae-Woo, subsequently announced free presidential elections and the release of opposition politician Kim Dae-Jung from house arrest. In this sense, Korea's transition was a key instance of popular pressure against authoritarianism. It is important, however, to place the Korean transition within the broader international context of the ongoing 'third wave of democracy' (Huntington 1991).

It has been argued, for example, that the People Power Revolution and demise of the Ferdinand Marcos administration in the Philippines forced Chun to drop his earlier insistence on transfer of power in accordance with the rules of the anti-democratic constitution of the Fifth Republic. Furthermore, the impending 1988 Seoul Olympics and the risk of a serious tarnishing of Korea's international reputation have been said to have worked against a military crackdown on the democracy protests (Cotton 1989, pp. 251–253). Nonetheless, there is evidence to suggest that on 18th June 1987, in the midst of the popular uprising, Chun was once again considering imposition of martial law and was in fact making preparations to mobilise the military. However, US President Reagan sent Chun a letter warning him not to use military force and to reopen negotiations with the mainstream opposition parties over the democratic transition (Katsiaficas 2012a, p. 294). Thus, just as Washington had been decisive in conferring legitimacy on Chun's rise to power and facilitating the bloody suppression of the Kwangju uprising, it had also played an equally important role in bringing Chun's dictatorship to an end.

In retrospect, however, the revision of the constitution and introduction of free presidential elections can be viewed as an instance of what Patrick Bond (2005) has referred in the South African context to an 'elite transition.' The Korean democratic aperture took the form of a compromise between Chun Doo-Hwan's political party and the opposition elites, to the exclusion of the political activists and student organisations that had led the struggle for democracy. Thus, this elite pact between the ruling and opposition parties limited the institutional reform of electoral procedures and voting rights, without dealing with issues relating to democratic consolidation, such as the removal of the antidemocratic apparatus and authoritarian social forces within state and civil society (Shin 2012). Less still did it seek to bring the emerging democratic political system to reflect the shifting of the power balance between labour and capital at the grassroots level, nor, as will be argued here, did it bring about an end to the repression of the labour movement. The elite-centred nature of this transition was even more apparent in the failure of the opposition camp to mobilise a credible opposition to the ruling party. Opposition politicians Kim Young-Sam and Kim Dae-Jung failed to agree on a single unified candidacy in the presidential elections of December 1987. With both candidates running, they split the vote, gaining 27.5 per cent and 26.5 per cent of the vote, respectively. As a result, General Roh Tae-Woo, one of the key figures behind the Kwangju massacre and Chun's nominated successor, won the presidency with only 35.9 per cent of the vote.

The process of democratisation in Taiwan was a more drawn-out process than it was in Korea. The one-party system meant that the establishment of the DPP in 1986 constituted a violation of the legal regulations governing political parties. This immediately posed the question of whether the KMT would deploy a strategy of repression or facilitate a transition toward democratisation. By July 1987, it became clear that the KMT had adopted the latter strategy as martial law and the ban on opposition parties were lifted. Free elections were subsequently introduced on a gradual basis over the coming decade. In 1991, elections were held for both the Legislative Yuan and the National Assembly, and the following year, further elections were held for the positions of provincial governorship and mayors of Taipei and Kaohsiung. Finally, in 1996, the first free presidential elections were held, in which KMT candidate Lee Teng-hui was elected president. However, the more gradual nature of democratisation in Taiwan meant that an opposition party did not come to power until 2000.

Again, however, Taiwan's democratic transition should be explained both as a result of domestic social pressure as well the changing geopolitical strategy of the United States. As in Korea, late industrialisation had brought forth new social forces that arose to contest authoritarian developmentalism. These social movements can roughly be separated into four distinct types. The first was oriented against the state's inaction in the face of new social issues, such as consumer protection, pollution, rising housing costs, and conservation. The second focused on state policies regarding ethnic groups and minorities' language rights, land control, and cultural identity and preservation, as well as issues relating more generally to disadvantaged groups. The third challenged the state's corporatist control over key social groups such as workers, farmers, students, women, teachers, and intellectuals, whereas the fourth challenged the rules surrounding politically sensitive issues, such as the ban on private contacts between Taiwan and mainland China, as well as human rights (Hsiao 1992b, p. 59). Each of these groups and the issues they raised had their origins in the specific nature of Taiwan's post-war passive revolution, such as the dominance of the industrialisation agenda over issues such as social wellbeing or equity, the ethnic basis of the post-war KMT state and its suppression of the non-mainlander ethnic groups, Leninist state corporatism and political authoritarianism, and more generally, the specific geopolitical context of Taiwan's industrialisation. However, as in Korea, the democratic transition also took place in the context of external US pressures. As a means of securing social stability, the American Institute Director James Lilley sought to convince Chiang Ching-Kuo that a transition toward democracy would be the best way to maintain stability and guide the country forward. Again, the impact of the People Power Revolution in the Philippines and the upheaval in Korea both motivated social movements and pressured the KMT to pursue pre-emptive democratic reforms (Katsiaficas 2012b, pp. 192–193).

Why had the United States shifted its broad geopolitical strategy toward that of democracy promotion? As has been well established in the literature, it was the rising social power of labour in both the West and in the Third World after the Second World War that strongly shaped the form of post-war US hegemony. This manifested in the international framework of embedded liberalism which in the West recognised core labour rights and provided for national-level social security systems. In the Third World, however, despite the anti-imperialist movements in which labour had often played a key role, New Deal ideals of high mass consumption and full employment were considered too expensive and inimical to both dependent capitalism across the Third World and to rapid industrialisation in East Asia. Instead, the United States promised national self-determination and opportunities for catch-up development for the developing world (Arrighi and Silver 2000, pp. 54–55). Thus, until the mid-1980s, the United States had followed a fairly consistent policy of supporting authoritarian strongmen in the Third World and in forestalling democratic movements that might upset US interests there (Robinson 1996). Indeed, as we have seen, the support for authoritarianism was a cornerstone of US Cold War policy toward Korea and Taiwan.

This global arrangement was, however, faced with deepening internal contradictions from the mid-1960s, when the manufacturing sectors in the advanced capitalist countries saw a marked decline in profitability (Duménil and Lévy 2004b, pp. 21–28). Part of the reason for this decline was that workers in the West were increasingly dissatisfied with the Keynesian class compromise. Whilst Fordism was an extraordinarily efficient regime of accumulation, it laid the foundations for its own demise. During the long boom of the 1950s and 1960s, there was a massive shift of employment from agriculture to industry, and the concentration of workers in factories and working-class neighbourhoods led to the emergence of new forms of class consciousness. The economic boom of the post-war years also meant that unemployment was low over a sustained period and management's prerogative was weakened as a result. Unemployment benefits were on the rise, and the economic consequences of losing one's job had a positive impact on workers' willingness to engage in collective action, leading to high rates of industrial unrest across the advanced industrial countries onwards (Glyn 2006, pp. 3–8). In addition to these emerging vertical contradictions between labour and capital, the advanced capitalist countries also faced heightened horizontal contradictions as a result of the rise of new economic powers such as West Germany and Japan. Whilst neoclassical economy theory would have predicted that in such conditions the less productive and thereby less profitable manufacturers in the United States would have exited the market, thus returning the economy to a 'natural equilibrium,' in reality, companies such as General Motors and Ford had invested huge amounts of money into plants and production lines and were thereby unwilling and unable to simply pull their money out and invest elsewhere. As a result, employers sought to repress workers' wages and make a profit on their circulating capital. The crisis was thus also a crisis of overproduction—that is, a situation whereby producers were not able to raise their prices up enough to make a profit (Brenner 1998).[1]

Initially, this global crisis of profitability presented itself in the form of an opportunity for East Asia. As Giovanni Arrighi (1996, pp. 6–8) has argued, the rise of East Asia as the most dynamic centre of processes of capital accumulation was a phenomenon of the 1970s and 1980s, namely after the onset of the world economic crisis. Though the bases of the developmental state were laid earlier, the region did not begin its specifically *catch-up* development, as measured in terms of global rankings of gross national product per capita, until after the onset of the crisis in the 1970s. Thus, it was specifically the regionalisation of East Asian economy that underpinned its developmental success. The reasons for this have already been discussed in the preceding chapters. The region was well situated geopolitically and had the requisite social conditions, including labour regimes based on the subordination of labour to be able to tap into flows of increasingly mobile international capital and launch a process of HCI. Yet, as Arrighi has also argued, it is also important to keep in mind the geopolitical context, particularly the dynamics of North-South relations during the Cold War. The crisis of profitability and the great stagflation of 1970s were deeply affected by the crisis of US hegemony, itself a result of the escalation of the Vietnam War and the US defeat there (Arrighi 2003, p. 67)—the latter of which was also, as argued previously, central to the industrialisation success of Korea and Taiwan, most significantly through military procurement contracts.

Nonetheless, as the global crisis of profitability deepened and the American economy experienced increasing trade deficits, the United States sought to restructure the terms of both the labour-friendly regimes of the West and the development-friendly regimes of the Third World. The promotion of democracy played a central role in this process. In the first instance, the shift toward support for democracy was a means of forestalling popular movements that might in turn threaten the mobility of transnational capital and the US-centred multilateral trading system. It can also, however, be viewed precisely as a means of dismantling the authoritarian developmental states that exerted increasing competitive pressure on the United States. As the United States sought to create a more 'level playing field,' its attitude toward authoritarian developmentalism thereby began to change. As noted above, democratisation would have the effect of allowing wage and production costs to rise, thus making East Asian exports less competitive, thereby reducing the US trade deficit. Domestically, democratisation became the means by which elites could re-legitimise their rule; as such, 'the same people remained in control beneath the surface appearance of democratic change' (Gills 1993, pp. 238–239). Indeed, US backing of post-authoritarian regimes remained conditional upon those nations not pursuing nationalistic economic programmes aimed at raising the standard of living for ordinary workers and achieving greater social equality (Amin 1993). Such programmes would immediately interfere with the United States's and the international business community's wider interests of extending the reach of transnational capital and ensuring the repatriation of profits. Furthermore, in order to facilitate the extended reach of global capital, Third World governments still needed to retain their coercive function and capacity to repress social forces, particularly the working class, in order to legitimise themselves from the point of view of international, and to a lesser extent, domestic capital (Gills *et al.* 1993).

Political democratisation and the labour surge

Following the democratic aperture, this dual nature of the democratic state was heightened by the extension of the democratic struggle to the economic sphere; as such, both Korea and Taiwan saw a strong surge in labour militancy in the late 1980s. In line with the relative differences between the countries, the labour surge in Korea was of a more dynamic and militant nature. As noted, the Korean developmental state had been responsible for imposing harsh restrictions on labour unions, allowing management to compel workers to work long hours, endure a high rate of industrial accidents, and receive low wages that did not keep up with gains in productivity (Park 2001, p. 63). This exploitative labour relations regime thereby failed to provide a sustainable basis for capital accumulation. As Bello and Rosenfield (1992, p. 44) have argued, 'by aligning itself with business to create a solid phalanx of opposition to labor in the thirty years of high-speed of industrialisation, the Korean state provided no significant safety valves for working class resentment.' Furthermore, the anticommunist and paternalistic Confucian ideology mobilised in favour of the repressive system of labour relations was ultimately counterproductive in that it served to encourage the emergence of a militant working-class consciousness (Koo 2001).

As a result, from the late 1980s, the Korean state and capital were increasingly unable to control labour unrest and, by extension, wage costs. Within two weeks of the 29th June declaration, workers went on to conduct the largest wave of protests and strikes in the country's history. Production was halted in the southeastern industrial cities of Pusan, Masan, Ch'angwŏn, and Ulsan and militant labour struggles broke out at many of the largest *chaebŏl*, including Hyundai, Daewoo, Lucky Goldstar, Kia, and Samsung. From the southeastern regions in which the heavy industries are concentrated, the unrest quickly spread to the rest of the country. This labour surge was not limited to workers in manufacturing, however, but also involved bus and taxi drivers, miners, fisherman, and office workers. Indeed, this workers' uprising bore striking similarities to the immediate post-liberation unrest in 1945, which saw an intense period of social organisation and protest. Between the months of July and September 1987 alone, a total of 3,111 cases of labour unrest, including work stoppages, wild cat strikes, and demonstrations, were recorded (Koo 2001, p. 157). As Table 4.1 shows, a total of 3,749 strikes took place in 1987, up from 276 the year before. It is important to note, however, that these struggles initially

TABLE 4.1 Unionisation and Strikes in Korea

Year	*Strikes*	*Density (%)*	*Year*	*Strikes*	*Density (%)*
1969	7	12.54	1989	1616	18.60
1970	4	12.63	1990	322	17.23
1971	10	12.67	1991	234	15.42
1972	0	12.87	1992	235	14.56
1973	0	13.20	1993	144	13.96
1974	58	14.76	1994	121	13.29
1975	52	15.79	1995	88	12.52
1976	49	16.45	1996	85	12.11
1977	58	16.71	1997	78	11.07
1978	102	16.90	1998	129	11.40
1979	105	16.79	1999	198	11.69
1980	206	14.67	2000	250	11.43
1981	186	14.64	2001	235	11.48
1982	88	14.39	2002	322	10.85
1983	98	14.08	2003	320	10.76
1984	114	13.24	2004	462	10.32
1985	265	12.39	2005	287	9.92
1986	276	12.28	2006	138	10.03
1987	3749	13.79	2007	115	10.57
1988	1873	17.77	2008	108	10.28

Source: Organisation for Economic Co-operation and Development, http://www.oecd.org/std/labour-stats/.

took place in a relatively permissive economic and political environment. Since 1986, Korea had been experiencing a period known as the 'three lows' (*sam chŏ*), which included a weak dollar relative to the yen, making Korea's exports more competitive and inducing an export boom to the United States; falling global oil prices, which reduced Korea's energy import costs; and low international interest rates, which helped Korea to reduce its foreign debts. Korean corporations were thus initially able to absorb the rapid wage increases of the late 1980s. Furthermore, with the impending presidential elections of late 1987, the government adopted a weak response to labour unrest for fear of negatively influencing the election's outcome (Kim 1997c, p. 1136).

These militant labour actions had several interrelated objectives. First and foremost, workers regarded inhumane treatment by management amongst their key concerns. Years of pent up *han* – a somewhat difficult-to-translate Korean cultural term referring to resentment caused by suffering, persecution, and injustice – underpinned these struggles. As one striking worker at Hyundai Heavy Industries was quoted as saying, 'My basic loyalty lies with the company. But we want equal treatment. We don't want the master–servant relationship that has been traditional in Korean companies' (quoted in Haberman 1987). Second, workers made demands for improvements in wages, which had remained repressed under the authoritarian labour regime. The success of these demands can be seen by the fact that wages increased by between 15 and 20 per cent in the months between July 1987 and the end of 1988. It was the workers in the heavy industries that made the greatest material gains, including those at Daewoo Shipbuilding and Heavy Industry, Daewoo Motor Corporation, and Daewoo Precision, despite the ban on strikes in the defence industries. Workers in nonunion companies such as Samsung Heavy Industries, Hyundai Heavy Industries, and Hyundai Engine Corporation also made significant gains (Deyo 1989, p. 81). The labour surge also constituted an attack against pro-company unions and the anti-union policies of management. The results can be seen in the fact that between 1987 and 1990, 45.6 per cent of existing union presidents stepped down, with 19.3 per cent of them forced to do so through votes of 'no confidence' by rank-and-file workers (Lee 1998, p. 351). Furthermore, the absolute number of unions rose from 2,742 in June 1987 to 7,883 in 1989 (Lee and Lee 2005, p. 5). Furthermore, the overall union density rate rose from 12.3 per cent in 1986, to 17.8 per cent in 1988 (see Table 4.1).

Perhaps most importantly, however, was the labour struggle against the state-corporatist labour laws that had still not been repealed despite the introduction of free presidential elections. An amendment of the labour laws on 28th November 1987 had granted basic rights to organise unions and engage in collective bargaining. However, unions were still banned from forming, cooperating with, or contributing to any political party. The prohibition of multiple unionism remained in place with the effect that monopoly status was granted to existing pro-management unions, preventing the legal recognition of independent unions. Restrictions against third-party intervention in collective disputes also remained in place, thereby deliberately hampering the formation of solidarity between labour and other social movements, such as the pro-labour religious organisations. Furthermore, public employees and workers in the defence industry continued to be denied the right to engage in collective action (Im 1992, pp. 13–14). The struggle for legal reform, however, immediately drew attention to the limitations of the enterprise union system and the need for increased solidarity between workers. The legacies of authoritarian labour relations were, as such, a key issue around which workers mobilised following the democratic aperture. Efforts to build new organisations began with the establishment of the Confederation of Masan-Ch'angwŏn Unions (*Mach'ang Noryŏn)* in December 1987. By the end of 1988, a total of eight regional federations had been established. White-collar workers similarly sought to establish occupational unions, reflecting the fact that white-collar workers in the same occupational or industrial category were often subject to similar market pressures and thus often had to deal with the government to protect their jobs. Therefore, by the end of the 1988, a total of eight occupational federations had been established (Koo 2001, pp. 177–178). Furthermore, these regional and occupational unions played a leading role in establishing national-level solidarity organisations aimed at labour law reform.

There had been some initial debate amongst independent unions over whether the appropriate strategy should be to seek the democratisation of the FKTU

FIGURE 4.1 Unit Labour Costs by Year, Korea
Source: US Bureau of Labor Statistics, http://www.bls.gov/data/#international.

(Im 1992, pp. 18–19). However, by January 1990, the independent labour movement had established its own national centre, *Chŏnnohyŏp* (the National Council of Trade Unions), which represented 600 members and 190,000 workers, mostly in the SME sector. Its founding statement argued (quoted in Katsiaficas 2012a, p. 342):

> We will struggle to achieve economic rights and unite with all democratic peoples' movements which fight for economic and social reform, achieve fundamental changes in the current situation of workers, and pursue our struggle for democracy, self-reliance, and peaceful national unification.

Whilst large enterprise and white-collar unions expressed solidarity with *Chŏnnohyŏp,* they remained affiliated with their own solidarity organisations. The organisational basis of *Chŏnnohyŏp* was therefore rather weak. Nonetheless, as Jin Kyoon Kim (2000a, pp. 493–496) argues, *Chŏnnohyŏp* played an important position within the history of the Korean labour movement, particularly with regards to the assistance it gave to collective bargaining and the struggle to reform the labour laws, as well as the role it played in resisting government repression of the labour movement. It organised, for example, the country's first general strike since the founding of the Republic of Korea in solidarity with the disputes at the Korean Broadcasting System and at Hyundai.

However, the Roh Tae-Woo government's hands-off approach to labour issues began to aggravate relations between state and capital. Initially, the *chaebŏl* had been able to absorb the cost of the wage increases won by labour. But when the period of the 'three lows' came to an end, the balance of trade shifted to negative and economic growth slowed. Central to this shift was the rapidly changing external context. Faced with its own economic problems, the increasing unwillingness of the United States to act as market of last resort led to aggressive attempts to liberalise the Korean economy. The revaluation of the *won* under US pressure in 1988 in particularly served to expose the lack of competitiveness of the *chaebŏl*. As Figure 4.1 shows, unit labour costs rose from US $74.80 in 1986 to US $125.60 in 1989. Furthermore, the challenge to Korea's competitive position was further exacerbated by the rise of newer low-wage competitor countries such as China and those in Southeast Asia. Korea experienced a marked slowdown in exports. Car exports to the United States, for example, which had accounted for 8 per cent of Korea's total exports to the United States in 1988, fell by 40 per cent in 1989 (Kihl 1991, p. 71). Labour unrest, however, showed no sign of abating. The Hyundai Group, in particular, was hit by a series of strikes in the late 1980s, and the company's management felt that the government was not dealing with labour unrest effectively. Indeed, it was this general dissatisfaction with the state's ability to provide favourable conditions for capital accumulation that led Hyundai founder Chung Joo Young to enter politics directly and participate in the presidential elections of 1992. Though Chung's candidacy was unsuccessful, it clearly demonstrated the radically transformed relationship between state and capital to that which had existed under the developmental state (Shin 2011, p. 14).

Following the onset of economic recession, the state abandoned its relatively hands-off approach to labour relations. On the very day that *Chŏnnohyŏp* was established, Roh Tae-Woo sought to overturn the minority position of the ruling party *(yŏsoyadae)* in the National Assembly by facilitating a merger with the two leading opposition parties in order to institutionalize majority conservative rule along the lines of the Liberal Democratic Party in Japan (Gills 1993, p. 247). Following this strategy of *trasformismo* toward the mainstream political opposition, the Roh Tae-Woo government adopted an intense campaign of repression against labour and *Chŏnnohyŏp* in particular. It launched inspections of the activities of its affiliated unions, put leaders on wanted lists, and promoted norms of 'no work, no pay' in order to deter financially weak unions from engaging in strike actions. Thus, no sooner had *Chŏnnohyŏp* been established, it was forced to engage in a struggle to defend both its own existence and that of the wider independent labour movement (Kim 2000a, p. 493). Though employers continued to adopt repressive strategies against workers, they also developed new personnel management strategies such as the introduction of performance-related pay to replace seniority wages. The *chaebŏl* also sought to scale back the most authoritarian aspects of their labour relations, including the abandonment of much-resented measures, such as regulation of hair length and compulsory physical exercise, in favour of more conciliatory approaches aimed at nurturing company loyalty amongst employees (Koo 2001, pp. 191–193). Whilst this combination of coercion and consent-based approaches did not lead to an end to resistance by labour, the fact that *Chŏnnohyŏp* was fighting a losing battle could be seen in the figures. Union density had by 1989 reached a peak at 18.6 per cent of the workforce, but declined to 17.2 per cent in 1990 and 15.4 per cent the following year (OECD, n.d.). Furthermore, whilst the labour surge had represented an organisational peak amongst male regular workers in large enterprises, by the early 1990s, many of the militant union leaderships were replaced by more conciliatory leaderships who explicitly eschewed militant tactics in favour of more co-operative approaches (Yu 1997, p. 123). As will be discussed in more detail in Chapter 5, this repression of militant unionism led to a more reformist tendency emerging within the labour movement, explicitly aimed at garnering wider public support.

With strong parallels to Korea, the KMT's lifting of martial law in 1987 opened up to Taiwanese labour a political space for heightened activism and expression of pent-up grievances. The surge was on a smaller scale, however. Between 1987 and 1989, the Taiwanese labour movement saw a wave of militant struggles involving eighty-eight major workers' collective actions. Many of these disputes, such as the railway worker and Miaoli bus driver strikes, as well as demonstrations by public utility employees, were aimed at the full enforcement of the LSL—particularly its stipulations relating to minimum wages and working hours, as well as pension, insurance benefits, and severance pay. A further key point of contention for labour was the government's policy of importing unskilled workers from Southeast Asia, which Taiwanese workers saw as a deliberate attempt to undermine their demands for improved labour conditions (Moore 1988a). More generally, however, these actions were aimed at challenging the authoritarian state corporatism and paternalistic management practices that had dominated Taiwan's labour relations over the post-war period (Hsiao 1992a, pp. 163–164). As in Korea, the surge saw the establishment of a number of solidarity organisations designed to overcome the enforced isolation inherent in the enterprise union system. In the early stages, such organisations took the form of clandestine arrangements under such designations as 'friendship organisations' and 'brotherhood associations.' The Tao-Chu-Miao Brotherhood, for example, was established in September 1987 and consisted of 13 unions in the Taoyuan, Hsinchu, and Miaoli counties (Chu 1996, p. 510).

Furthermore, in 1988, the National Federation of Independent Trade Unions was established. Although such organisations were in effect illegal as a result of the proscription of multiple unions, the KMT tolerated them as it did not wish to take actions that might further estrange workers from the party or provoke sustained labour unrest (Chen *et al.* 2003, p. 326). Indeed, as the election of the two anti-KMT worker functional representatives in the 1986 Legislative Yuan elections demonstrated, the KMT was fully aware of the threat of an alliance between labour and the DPP; as such, the KMT responded with conciliatory measures. For example, the KMT sought to improve its standing vis-à-vis workers and at the same time increase its capacity to effectively deal with labour issues by replacing the hitherto insignificant Division of Labour with a separate ministerial-level Council of Labor Affairs (CLA). The CLA was responsible for the administration of labour laws, the resolution of disputes, occupational health and safety matters, and social welfare legislation. Such measures did not, however, imply a relaxation of control over the labour movement but were aimed at its incorporation (Chen *et al.* 2003, p. 325). Management also responded with new methods of co-opting workers. For example, expansive banquets and gifts were given to unionists in order to encourage them to form pro-company unions and to dominate their executives. If such attempts at co-optation failed, however, more coercive methods were used, such as obstructing the formation of independent unions, subverting strikes, and sacking those workers considered to be troublemakers (Chu 1996, p. 507).

Again, as in Korea, the KMT government's relatively conciliatory approach was abandoned when it became clear that the labour surge was serving to undermine capitalist profitability and managerial prerogative. The first wave of labour struggles in 1988, for instance, had enabled workers from more than thirty companies to receive up to a 25 per cent increase in their year-end bonus. As Figure 4.2 shows, unit labour costs increased from US $79.90 in 1986, to US $129.50 in 1989. There was as a result increasing criticism of the government by a number of prominent capitalists for failing to tackle this rising unrest; they threatened to withhold investment and engage in a capital strike. Founder and owner of the Formosa Plastic Group, Wang Yong-Ching, for example, threatened to abandon plans for the building of an oil refinery in Taiwan and to build the plant in mainland China instead. Such threats thus compelled the government to deal with the unrest, and from the early 1990s, the KMT adopted increasingly repressive labour policies (Huang 2002, pp. 307–308). Upon entering office in May 1990, Premier Hau Pei-Tsun adopted a confrontational approach toward the ongoing social turmoil labelling activists as 'bullies' and vowing to put them behind bars. Leaders of the farmers, labour, and environmental movements were jailed, and the KMT moved to revise labour laws that were deemed 'too friendly' to workers (Ho 2010, pp. 9–10). The labour surge in Taiwan was thus brought to an end. Indeed, there had been significant labour defeats as early as 1989. In May of that year, a strike had broken out at

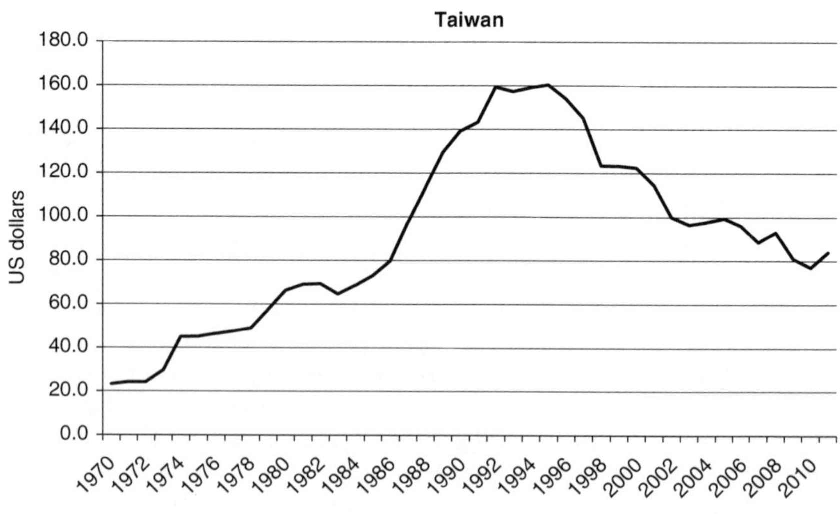

FIGURE 4.2 Unit Labour Costs by Year, Taiwan
Source: US Bureau of Labor Statistics, http://www.bls.gov/data/#international.

TABLE 4.2 Unionisation and Disputes in Taiwan

Year	*Disputes*	*Density (%)*	*Year*	*Disputes*	*Density (%)*
1965	15	NA	1998	4,138	41.1
1970	92	NA	1999	5,860	40
1975	458	NA	2000	8,026	38.5
1980	626	NA	2001	10,955	39.4
1987	1,609	34.2	2002	14,017	38.5
1988	1,314	37.6	2003	12,204	38.4
1989	1,943	38.1	2004	10,838	37.8
1990	1,860	43.3	2005	14,256	37
1991	1,810	48	2006	15,464	36
1992	1,803	48.1	2007	19,729	35.8
1993	1,878	49.5	2008	24,540	36.1
1994	2,061	48.9	2009	30,385	37.8
1995	2,271	46.6	2010	23,865	37.3
1996	2,659	44.6	2011	22,618	34.8
1997	2,600	42.2			

Note: These data do not reveal whether work stoppages actually took place and reveal little about illegal wildcat stoppages (Kleingartner and Peng 1991, pp. 436–437.)
NA, not available.
Source: Council for Labor Affairs, http://statdb.cla.gov.tw/html/nat/natehidx08.htm.

the Far Eastern Chemical Factory as a result of attempts by management to transfer union cadres to distant posts. The strike was the largest in post-war Taiwan, involving 2,000 workers, but was defeated through police repression, with union officials and its leader Lo Mei-Wen dismissed and prosecuted. The strike thus achieved very little, and what had been the most well organised and strongest union in the private sector was crushed overnight. After this setback, strikes became a less popular means of addressing workers' grievances; they were replaced by street demonstrations and efforts to lobby politicians for revisions to the labour laws. The defeat also saw a shift in the locus of the movement from the private sector to the unions of state-owned enterprises (Liu 2011, p. 36).

However, the key event that marked the final demise of the labour surge in Taiwan was the 1992 Keelung Bus Company strike. This strike over union independence and improved wages and working conditions lasted for 40 days in the summer of 1992. The strike was thereby one of the longest in Taiwan's post-war history and was distinctive in terms of the high degree of mobilisation by male strikers' spouses, who regularly organised and attended picket lines. However, the company utilised provisions in the LSL, the Labour – Management Dispute Settlement Law, and Labour Union Law, which effectively made it possible for the company to outlaw almost any strike. Thus, the Keelung Bus Drivers' Union, previously considered to be one of vanguards of the labour movement, was defeated, and the drivers returned to work having achieved virtually nothing (Minns and Tierney 2003,

p. 115). These defeats, along with the repressive approach of Premier Hau, marked the onset of the decline of the independent labour movement. The KMT subsequently sought to revise the legal system governing labour relations in line with the interests of management. These revisions included the removal of compulsory union membership, the legalisation of multiple unions in the same workplace so as to undermine existing unions, banning unions from certain industries, and requiring a higher level of consultation with union members regarding any planned industrial action (Ho 2006a, pp. 114–115). As a result of these changes, the number of workers involved in labour disputes reached a record high of 62,391 in 1989 and fell to 12,696 in 1991. Labour unrest did not rise again until the East Asian financial crisis in 1997 and 1998, when large numbers of workers were faced with the effects of the regional economic downturn as well as the government's policy of privatisation of SOEs. As such, the KMT's response bore striking similarities with that of the Korean government's: an initial strategy aimed at co-optation of labour in the context of a relatively favourable international economic climate quickly gave way to a more repressive approach when it was deemed that independent labour militancy threatened management's prerogative.

Conclusion

The rise of East Asia in the post-war era was from the outset established on a set of mutable social and geopolitical underpinnings. As I have argued, the end of the Second World War and the Japanese surrender left East Asia at a revolutionary juncture. The incorporation of the region into the ascendant US hegemonic order was based on the prior establishment of a specific configuration of state–society relations through a process of region-wide passive revolution. As we have seen in this chapter, however, the East Asian developmental regimes of Korea and Taiwan were subsequently challenged from within by the rising social power of labour. Workers were part of a broad social coalition that pushed for democratic transition, and this democratisation was itself indicative of the decline of the apparent autonomy of the state from society.

Yet, as I have also argued, democratisation cannot be explained without reference to challenges to US hegemony in the latter quarter of the twentieth century. This crisis of the US economy stemmed in part from the inherent instability in its relationship with East Asia. Whilst neoclassical economics argues that trade is theoretically a positive-sum game, the influx of manufactured goods from the authoritarian East Asia developmental states created tensions with particular domestic constituencies within the United States. At the same time, the inability of the United States to police the geopolitical boundaries of the East Asian region ultimately led to the re-admission of China into the regional and world order. Furthermore, from the mid-1980s, the United States responded to these challenges by seeking the liberalisation of East Asia's neomercantilist states. This countermovement would have important implications for workers because it would greatly facilitate the transition away from national developmentalism toward a more fully transnationalised regional production network—a trend that was exacerbated by wage rises and ensuing capital flight. Neoliberalism thus emerged in the United States as a means of both state and capital to reassert its position against labour domestically and its economic competitors globally.

Within this broad process, one of the most remarkable features of the Korean and Taiwanese cases has been their similarity in terms of the path of their historical development. Labour repression underpinned the post-war developmental paradigm, but the very process of rapid industrialisation served to undermine that system. In the context of increasing labour shortages, workers gained the structural power with which to challenge labour repression and to push for improvements in wages, working conditions, and labour rights more broadly. Labour formed an important axis in the broad social coalition that emerged to challenge authoritarian developmentalism, and the democratic aperture that both countries experienced in the late 1980s further provided the space for workers to mobilise a more coordinated attack on the authoritarian labour regime. Favourable international conditions led both the Korean and Taiwanese governments to initially adopt a noninterventionist approach to this labour activism. Yet, as economic conditions worsened at the end of the 1980s, this noninterventionist approach became a threat to the legitimacy of the state as business threatened to withhold investment. Amidst the repression in the early 1990s, organised labour was forced to rethink its strategy and, in both case's, was faced with the question of how to directly enter the formal political realm in order to directly influence the process of reform of labour relations.

Note

1 Whilst these vertical and horizontal explanations of the crisis of Fordism have been presented as mutually exclusive (see Brenner 1998, pp. 13–26), they are in fact, as Crotty (1999) argues, compatible. The greater share of profits to labour only negatively impact profitability when the competition between capitals prevents corporations from raising prices to compensate. Furthermore, the very premise that an inexhaustible reserve army of labour makes the labour–capital dynamic irrelevant to global capital profitability is directly challenged by the analysis offered in the pages of this book (see also Arrighi 2003, p. 31).

5

LABOUR, NEOLIBERALISM, AND THE REFORMULATION OF EAST ASIA'S PASSIVE REVOLUTION

Much has been written on the transition toward neoliberalism in East Asia and how politicians and policymakers in the region came under the increased influence of the global neoliberal *zeitgeist*. For the most part, the focus has been on how developmental states, understood as autonomous bureaucracies formulating industrial policies for the wider purposes of national development, came under the influence of neoliberalism, either through increased consent toward changing global economic norms or through the coercive role of the international financial institutions (IFIs) and outside powers such as the United States (Chang *et al.* 1998, Wade and Veneroso 1998). As I argue in this chapter, however, it is important to give due consideration to the constitutive role of labour within this neoliberal transition, both at the global level and within the East Asian developmental states themselves. Whilst the world economic crisis of the 1970s initially served as an opportunity for broader regional catch-up industrialisation, the 'neoliberal counterrevolution' (Duménil and Lévy 2004a) led the United States and IFIs to pressure East Asian developmental regimes to liberalise their economies and reduce barriers to entry by transnational capital. In addition, however, the East Asian countries also came under internal domestic pressures for reform. In Japan, for example, the 1985 Plaza Accord and the ensuing 'high yen crisis' significantly decreased Japan's competitiveness in terms of labour costs and led to a renewed round of domestic restructuring and internationalisation of Japanese production (Steven 1990, p. 40). By the late 1980s, the rise of labour in Korea and Taiwan had also undermined their existing niche in low-wage production and produced the same impetus toward neoliberal restructuring as had existed in the industrial heartlands of Western capitalism (Chang 2001). As such, East Asian capital became increasingly transnational, thereby undermining the national developmental model and the supervisory capabilities of the developmental state. As in the West, the rise of neoliberalism as a political project was also very much about seeking to reverse the gains made by labour.

In the midst of these domestic and international pressures, one of the key tasks of East Asian states has been that of formulating a new strategy of passive revolution to secure the acquiescence of labour in a more flexible neoliberal economy. Whilst East Asian labour regimes traditionally took the form of state-corporatist institutions and the mobilisation of nationalist and anti-communist ideologies for the purposes of catch-up industrialisation, more recently this has occurred through more liberal labour relations frameworks alongside the rhetoric of 'national competitiveness' under conditions of globalisation. In this chapter, I argue that attempts by organised labour to contest restructuring must be understood within the context of a new neoliberal passive revolution. As Antonio Gramsci argued, a key feature of passive revolution was the strategy of *trasformismo*. This originally referred to the nature of Italian party politics in the aftermath of the *Risorgimento,* whereby the right-wing Moderates led by Count Camillo Cavour and the Republican Party led by former 'radicals' Giuseppe Mazzini and later Giuseppe Garibaldi largely adopted identical programmes of industrial modernisation, political reform, and imperial expansion (Jones 2006, p. 14). As such, *trasformismo* describes the absorption of potentially opposing forces that may disrupt passive revolution, involving the incorporation of cultural, social, economic, and political leaders into elite networks (Moore 2005, p. 45). With regard to labour, *trasformismo* involves the promotion by elites of the 'politics of reform.' The acceptance of certain demands from below serves to encourage the working class to restrict its struggle to the economic-corporative domain. This forms part of a wider attempt to preserve the hegemony of the dominant class whilst changes in the world of production are accommodated within the current social formation (Sassoon 1982, p. 133).

As I will argue, in Japan, conditions of global neoliberalism have led to the increased consolidation of the labour movement at the national level and greater scope for labour's participation in national-level policymaking. However, this participation has taken place amidst the ongoing flexiblisation of labour and a weakening of organised labour at the grassroots level. For the most part, however, there has been a remarkable degree of continuity in the Japanese labour regime, which is a testament to the thorough political defeat of the working class in Japan in the immediate post-war era. Whilst resistance to neoliberal restructuring in Korea and Taiwan has been greater and more sustained, similar trends of co-optation have occurred. Both countries have seen a marked transition from the repressive labour regimes that remained in place until at least the late 1980s toward the more liberal institutions that accompanied formal democratisation. Unions too have adapted to these new institutions and have sought to use them in their resistance to the vestiges of authoritarian developmentalism and to deepening neoliberal restructuring. In contrast to the Western European experience, however, neoliberalism in Korea and Taiwan should not be understood simply as the destruction of the welfare state, the undermining of labour rights, and the flexiblisation of labour but also as the establishment of new institutions and legal frameworks. The dual nature of this transition from authoritarian developmentalism to neoliberal democracy had played a specific role in the continuation of the East Asian passive revolution, particularly through strategies of *trasformismo* vis-à-vis labour.

Japanese labour and the rise of neocorporatism

There has been much debate surrounding the extent to which Japan and other East Asian developmental states have undergone transitions toward neoliberal state forms in recent years. Linda Weiss (2003) and Mark Beeson (2004) have both argued, for example, that arguments of global convergence toward neoliberalism notwithstanding, the Japanese state retains strong developmental characteristics. However, they draw quite different conclusions regarding the implications of such continuity for the future of the Japanese economy. Weiss argues that whilst there has been no retreat of the state in Japan, the successful industrialisation of the Japanese economy has meant that there is no longer any need for Japan's pilot agency, the Ministry of International Trade and Industry, to take an active role in promoting exports or presiding over industry creation. Whilst the state has abandoned many of its former policy instruments such as capital, foreign exchange, and licensing controls, it has created new tools more suited to the internationalisation of Japanese capital. These tools include the support of self-governing cartels in basic materials, the promotion of technological innovation through cooperative arrangements, and the facilitating of the internationalisation of corporate activity through the use of overseas developmental aid (Weiss 1997, p. 18). Beeson (2003) argues, on the other hand, that Japan's failure to overcome the crisis is precisely a result of the failure to reform the developmental state and, in particular, its ossified institutionalised relationship between business and the bureaucracy. A key example of how features of the developmental state have become inimical to further growth is the practice of *amakaduri* or 'descent from heaven' (see Colignon and Usui 2003). Upon retiring, Japanese government officials would obtain positions on boards of private corporations, thereby enabling the bureaucracy to monitor and respond to changing business conditions, as well as to construct and implement policies. Over time, however, this practice has become increasingly characterised by cronyism, collusion, and self-serving and opaque practices. This can be seen clearly in the construction industry, where government funding of infrastructure projects often goes to building companies with political connections (Beeson 2003, pp. 8–9).

For both Weiss and Beeson, the developmental state is understood to denote a close relationship between business and the bureaucracy. However, Weiss sees that relationship as productive, whereas Beeson regards it as dysfunctional and characterised by corruption. It is necessary, however, to extend the analysis of changing state forms beyond relations between business and the bureaucracy toward underlying social changes in Japan's labour regime. In this sense, the origins of neoliberalism in Japan can be seen as extending back several decades. During the 1960s, Japan's emphasis on the heavy industrial sector had created excessive dependence on energy- and resource-intensive technologies. Between 1970 and 1974, rapid rises in primary product prices led to an overall worsening of Japan's terms of trade by 32 per cent in those years. Furthermore, overaccumulation of capital in relation to the country's working population led to rises in real wages of 31 per cent between 1970 and 1973, thereby leading to an inflationary crisis. Japan was thus fully exposed to the global crisis of profitability. The quadrupling of world oil prices posed a particular problem for Japan, dependent as it was on imports for over 90 per cent of its energy (Itoh 1994, pp. 33–34). These events thus induced an outward expansion of Japanese capital in order to secure raw material inputs, including basic materials industries such as steel, nonferrous metals, petrochemicals, pulp, and paper. Domestically, the focus of the economy shifted toward machinery, final processing, and final assembly, particularly in the high-tech industries (Steven 1990, pp. 74–75)

The government placed pressure on domestic industries to rationalise their operations and put labour on the defensive through tight monetary and fiscal policies in 1974 and 1975. However, it did not intervene directly in the restructuring process. It was Japanese corporations, particularly in the heavy and chemical industries, that took the initiative by launching a wave of restructuring. For the most part, these corporations retained the lifetime employment system; as a result, corporate restructuring did not lead to higher levels of unemployment. Instead, Japanese corporations adopted strategies such as the reduction of overtime and reassignment of workers to affiliated companies within the same *keiretsu,* particularly to subcontracting companies (Otake 1999, p. 376). This latter strategy, known as *shukko*, has been a key means whereby Japanese companies have been able to cut personnel expenses whilst avoiding layoffs by transferring employees from large enterprises to small and medium enterprises (SMEs). Whilst this approach was arguably more favourable to workers' interests, the failure to decisively reduce manpower levels served to exacerbate capital's problem of excessive labour power and physical capacity in Japanese corporations and thereby oppressed the recovery of the rate of profit (Itoh 1994, pp. 43–44). Yet, although there were no significant layoffs, there was nonetheless a general attack on the livelihood of the working class. The introduction of new technologies served to exploit the parallel intensification of the temporary labour and subcontracting systems and played a central role in raising Japan's competitiveness in machine industries, to the extent that it surpassed the other leading advanced industrialised economies. Indeed, it was this increased exploitation of labour that enabled Japanese corporations to keep wage costs from rising in the latter half of the 1970s (Steven 1990, p. 15).

These structural changes resulting from the crisis of the early 1970s also brought about a broader change in the political strategies of the Japanese labour movement. Japan has in the past been characterised as a case of 'corporatism without labour' (Pempel and Tsunekawa 1979). The labour movement was excluded from participation in policymaking at the national level and was weakened and co-opted at the enterprise level. The Japanese labour regime has not remained static, however. As the crisis led Japan onto a 'medium growth path' (Yoshitomi 1976), labour unions began to reconsider their reliance on the *Shuntō* Spring Offensive as the primary means by which workers conducted wage bargaining. A key weakness of the *Shuntō,* at least from the perspective of state and capital, was that wage demands did not take into account the health of the wider economy. In 1974, for example, when Japan experienced an unprecedented negative growth rate, the *Shuntō* was as aggressive as ever.

As Table 5.1 shows, the annual number of strikes rose to 5,211, more than double the rate of 2,498 just two years earlier. The achievement of wage increases far in excess of the rate of inflation led to heightened public disquiet regarding the perceived selfishness of the labour unions. As a result, government, business, and the more moderate labour unions sought to establish new mechanisms whereby labour could participate in national policymaking alongside business and government (Taira 1988, p. 161), thereby shifting the emphasis away from the wage struggle at the grassroots level. Moderate labour unions, particularly those belonging to the International Metalworkers Federation–Japan Committee, took the lead in this reorientation toward national-level corporatist policymaking. These unions were

TABLE 5.1 Unionisation Rates and Strikes in Japan

Year	*Density (%)*	*Strikes*	*Year*	*Density (%)*	*Strikes*
1958	32.7	903	1986	28.2	620
1959	32.1	887	1987	27.6	474
1960	32.2	1,063	1988	26.8	498
1961	34.5	1,401	1989	25.9	362
1962	34.7	1,299	1990	25.2	284
1963	34.7	1,079	1991	24.5	310
1964	35.0	1,234	1992	24.4	263
1965	34.8	1,542	1993	24.2	252
1966	34.2	1,252	1994	24.1	230
1967	34.1	1,214	1995	23.8	209
1968	34.4	1,546	1996	23.2	193
1969	35.2	1,783	1997	22.6	178
1970	35.4	2,260	1998	22.4	145
1971	34.8	2,527	1999	22.2	154
1972	34.3	2,498	2000	21.5	118
1973	33.1	3,326	2001	20.7	90
1974	33.9	5,211	2002	20.2	74
1975	34.4	3,391	2003	19.6	47
1976	33.7	2,720	2004	19.2	51
1977	33.2	1,712	2005	18.7	50
1978	32.6	1,517	2006	18.2	46
1979	31.6	1,153	2007	18.1	54
1980	30.8	1,133	2008	18.1	52
1981	30.8	955	2009	18.5	48
1982	30.5	944	2010	18.5	38
1983	29.7	893	2011	N/A	28
1984	29.1	596	2012	17.9	38
1985	28.9	627			

Sources: Ministry of Health, Labour and Welfare, http://www.mhlw.go.jp/english/database/db-l/index.html; OECD Labour Stats, http://www.oecd.org/std/labour-stats/.

more exposed to international competition and consequently had greater concerns regarding the linkage between wage increases and inflation.

Union leaders thus argued that it was no longer possible to maintain a sole focus on nominal wage gains and that demands had to take into account the international competitive position of the exporting metal industries. They also argued that focusing on real rather than nominal wage increases required unions to participate in the formulation of government policies relating to price controls (Inagami 1996, p. 176). As such, these unions began to tie their wage demands to growth in national productivity in order to prevent stagflation. At the same time, they increasingly made demands for improvements in social welfare provisions and income tax cuts; by their very nature, these demands could not be addressed at the enterprise level but required labour's participation in national policymaking (Carlile 1994a, pp. 610–612). Japan's labour regime thereby underwent a transition from a wage-bargaining system centred round the *Shuntō* Spring Offensive to one more properly resembling a corporatist structure.

Participation in national-level policymaking can also be seen as addressing a key shortcoming in labour's hitherto more pluralistic mode of engagement with the political sphere. Hitherto, the labour movement's political activities had been channelled through *Sōhyō* and *Dōmei* to the Japanese Socialist Party (JSP) and the Democratic Socialist Party (DSP), respectively. However, aside from the JSP's brief eight months in power in 1947 under Tetsu Katayama and the DSP's participation in a short-lived coalition government in 1993, both parties had been excluded from power for most of the post-war era, thereby presenting a barrier to labour's attempts to achieve their political aims. More meaningful participation by labour in national policymaking would first require the establishment of new organisations that would enable the labour movement to speak with a unified voice.

Following the failed attempts by the leadership of the postal workers' union in the late 1960s to unify labour's political representation through the merger of the JSP and DSP, the private sector unions took the lead in establishing the Labour Union Policy Roundtable (LUPR) in 1976. The LUPR declared at its formation that it would emphasise economic policy, employment, prices, and tax reform, as well as social security, housing, education, and medicine. This turn to 'economic realism' was one that unsurprisingly was met favourably by both employers, because they too were seeking to keep down nominal wage increases without alienating the labour force and provoking resistance (Whittaker 2003, p. 287). Formal tripartite consultations and informal negotiations were thus frequently held in order to reach consensus among labour, business, and government about how to allocate economic benefits in the context of a more sluggish national economy. Industrial restructuring and the increased role of national corporatist arrangements also led to changes at the enterprise level. In response to the achievement of some degree of consensus, labour increasingly moderated its demands at enterprise-level collective bargaining (Kume 1988, p. 660).

However, despite the formation of this LUPR, the fractious nature of Japan's labour federations inhibited labour's influence. As noted in Chapter 2, for much of the post-war era, the national-level labour movement in Japan was divided into *Sōhyō,* which represented public-sector unions and was politically aligned with the JSP, and *Dōmei,* which represented private-sector unions and was aligned with the DSP (Broadbent 1990, p. 43). The merger of *Sōhyō* and *Dōmei* in 1987 to form *Rengō* in 1987 was, as such, a milestone in the development of the Japanese labour movement. It did not fully unify the labour movement as the formation of *Rengō* was opposed by the more militant Japanese Communist Party-aligned *Zenrōren* and the smaller *Zenrōkyō,* the latter of which was established in 1989. Nonetheless, despite these continued divisions, *Rengō* contained 60 industrial federations and 20 affiliate federations, representing 60 per cent of organised labour in Japan (Whittaker 2003, p. 287).

This merger of *Sōhyō* and *Dōmei* was made possible by the decreasing salience of ideological divisions that had characterised the labour movement throughout much of the post-war era. The ideological outlook of the *Sōhyō* and *Dōmei* leadership had been formed during the turbulent occupation years. It was not until the 1970s that the leaders of these organisations began to retire, thereby paving way for a new generation of leaders whose views were shaped in the context of declining political polarisation and increased economic prosperity and employment security. The formation of *Rengō* can thus be seen as a watershed moment, whereby this new leadership achieved hegemony over the mainstream labour movement (Carlile 1994a, p. 609). For the most part, however, *Rengō* has adopted a conservative line toward labour issues. It was the unions affiliated with the International Metalworkers Federation–Japan Committee and supported by *Dōmei* that took the leading role in the organisation's establishment. These were the unions at the core of the Japanese economy and were thoroughly committed to maintaining and promoting the international competitiveness of the large corporations in which they were located. Indeed, this included unions that had even supported the privatisation of public-sector corporations in the mid-1980s, such as the Japan Salt and Tobacco Company, Nihon Telephone and Telegraph, and the Japan National Railway (JNR). After its foundation, *Rengō* offered no support to the ongoing struggle against the privatisation and division of JNR. This was despite the fact that the privatisation of the JNR had particularly anti-worker implications. As a result of the privatisation, the National Railway Workers' Union, JNR's most militant union, saw a decline in membership from 500,000 to 40,000 (Broadbent 1990, p. 43).

In the first half of the 1990s, efforts made by *Rengō* to participate in national policymaking were met with some success. Attempts to reform Japan's tradition of long working hours (see Figure 5.1), for example, showed some progress, with *Rengō* making demands through negotiations for a five-day working week as a primary means through which to reduce working hours. This political pressure from labour, however, was aided by widespread international criticism of the role of long working hours in underpinning the competitiveness of the Japanese economy, and the Japanese government itself was thus consequently eager to deflect such criticism. As a result, a forty-working-hour week was implemented in April 1997, and overall, working hours fell from a yearly average of 2,052 in 1990 to 1,879 in 1998 (Inoue

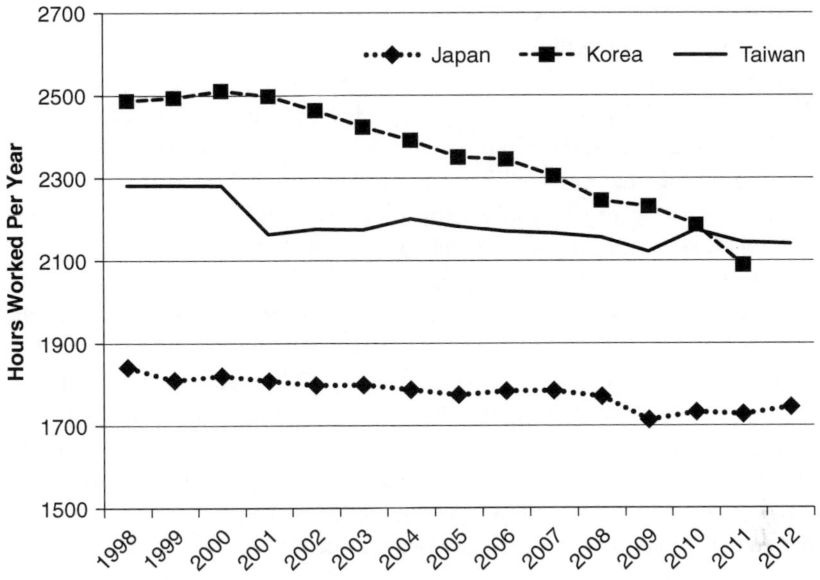

FIGURE 5.1 Hours Worked Per Year in Japan, Korea, and Taiwan
Source: OECD Labour Stats, http://www.oecd.org/std/labour-stats/.

2002, pp. 36–37). Whilst this reduction in working hours was a significant victory for *Rengō,* the mechanisms by which labour has participated in policymaking have been weakened in recent years. Prior to the mid-1990s, labour law revision bills were typically submitted to the Diet only after they were negotiated by government, business, and labour in the Deliberation Council in the Ministry of Labor. Since 1996, however, the initiative for labour law revisions has passed to the Deregulation Subcommittee in the Cabinet. This subcommittee now takes the leading role in setting agendas and determining the overall direction of revisions. Once the Cabinet approves the proposed revisions, only then are they passed to the Deliberation Council; the Council is no longer a forum for discussing and shaping revision bills through consensus. Bills can only be discussed once they are handed down from above. As such, the Deliberation Council found itself unable to challenge neoliberal revisions to the Labour Standards Act in 1998 and 2003 or the Worker Dispatch Law in 1999 and 2003. In these instances, *Rengō* found itself only able to resist amendments in partnership with sympathetic political parties, but has itself been unable to proactively promote amendments (Nakamura 2007, p. 11).

On the one hand, the formation of *Rengō* did represent the end of a debilitating split in the Japanese labour movement and the achievement of unparalleled unity at the national level. Yet, *Rengō*'s role in policy participation, inevitably perhaps, led to a debate over whether *Rengō*'s new role amounted to participation or incorporation. As Whittaker has argued, *Rengō* has only been successful to the extent that its proposals are in line with wishes of government and business, raising the question of whose interests *Rengō* actually represents. Whilst *Rengō* claims that it represents 'working people,' it is in reality dominated by the moderate large private-sector unions and has often been criticised for failing to represent the interests of workers in smaller enterprises (Whittaker 2003, p. 288). Indeed, here can be seen the true essence of Japan's famed 'harmonious' labour relations. Whereas enterprise unions together with management created harmonious labour relations at the shop-floor level, the goal of *Rengō* was to create harmonious relations amongst government, business, and labour at the national level. At the same time, however, this 'co-operative' labour movement became an agent of social control and suppression of conflict. Although *Rengō* was invited to participate in national discussions as the recognised representative of labour, the unequal distribution of power served to reinforce class domination, enabling government and business to institute industrial, economic, social, and military policies without resistance (Broadbent 1990, p. 47). Indeed, it is important to note that advances in terms of representation at the national level have done little to reverse the declining strength of the labour movement at the grassroots level. The unionisation rate has declined from 34.7 per cent in 1975, to 28.9 per cent in 1985, to 23.8 per cent in 1995, and to 22.4 per cent in 1998 (Kwon 2004, p. 340).

No doubt these trends of organisational decline are a reflection of the sustained process of restructuring in the Japanese economy from the mid-1980s caused by currency realignments and the ensuing high yen crisis. In the early 1980s, Japan's export success in high value-added products had been seen by many in the United States as underpinning the latter's growing trade deficits and deindustrialisation. The United States thus pressured Japan to take part in the international negotiations that led to the September 1985 Plaza Accord, which sought to use exchange-rate adjustments to bring about a more even trade relationship between the United States and its economic partners. As a result, the Japanese yen appreciated by 46 per cent within three years of the Accord, leading to a decline in Japan's export competitiveness (Burkett and Hart-Landsberg 2000, p. 116). Furthermore, as Figure 5.2 shows, these currency realignments meant that unit labour costs in Japanese manufacturing rose from $56.7 dollars in 1985 to $106 dollars in 1988. The high yen crisis thus led to another relocation of industry offshore, particularly to Southeast Asia and China (Bernard and Ravenhill 1995), as well as a hollowing out of the domestic economy (Bailey 2003).

In the industries that maintained domestic production, there was a degree of rationalisation and retrenchment. The shipbuilding industry, for example, reduced its workforce from 60,000 to 40,000 workers. Kawasaki Steel implemented a five-year plan in 1985 to reduce the workforce by 4,500. The closure of coal mines in Kyushu and Hokkaido led to mass migration out of towns previously reliant on the industry (Broadbent 1990, p. 43). Furthermore, the bursting of the Japanese bubble economy and ensuing lost decade(s) of Japanese growth continued to exert a deleterious impact on labour. As Figure 5.3 shows, although still relatively low in comparative terms, Japanese unemployment increased from 2.1 per cent in 1990 to 3.2 per cent in 1995, and again to 4.7 per cent in 2000. However, throughout this

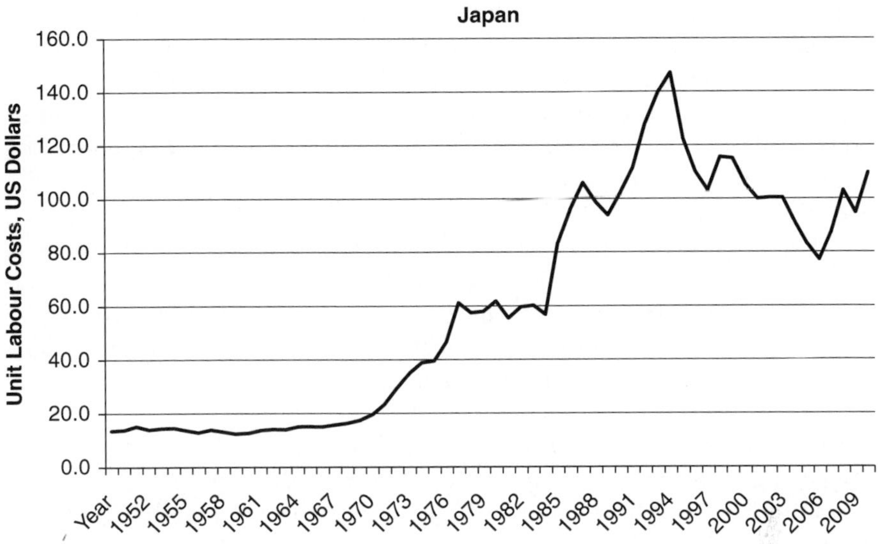

FIGURE 5.2 Unit Labour Costs by Year, Japan
Source: US Bureau of Labor Statistics.

era, the dominant response on the part of Japanese management remained not that of layoffs but transferring workers to the secondary labour market consisting mainly of peripheral, temporary, and part-time workers (Otake 1999, p. 377).

As a result, there has been much discussion in recent years as to the extent to which this constant process of restructuring has led to the broader decline of the distinctive 'three pillars' of the Japanese employment system amidst alleged

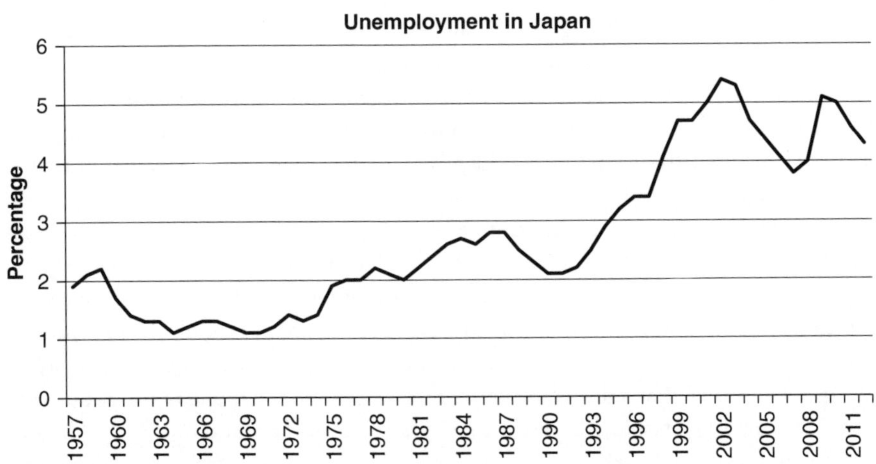

FIGURE 5.3 Unemployment in Japan
Source: OECD Labour Stats, http://www.oecd.org/std/labour-stats/.

tendencies toward convergence under global neoliberalism. It has been suggested, for example, that Japan's distinctive employment practices have been more resilient than we might otherwise expect (Watanabe 2000). One response of Japanese corporations to the ongoing economic malaise, as noted above, has been that of maintaining the lifetime employment guarantee by loaning workers out to subsidiaries. As a *Rengō* official was quoted (Whittaker 2003, p. 289),

> Firms still do their best to avoid redundancies by relying on reduced overtime work, transfers to new positions within the company, and 'loaning' some workers to firms within the same corporate group. When redundancy is unavoidable, management goes about trying to find a new job for the prospective job loser so that no interim unemployment occurs.

There is evidence to suggest, however, that the implicit job security guarantee is beginning to unravel. According to Hamaaki *et al.* (2012, p. 811), most of the studies that have argued for continuity in Japanese employment practices, particularly in its key features of seniority wages and lifetime employment, were conducted in the 1990s and early 2000s. However, it was only in the late 1990s that employers started to downsize their workforces by laying off employees – a process that has been reflected in the higher unemployment rate in the early 2000s. Indeed, in the past decade, government surveys have shown an intensification of workforce reduction. The percentage of companies that have carried out workforce reductions have increased by 1.3 per cent in 1995, 3.8 per cent in 1999, 2.3 per cent in 2000, 3.8 per cent in 2001, and 4.5 per cent in 2002. By 2002, unemployment levels in Japan reached an unprecedented high of 5.4 per cent (see Figure 5.3). This is not enough to pronounce the end of lifetime employment per se, because comparatively more companies still choose overtime restrictions and *shukko* reassignments. Outright layoffs are still far below what is typical in Western industrialised countries. Nonetheless, the figures do suggest that the lifetime employment system is gradually being weakened (Jung and Cheon 2006, p. 461). There has also been a decline in the weight given to seniority in wages and an even greater emphasis given to the evaluated component of remuneration packages with greater emphasis on results, leading to a more individualised human resources management-style approach (Whittaker 2003, p. 289).

In any case, it does appear that change in the Japanese labour regime has occurred at rather a slow pace, which serves to confound expectations surrounding convergence under global neoliberalism. Such continuity seems at first sight to be counterintuitive. One argument has been that this continuity has much to do with the fact that, in conditions of intense competition under globalisation, Japanese corporations have found that success in the market increasingly depends on tightly coupled production networks, including just-in-time production, and highly coordinated supplier links. In addition, the predictability of the shop floor and active cooperation of the workforce to produce at high quality and on a just-in-time basis has led to an intensification of cooperation with workers and traditional protections (Thelen and Kume 1999, p. 478). However, if the Japanese labour regime is understood as one that is predicated upon the subordination of labour, then the resilience of the 'three pillars' becomes even less surprising. This continuity should therefore be understood in relation to the fact that the Japanese labour regime was, as argued in Chapter 2, from the outset oriented toward the hyper-exploitation of labour. Whilst productivity in Japan has seen a continuous increase – increasing 2.17 times between 1975 and 1985 – real wages have by contrast risen by only 5.9 per cent over the same period. The social position of enterprise unions have been weakened and, as noted above, unionisation has declined with the increase of various types of irregular unskilled part-timers, casual employees, and detached workers. The increased utilisation of cheaper labour from abroad has also been detrimental to Japanese workers, who have been largely unable to bargain for higher wages. Despite gains in productivity, the number of deaths through overwork (*karoshi*) number at approximately 23,000 per year, whilst the birth rate in Japan has declined to an historical low, leading to a failure of the labour force to reproduce itself (Itoh 1994, pp. 45–47).

Labour and neoliberalism in Korea

The trend toward the growing incorporation of labour alongside sustained neoliberal restructuring has also been apparent in Korea. On the one hand, this restructuring came about as a result of heightened external pressure on the Korean government for economic liberalisation. The US government succeeded in forcing Seoul to upwardly revalue the won by 16 per cent in 1988 alongside greater market access for US products (Hart-Landsberg 1993, pp. 237–238). Furthermore, the 'Clinton Doctrine' in the 1990s was an aggressive foreign economic policy aimed at promoting exports and opening targeted economies, such as Korea's, to American goods and investment (Cumings 1998, pp. 51–52). One of the reasons that the United States possessed the capacity to force adjustment on the East Asian states, such as Korea, was the historical fact of the latter's excessive dependence on US markets as an external source of demand—a level of dependence on US markets surpassed only by Canada and Mexico. The Clinton administration thus used this leverage to open up the East Asian states' domestic markets to American products and investments and to restrict certain exports to the United States (Pempel 1999, pp. 177–178).

However, the role of external coercion is in itself insufficient as an explanation for the neoliberal transition in Korea. Much of the impetus for liberalisation came from within the country as a response to the growing contradictions in Korea's developmental model. Rising wages played an important role in this process. As noted in Chapter 4, following the transition to formal democracy and the lifting of the most stringent restrictions on independent union organising, workers were able to make significant gains in wages and working conditions. Wages increased by 19.6 per cent in 1998, 25.1 per cent in 1989, and 20.2 per cent in 1990 (Van Hoesel 1998, p. 127). These wage rises played an important role in the decline of the average rate of profit in the Korean economy, which had already fallen from 21.4 per cent in 1972 to 14.7 per cent in 1985. By 1996, the year before the outbreak of the economic and financial crisis, the profit rate had fallen again to 6.7 per cent. Whilst the profit rate did increase somewhat following the economic and financial crisis in 1997, the profit rate in 2007 was still only 11.3 per cent, less than half the rate in 1972 (Jeong 2005, pp. 17–18). Wage rises in turn had a negative impact on the country's competitive position. As Bello and Rosenfield (1992) have argued, rising wages in the 1980s intensified the 'structural squeeze' whereby Korea found it increasingly difficult to compete with the lower-wage economies of Southeast Asia and China, and with the higher-technology economies of Japan and the United States.

The liberalisation of the *dirigiste* political economy had been an active goal of the Kim Young-Sam government (1993–1997) under the slogan of 'globalisation' (*segyehwa)* (Gills 1996). Liberalisation thus involved a drastic scaling back of key developmental tools, such as the policy loans directed at strategic industries, and the privatisation of the domestic banks that had been the main conduit of capital to the *chaebŏl*. The latter also sought access to cheaper international capital and expanded production overseas to counteract rising labour costs at home and increased uncertainty surrounding overseas market access. Whilst the role of the authoritarian developmental state had traditionally been to nurture the *chaebŏl* through the provision of policy loans via the state–bank–business nexus, the Kim Young-Sam government responded to the decline of profitable investment opportunities within the domestic economy by facilitating this global expansion strategy. However, the liberalisation of short-term capital flows and continuing restrictions against long-term inflows and equity participation reflected what was in fact a reformed mercantilist strategy of selective liberalisation in such a manner as to allow the *chaebŏl* to directly finance their overseas expansion through access to global credit flows, whilst at the same time maintaining barriers to foreign direct investment in the Korean economy (Kalinowski and Cho 2009, p. 233).

However, the crisis that erupted in late 1997 unleashed an even more thoroughgoing process of liberalisation, privatisation, and flexiblisation. The bailout agreement signed between the Korean government and the International Monetary Fund (IMF) on 5th December 1997 led to a series of reforms in the area of monetary policy, financial regulation, corporate governance, regulatory reform, industrial policy, public services, and labour market regulation. All of these reforms served to profoundly increase the role of market competition in the Korean economy (Pirie 2005, p. 36). Measures to facilitate greater labour market flexibility were viewed by the IMF and the incumbent Kim Dae-Jung government (1998–2003) as essential in improving the country's international competitiveness. Specifically, labour flexibility was to be achieved by expanding the legal scope for layoffs, the hiring of substitute workers during strikes, the diversification of job categories, flexible wage systems, the strengthening of job placement efforts, and improvements in occupational training. However, after the crisis, it seems unlikely that the restructuring demanded by the IMF would have proceeded to the extent that it did were it not for the fact that the liberalising objectives were supported by key elite sections of the Korean state and capital, including Kim Dae-Jung himself. His explicit attempts to increase the entry of foreign capital into Korea, often at the expense of the domestic *chaebŏl,* could not have been more different from the policy direction of Kim Young-Sam.

Far from being a reluctant facilitator of IMF reforms, the Kim Dae-Jung government enthusiastically embraced them and, in some cases, went further than IMF demands. Rather than simply comply, for example, with the IMF demands that the ceilings on aggregate foreign equity ownership be raised to 55 per cent by the end of 1998, the Korean state abolished the ceilings altogether. Similarly, rather than simply remove restrictions on foreign ownership of key banks, the Korean state actively sought to encourage foreign ownership whilst restricting ownership by domestic investors (Pirie 2008, pp. 141, 155). Thus, whereas Kim Young-Sam had sought to promote the interests of the domestic *chaebŏl* in an increasingly globalised economy, the Kim Dae-Jung government represented a more fundamental break with the country's neomercantilist past by promoting the interests of foreign investors. This somewhat surprising alliance between Kim Dae-Jung and the interest of foreign capital can be explained with reference to the former's social support base. Kim Dae-Jung originated from the traditionally underrepresented Chŏlla province and was the first opposition leader to be elected president. Kim's rise to power thus served to break the monopoly of the conservative political forces based in the more developed Kyŏngsang province. Whilst his electoral success was certainly an indicator of the growing maturity of the country's democratic political system, Kim Dae-Jung's political position remained fragile because his party, the National Congress for New Politics, held only 78 seats out of a total of 299 in the National Assembly. Kim sought to consolidate his position through drawing on two bases of social support outside of the authoritarian developmental state. These included, on the one hand, labour and the new civic organisations that had emerged following the transition to democracy, and on the other, that of the IFIs and foreign investors. Kim viewed the entry of foreign capital as a means with which to discipline the *chaebŏl* and tackle the government–business collusion, which many had held responsible for bringing about the crisis in the first place (Kalinowski and Cho 2009, pp. 234–235).

Though the Korean labour movement has often been cited as a case of resistance to neoliberalism, the actual record is more complicated. Despite the liberalisation of the labour laws following the 1987 transition, there remained strict limits within which state and capital were prepared to tolerate independent labour activism. The economic slowdown of the early 1990s led to an increasingly repressive approach on the part of state and capital toward the militant labour movement, and in particular, toward *Chŏnnohyŏp*. However, formal democratisation also brought new opportunities for the institutionalisation of the labour movement. This combination of coercion with opportunities for participation in policymaking provoked a debate amongst labour academics and activists about how to respond to this perceived 'crisis of labour.' Though an unfavourable economic climate along with repression by state and capital were the immediate challenges faced by labour, it was argued by some in the movement that the deeper causes of the crisis of labour were triggered by failure of the unions to adapt to the new context of political liberalisation and increased opportunities to work within the system. The crisis was, it was argued, caused by adherence to a militant strategy which not only served to invite increased repression but also alienated workers and the public more generally (Choi 1992, Pak 1992, Kim 1997b). Instead, it was argued that solidarity with the burgeoning 'civic movements' (*shimin undong*) and the middle class more generally was essentially for the continued development of the labour movement (Choi 1992, pp. 245–246; Chŏng 1992, p. 293). As an alternative, labour should pursue issues in the public interest and strategically utilise new opportunities for participation in government policy-making forums (Im 1992, p. 21).[1]

Initially, the government sought to restrict labour's participation in policymaking to the official Federation of Korean Trade Unions (FKTU). In February 1993, the FKTU together with business representatives reached the 1993 Labour–Management Agreement on Wage Adjustment, which aimed to keep wage increases between 4.7 and 8.9 per cent. However, the agreement was strongly opposed not only by *Chŏnnohyŏp* but also by many of the FKTU's own member unions, who argued that the wage increase was far below expectations. Independent unions in turn further argued that the FKTU did not have the authority to represent them. In any case, the government and employers reneged on the agreement, thereby undermining the FKTU's claim that it was able to negotiate meaningful deals on behalf of its members. In response, the FKTU embarked upon a process of internal reform in order to halt the exodus of unions from its ranks. This included a proposal for a 'grand unity of labour' through partnership with *Chŏnnohyŏp,* an overture that was rejected by the latter (Chang 2008, pp. 108–109). The failure of social agreement politics in the early 1990s meant, however, that the Korean state and capital's strategy of exclusion of the independent labour movement was increasingly unviable.

Chŏnnohyŏp was, however, a problematic partner for social agreement politics because its membership was limited mainly to the SME unions in manufacturing, which had been at the forefront of the militant labour struggles the late 1980s. The *chaebŏl* and white-collar unions remained affiliated to their own solidarity organisations. Furthermore, the militant character of *Chŏnnohyŏp* exposed it to the full force of state repression, to the point where it had almost ceased to function by 1993. The mid-1990s, however, saw the emergence of a more inclusive labour federation in the form of the Korean Confederation of Trade Unions (KCTU). The KCTU represented the SME unions in the manufacturing sector, the white-collar unions, and most significantly, the *chaebŏl* unions. Though the KCTU was in many respects the successor of *Chŏnnohyŏp*, it was an organisation that in its founding platform explicitly sought to adapt to the new capitalist democracy. The KCTU remained technically illegal under the country's semi-corporatist labour laws, but two of its key stated objectives were the building of industrial-level unions along with the 'political empowerment of the workers' (*nodongja chŏngch'i saeryŏkhwa*) through the establishment of a broad-based labour party. Furthermore, the KCTU placed more emphasis on working with the new middle class–oriented civic movements rather than the older *minjung* organizations, conceptualising itself as pursuing a 'labour movement together with the people' (Kim 2002, pp. 36–38). As such, the KCTU aspired to a social democracy in which labour was recognised as a legitimate partner in policymaking alongside state and capital.

The KCTU thus reflects the tensions present in the dual transition from authoritarian developmentalism toward neoliberal democracy. Participation in the policymaking was seen as a key means whereby labour could increase its influence, yet the organisational weakness of labour and lack of a political party meant that the KCTU was relatively powerless to exert a decisive influence vis-à-vis state and capital. As a result, social agreement politics in Korea did not take the form of, for example, wage restraint in return for full employment and social welfare policies but was rather a *quid pro quo* in which state and capital held out the opportunity of full legal recognition to the independent labour movement in return for the latter's acquiescence to neoliberal labour market reform. The problem was, however, that neoliberalism served to undermine the livelihood of workers and ultimately the organisational basis of the labour movement. Formal recognition of organised labour would in itself do little to halt the worsening social inequality and undermining of wages and working conditions.

Shortly after the KCTU was established, for example, the Kim Young-Sam government made renewed efforts to incorporate labour into the policymaking process through the establishment of the Presidential Committee for Industrial Relations Reform. This forum brought together government, business, and labour, along with other interested parties, to discuss the reform of the labour law. Through these negotiations, the KCTU sought to lift the continued restrictions on third-party intervention, multiple unionism, and the participation of labour in formal politics. Government and business, however, were more interested in pursuing more flexible labour markets as part of the wider imperative of raising the country's international competitiveness. These divergent views over the direction of labour reform led to a collapse of negotiations, to which the ruling party responded by 'railroading' a set of neoliberal labour laws through the National Assembly at an early morning session on 26th December 1996, with no opposition party members present. For the following three weeks, the KCTU responded by successfully leading the largest strike in Korea's history, thereby bringing the country to a halt and forcing the ruling party to agree to revise the laws. Though the strike has been regarded as representing a 'late blooming' of the Korean labour movement (Sonn 1997), this largely spontaneous mass mobilisation of the country's workers with the support of the civic organisations and the public more broadly was not a feat that could be easily reproduced at will. When the ruling party dragged its feet over its subsequent promise to revise the laws and proposed a set of laws little different to those originally passed, the KCTU found it difficult to revive the mass movement against neoliberalism as a result of the worsening economic situation of 1997.

Whilst Kim Dae-Jung aggressively pursued neoliberal reform, his status as Korea's best known opposition politician enabled him to present himself as a potential ally to labour and other social movements. His rise to power thus presented itself as an opportunity for organised labour to pursue its interests through participation in policymaking forums. In order to negotiate the terms of the IMF-mandated restructuring, the KCTU and the FKTU leaderships thus entered into negotiations with government and business in the newly established Tripartite Commission. On 6th February 1998, after three weeks of negotiations, labour, government and business reached the First Tripartite Accord. Essentially, the Accord represented the KCTU and FKTU's agreement to labour flexibilisation and corporate restructuring in return for the guarantee of labour rights, including the legalisation of the KCTU alongside the strengthening of Korea's social security system. For many of the independent grassroots unions, however, the Accord was regarded as a serious threat to workers' livelihood by increasing the scope for redundancies at a time of economic crisis. The labour market flexibility measures contained within the Accord portended the expansion of irregular labour, which would serve to threaten the organisational basis of the labour movement. On the one hand, the KCTU's agreement to these measures represented the considerable pressure placed on organised labour. The crisis had created an atmosphere of existential questioning over the future of Korean economic development. Nonetheless, in contrast to the labour struggles of the preceding winter, the sense of national crisis and hostility of public opinion toward industrial action made a sustained campaign against IMF-led neoliberal restructuring much more difficult to achieve (Noh 2002, p. 2). Nonetheless, upon hearing of the agreement, KCTU delegates rejected the agreement, which led to the resignation of the KCTU leadership and the withdrawal of the organisation from the Tripartite Commission. However, the government proceeded with its restructuring plan in accordance with the Accord and organised labour was relatively powerless to stop it.[2]

The Tripartite Accord thereby served as testament to the labour movement's willingness to participate in the new capitalist democracy as well as its lack of concrete influence in policymaking. These failures gave added impetus to the KCTU's founding aims of establishing industrial-level unions along with a labour-oriented political party. Such strategic goals were seen to be essential in halting the steady decline of the labour movement. Indeed, throughout the 1990s, labour union density had experienced a decline, from a peak of 18.6 per cent in 1989 to 11.1 per cent in 1997 (OECD, n.d.). This decline was a result of both ongoing industrial restructuring with relocation of manufacturing jobs abroad as well as an aggressive campaign of repression against militant unions by state and employers. The Korean labour market also experienced increased polarisation and a relative shift of workers toward difficult-to-organise sectors and employment relations. Many unions thus felt that enterprise unionism was ineffective in defending and enlarging their membership in these unfavourable conditions, and indeed, that enterprise unionism itself was responsible for the growing wage gap between companies. The wage gap between employees in companies with more than 500 employees and those with between ten and twenty-nine employees increased from less than 10 per cent in the late 1980s to more than 30 per cent in the late 1990s. Contingent workers tended to be excluded by these enterprise unions, and the 1997 legislation prohibited company payments of wages for full-time union officials, thereby raising questions about the continued financial viability of enterprise unions (Lee and Yi 2012, p. 481). There have been some successes in building industrial-level unions, such as the Korean Health and Medical Workers Union. Other industrial-level unions have experienced more difficulties, however. When the Korean Metal Workers Union (KMWU) was established in 2001, it initially only attracted the participation of unions in smaller firms, amounting to only 21 per cent of the membership of the KMWU's organisational predecessor, the Korean Metal Workers Federation. Nonetheless, the KMWU successfully carried out national-level collective bargaining with employers in 2003, and three years later in 2006, several of the large enterprise unions made the decision to join the KMWU. Whilst this greatly expanded the KMWU's membership, it has also brought an unparalleled degree of divergent interests and factionalism into the union's internal politics. The unionists at the larger enterprises, for example, have been obstructive toward organising contingent workers for fear that this would directly damage their material interests (Lee and Yi 2012, pp. 487–488).

Attempts to build a labour-oriented political party have seen similarly mixed results. Established in January 2000, the Korean Democratic Labour Party's (KDLP) first electoral breakthrough came in the local elections of 2002, in which it received 8.3 per cent of the vote. The KDLP built on these gains in the 2004 general elections by getting ten lawmakers elected, giving the KDLP the third largest presence in the National Assembly. This electoral success was aided by a prior campaign led by the KDLP and a number of civic organisations against what was deemed to be an unconstitutional electoral system. As a result, the electoral law was reformed into a two-vote mixed system, providing a greater degree of proportional representation (Lee and Lim 2006, pp. 319–323). The electoral success of the KDLP also took place, however, amidst heightened public dissatisfaction with the mainstream political parties (Steinberg and Shin 2006, p. 531). President Roh Mu-Hyun's (2003–2007) reputation for his 'impeccable personal integrity' had been tarnished by a corruption scandal, whilst his pursuit of neoliberal free trade agreements, particularly with the United States, alienated his support base in labour and the social movements (Lee 2004). Furthermore, Roh disappointed sections of the voting public, who had hoped for a foreign policy more independent of the United States. Widespread protests surrounding the killing of two high-school girls in an accident involving a US-armoured vehicle in July 2002, along with Roh's unpopular decision to send Korean troops to Iraq in 2003, saw a wave of anti-Americanism that extended beyond the radical student and *minjung* movement toward the wider public, thereby underpinning the KDLP's electoral success (Sonn 2006, p. 214).

However, the KDLP suffered from rising internal tensions, reflecting the fractious nature of Korean social movement circles. The KDLP was established as a broad united-front party consisting of labour as well as other mass social movement organisations and progressive nongovernmental organizations. However, this 'broad unity' was belied by latent divisions dating back to the 1980s student movement.

These included divisions between those who were influenced by dependency theory and North Korean *Juche* philosophy and favoured a united front cross-class coalition aimed at national liberation from US imperialism (the National Liberation line), and those who favoured a more directly Marxist-influenced strategy based on class struggle, thereby privileging the labour-capital contradiction rather than that of imperialism (the People's Democracy line). These factional differences formed a constant point of tension within the KDLP. In 2008, following the party leadership's refusal to expel two party officials convicted of spying for North Korea, a breakaway faction led by former student turned labour activist Roh Hoe-chan left the party to form the New Progressive Party (Bae 2009). Whilst this created the potential for a debilitating split in the leftist vote, the KDLP, reformulated as the United Progressive Party in advance of the April 2012 general elections, managed to maintain its position as Korea's third political party with 10 per cent of the vote, although down from the 17 per cent of 2004. The New Progressive Party, on the other hand, performed badly with 0.5 per cent of the votes and no seats.[3] Yet, the achievements of the KDLP/United Progressive Party (UPP) notwithstanding, the electoral gains pale in significance to the size of the working class in Korea, suggesting that the labour movement has largely failed to reorient voting along class-based lines (Lee 2011, p. 78).

It is highly questionable to what extent such mixed achievements have ameliorated the negative impacts of neoliberal restructuring on wages and working conditions in Korea. As noted, one of the key responses of business to the economic and financial crisis was to launch a sustained attack on the Korean working class. The immediate impact of the crisis was severe enough. First and foremost was the increased levels of labour exploitation in the context of greater job insecurity. In manufacturing, the average number of hours worked per week in 1999 was 51.1 hours, up from 50.7 hours per week two years previously (OECD, n.d.). This increased intensity of work was combined with a marked increase in the number of industrial accidents. Whilst this had always been historically high in Korea, it had been on the decline in the early 1990s. Following the onset of the crisis, however, it rose from approximately 50,561 annual cases in 1998, rising to a total of 92,267 cases in 2003, with 2,923 deaths and 92,001 workers injured (Korean National Statistical Office, n.d.). Until 1998, Korea's labour laws, whilst notorious for their pro-business tendencies, had nonetheless prohibited layoffs. 'Flexibility' henceforth became a keyword for management wishing to freely lay off workers, and unemployment rose from 2.1 per cent in 1996 to a 30-year high of 7.2 per cent in 1998 (see Figure 5.4). The number of employees in public corporations, financial institutions, and the top 30 *chaebŏl* dropped from a peak of 1.55 million in October 1997 to 1.22 million in October 2002 – a decline of 21 per cent in just five years (Kim and Park 2006, p. 441).

At the same time, capital adopted a strategy of nurturing a relatively privileged core of unionised workers in the heavy industries whilst encouraging the expansion of contingent nonunionised workers. This strategy took place against the background of several longer-term structural trends. For example, the linkage effects

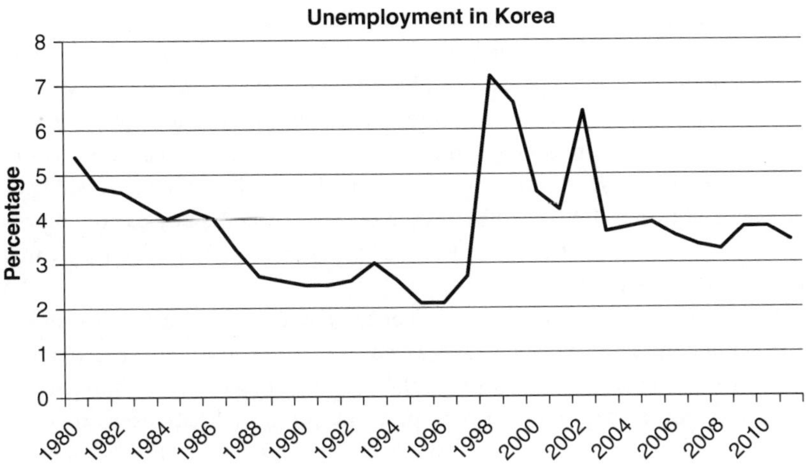

FIGURE 5.4 Unemployment in Korea
Source: OECD Labour Stats, http://www.oecd.org/std/labour-stats/.

among different industries were weakening as a result of the shift in the locus of the economy toward the information technology industry and services, both of which have lower than average backward linkages. The Korean economy's increasing interdependence with that of China has contributed toward the disruption of the hitherto close relationship between the *chaebŏl* and the SMEs. Thus, although Korea's *chaebŏl* have performed well in export markets, these benefits were not passed on to Korea's SMEs (Ok and Yang 2011, p. 227). Korean SMEs, furthermore, have been highly sensitive to competition from Chinese SMEs. In 2000, around 60 per cent of Korea's exports were under direct or partial threat from China's exports, particularly with regards to low-technology products, which are the typical preserve of the country's SMEs (Lall and Albaladejo 2004, p. 1453). Prior to the crisis, therefore, there had been a more symbiotic relationship between Korea's *chaebŏl* and SMEs, whereas since the crisis, there has been an increasing polarisation between the two. Profitability rates for the *chaebŏl* have continued to increase throughout the 2000s, whilst for the SMEs they have declined (Ok and Yang 2011, pp. 224–227).

As such, Korean capital's strategy has involved retaining regular workers for activities related to the firm's core competencies whilst relying on outsourcing and non-regular workers for non-core activities. Often this has involved the use of *de jure* independent but in reality *chaebŏl*-controlled subcontracting firms, who dispatch workers to the production line to work alongside regular workers (*sanae hach'ŏng*). As Tat Yan Kong has argued, compared with Japan, Korean non-core workers have tended to be substitutional in that they usually do the exact same work but for less pay. This dual strategy has partly been shaped by the need to accommodate the strength of organised labour in the large heavy industries rather than attacking it directly. It involves appeasing unionised workers whilst seeking to restrict job creation to the nonunionised sector. This has meant that the more powerful *chaebŏl* unions have effectively been complicit in the expansion of contingent labour. A key watershed in this trend was the massive strike at Hyundai Motors in 1998, whereby management had sought to impose compulsory redundancies on the company's workers. The strong resistance this provoked demonstrated the risks to capital of a directly confrontational approach (Kong 2013, pp. 631–633). As a result, neoliberalism did not see the implementation of US-style liberal employment practices because the involuntary workforce reduction of unionised regular workers remains difficult in Korea (Jung and Cheon 2006, p. 467).

The strategy of expanding the pool of contingent workers has unsurprisingly had a detrimental impact on working-class solidarity in Korea. Workers based in the *chaebŏl* have largely been able to protect their own job security against labour market uncertainties as they have become part of a privileged 'labour aristocracy' (Lee and Frenkel 2004; Nichols *et al.* 2004; Kim 2013, pp. 589–591). Though the KCTU has been increasingly vocal about the problem of contingent labour, it has failed to significantly extend its constituency beyond that of largely male regular workers in large enterprises. As Park Young-Sam, head of the policy department for the Korean Contingent Workers Center has argued, the KCTU failed to take effective action against capital's 'divide and rule' strategy of achieving labour flexibility. Organised workers in large enterprises, mainly affiliated with the KCTU, were reluctant to engage in solidarity actions with the new marginal workers of subcontracting firms or atypical workers in the same factory. Instead, organised regular workers barred contingent workers from joining their unions and interfered with the regular workers' organising process for fear of losing their own jobs. Voices for progressive social reform, such as a shorter working week, grow weak whilst organised workers demand more overtime to tackle inflation and decreasing incomes. Thus, workers are pursuing short-term rather than medium or long-term interests (cited in Lim 2002, p. 171).

Job creation, to the extent that it has taken place, occurs mainly in the realm of contingent labour. Total employment grew by 5 per cent between 2001 and 2004, yet the number of non-regular workers grew by a massive 48.3 per cent (Yun 2009, p. 271), with the result that contingent workers reached a peak of 51 per cent of the total labour force in March 1999 (Kim 2004). The most serious problem for these contingent workers is that of low wages. In 2004, the average wage of contingent workers was between 50 and 70 per cent that of regular workers. Furthermore, contingent workers experience heightened job instability and do not receive welfare benefits, such as unemployment and work injury insurance, because employers and employees alike have a shared interest in avoiding welfare contributions despite their legal requirement to do so (Shin 2011, pp. 17–18). Although this has been described by some observers as a 'government policy failure' (Yun 2009), official flexible labour policies have in fact been in line with capital's strategy. Furthermore, whilst the reform and expansion of social welfare has been the most noticeable achievements of the KCTU's participation in social corporatist institutions, the expansion of social welfare that was supposed to compensate for this had a negligible effect on raising the social protection for contingent workers. In August 2002, only 23.2 per cent, 21.6 per cent, and 24.9 per cent of irregular workers were covered by the Employment Insurance Scheme, the National Pension Scheme, and the National Health Insurance, respectively (Yi *et al.* 2003). Whilst the government established active labour market policies, such as the Employment Stabilisation Programme (part of the Employment Insurance System), they have been poorly implemented. Around 70 per cent of workers remain ineligible for its benefits, and much of the programme's reserves remain to be invested. The Job Skill Development Training Project was similarly underutilised, and those funds that were invested were directed more toward workers in large enterprises (Yun 2009, pp. 273–288).

In 2006, following years of pressure from civil society over the expansion of contingent labour, the government legislated a law ostensibly designed to provide increased protection for contingent workers by restricting the kind of jobs for which they could be hired. Enacted in 2007, the law required employers to change the employment status of irregular workers to that of regular workers following two years of employment. Predictably, however, employers simply laid off workers approaching the 2-year limit and then replaced them through dispatch firms or outsourcing (Shin 2011, p. 20). Labour unions demanded the withdrawal of the law, though as Lee *et al.* suggest, regular workers, who comprise the majority of the KCTU and FKTU membership, are also concerned that their own membership may shrink with increasing labour protection for contract job workers (Lee *et al.* 2008, p. 125).

An even more marginalised group of workers whose numbers have expanded in recent years are those that do not even enjoy proper 'worker' status. Jennifer Chun (2009, p. 537) argues that there is a 'legal liminality' surrounding contingent employment – a state of institutional exception in which workers are neither fully protected nor fully denied the rights of formal employment. Their activism frequently takes the form of classification struggles aimed at redefining the terms and conditions of the employment contract. There have been numerous important struggles taking place around irregular labour in Korea, including that of KTX train attendants, golf game assistants, private tutors, insurance salespeople, cafeteria workers, janitors, hotel cleaners, and retail cashiers. Exclusion of the contingent workers from organised labour thus occurs at the level of the national centre through failed policy, but also at the enterprise-union level through indifference and self-interest. Needless to say, this trend of the sustained expansion of contingent labour has had a negative impact on Korea's overall unionisation rate. As Table 4.1 shows, union density fell to 10.28 per cent in 2008, down from its previous height of 18.6 per cent in 1989.

Labour and neoliberalism in Taiwan

The Taiwanese developmental state underwent a similar process of economic and political liberalisation as a result of both changes in domestic state–society relations and, for Taiwan, a radically transformed geopolitical climate. As with Japan and

Korea, Taiwan was subject to external pressures to liberalise as the United States sought to address its trade imbalance and establish a more level playing field with East Asia. Taiwan's trade surplus with the United States had risen from US $2.1 billion in 1980 to US $16 billion in 1987 (Council for Economic Planning and Development 2009, p. 222). A key element of this rebalancing was the 1985 Plaza Accord, whereby the United States sought to tackle its own declining competitiveness through an agreement with the major capitalist economies to lower the value of the dollar. As part of the subsequent process of monetary realignments, the New Taiwan dollar appreciated by around 50 per cent between 1987 and 1989. This upward revaluation was combined with continued pressure over Taiwan's neo-mercantilist practices. The United States pressured Taiwan to restrict certain exports to the United States reform Taiwan's foreign exchange rules along more market-oriented lines, thoroughly implement labour protection laws as a means of reducing the country's cheap labour advantage, import more US goods by reducing import tariffs and removing nontariff barriers, liberalise inward foreign direct investments, and protect intellectual property rights more thoroughly (Huang 2009a, pp. 44–45). These demands were backed up by threats to use Super 301 legislation and remove Taiwan's status as an MFN partner under the GSP (Moore 1988b). Given Taiwan's diplomatic isolation and economic dependence on the US market, the country was faced with little choice but to comply. Indeed, it was Taiwan's weakness in its bilateral relationship with the United States that led it to seek membership in the World Trade Organization, a goal that was achieved in 2002. Yet even here, the United States managed to set strict conditions on entry, which led to concessions involving further economic liberalisation (Huang 2009a, p. 53).

However, this programme of liberalisation was, for the most part, supported by the Taiwanese capitalist class. As noted in Chapter 4, the country experienced rapid wage rises in the 1980s that undermined its reliance on labour-intensive export-oriented industrialisation. The year 1988, for example, saw wage increases of 10.9 per cent, followed by a further 4.6 per cent increase in 1989 and a 13.5 per cent increase in 1990 (Van Hoesel 1998, p. 127); as such, labour costs in Taiwan reached five times that of mainland China. These rises were also symptomatic of deepening labour shortages and a more relaxed political environment. Therefore, they were qualitatively different to wage rises experienced in 1960s Japan, which were underpinned by strong productivity growth in the capital-intensive industries (Tolentino 2000, p. 216). These wages rises, combined with a serious speculative bubble in the late 1980s, thereby created a domestic impetus for reform. Indeed, pressures for liberalisation also came from Taiwanese corporations who wished to both relocate production processes abroad, primarily to mainland China, as well as access cheaper international credit to invest in upgrading domestic production. Economic liberalisation, and particularly privatisation, also opened up lucrative opportunities for Taiwanese capital in areas of the economy that had long been dominated by state-owned enterprises (SOEs; Tsai 2001, p. 366).

As with Japan, a number of authors have argued that the Taiwanese state has not undergone a neoliberal transition but has retained developmental characteristics

(Thurbon 2001; Zhang 2002; Dent 2003; Weiss 2003, pp. 258–266). In reality, however, there has been a radical shift in the nature of government-business relations in Taiwan in a manner that questions the continued utility of the notion of an autonomous developmental bureaucracy directing investment into strategically important industries. Perhaps the most telling sign of the decline of the developmental state has been Taiwan's deepening economic integration with mainland China. Given their geographical, cultural, and linguistic proximity, the Chinese coastal provinces have been the primary beneficiaries of this relocation of Taiwanese production. Cross-straits trade and investment grew quickly as a result of China's economic reforms (Tung 2005, pp. 625–628) as well as the push factor of Taiwanese wage rises in the late 1980s.

It is difficult to understate the challenge that this capital flight poses for a state with such a precarious geopolitical existence as Taiwan. Successive administrations sought to stem this flow of capital, particularly with regards to the strategically important high-tech sector. However, neither Lee Teng-Hui's 'no haste, go slow' policy, nor Chen Shui-Bian's 'active management, effective opening' policy, met with much success. This continued failure of the Taiwanese government to stem the flow of capital to the mainland is a clear situation in which, to use David Harvey's (2003, pp. 33–36) terminology, the capital logic of power is in ascendance over the territorial logic of power. The fact that domestic business holds a clear preference toward investment on the mainland in direct contradiction to the government's wishes makes the notion of a reformed developmental state on Taiwan rather meaningless. Whilst much has been made of the Taiwanese government's role in the successful transition toward high-technology industries (Amsden and Chu 2003, Dent 2003, Weiss 2003), as Yu-Shan Wu (2007, p. 998) has argued, increased Taiwanese investment on the mainland shows how little the government can do to alter the profit-seeking decisions of business. The state's loss of control over the investment decisions of Taiwanese capital thus contrasts sharply with the developmental state of the past, whereby close cooperation with capital ensures fulfilment of the state's investment goals.

In addition to capital flight, a key manifestation of the retreat of the developmental state in Taiwan has been the significant reduction in the size of the state sector. The Taiwanese political economy had been distinctive in that it had possessed one of the largest state sectors in the capitalist world. In 1952, for example, 56 per cent total industrial production (value added at 1966 prices) and 56 per cent of manufacturing production were accounted for by SOEs. Although a small number of these were subsequently transferred to dispossessed landlords following the 1953 land reform, state ownership remained significant throughout the course of Taiwan's post-war industrialisation. It was particularly prominent in the heavy machinery, steel, aluminium, shipbuilding, petroleum, synthetics, fertilisers, and banking sectors (Amsden 1979, pp. 367–369). The state's share in industrial production/gross domestic product declined somewhat during the 1980s due to the rise of private business groups, but it nonetheless remained far higher than in other East Asian capitalist countries. However, in the 1980s, the Uruguay Round of the General Agreement on Tariffs and Trade coincided with heightened US criticism of Taiwan's monopolies and trade-constraining behaviour (McBeath 1997, p. 1150), and in 1989, privatisation became an explicit policy of the KMT. The Executive Yuan's Economic Reform Committee called for a programme of 'economic liberalisation, internationalisation, and systematisation' involving a reduction in size of the state sector and greater private participation in selected areas of the economy (McBeath 1997, pp. 1145–1146). The impact of privatisation can be seen in terms of the share of public-sector employment within total number of employees and combined revenue as a share of gross national product (GNP). Between the 1960s and the 1980s, employment in the top 100 business groups remained fairly constant at around 5 per cent of the total employed workforce. Their combined revenue amounted to between 25 and 33 per cent of the GNP during the same period. However, the 1990s saw a rapid rise in both employment and revenue in the private sector. By 2010, the top 100 business groups had 3.36 million employees (albeit with about 40 per cent of these in mainland China), whilst their combined revenue since 2008 has reached over 140 per cent of the GNP (Chen 2012, pp. 7–8).

The KMT's privatisation policy did not take place without resistance from labour, however. The majority of public-sector unions strongly opposed privatisation because it threatened the greater employment security, higher salaries, and better benefits enjoyed by SOE employees compared to private-sector workers. SOE unions, such as those in the Chinese Petroleum Company, and those in newly privatised companies, such as Chunghwa Telecom, made demands for the protection of workers' jobs and benefits as well as for greater industrial democracy through workers' participation in management decision-making (Chen *et al.* 2003, p. 330). Furthermore, this anti-privatisation struggle led to qualitative development of the labour movement and the formation of new solidarity organisations such as the Public Sector Unions Coalition in 1995, although such alliances tended to be short-lived due to their ultimate failure to halt the privatisation policies (Lee 2007a, p. 11). However, the opposition to privatisation by SOE workers was problematised by the manner in which the specificities of Taiwan's post-war passive revolution meant that the privatisation issue was inseparable from that of democratisation. As Hsin-Hsing Chen (2012, p. 17) has argued, the origins of this idiosyncratic framing of the privatisation issue could be seen clearly in the arguments made by journalist and commentator Nanfang Shuo (Wang Hsin-Ching) in his 1986 article 'Auction off the Republic of China.' In this article, Nanfang Shuo drew on a range of leftist authors such as John Urry, James Petras, Claus Offe, Antonio Gramsci, as well as neoliberal economists Lester Thurow and Milton Friedman, to argue for the replacement of the crisis-prone state with a vibrant civil society. Privatisation in the United Kingdom under Margret Thatcher and decentralisation in the Soviet Union under Gorbachev had, it was argued, shown that dismantling the overgrown state was a goal embraced by all advanced countries across the ideological spectrum. Thus, for genuine democratisation to take place, Taiwan had to sell off state assets and outsource as many state functions as possible.

It was in this vein that the Democratic Progressive Party (DPP) became one of the earliest supporters of privatisation in Taiwan, recognising as it did the role of the SOEs in forming a key element of the KMT's power base (McBeath 1997, p. 1150). However, these political cleavages along sub-ethnic lines also problematised labour's framing of the *anti*-privatisation struggle. When labour adopted a strong anti-privatisation stance, the issue was often framed around the KMT betraying workers through the selling-off of state properties. At the same time however, there was a failure by labour to mount any effective critique of the rhetoric of 'efficiency' that underpinned the privatisation programme. Instead, attention was directed toward the alleged danger of opening Taiwan's SOEs to foreign ownership and, in particular, to mainland capital. For example, when thousands of workers protested against privatisation outside the Legislative Yuan in 1989, one of the participating labour organisations brought a model missile to instigate the mainland phobia. As such, for labour, the anti-privatisation struggle was reduced to a dichotomous choice between unification or independence without developing a more fundamentally anti-capitalist, pro-worker position (Chen and Wong 2002, pp. 42–43).

Democratisation in Taiwan more generally was a contradictory process that both offered opportunities for labour's increased participation in politics but also served to suppress an independent workers' stance on many of the key issues facing labour. On the one hand, labour made a number of organisational advances at the national level through its alliance with the DPP. In 1994, for example, the first county-level autonomous confederation of trade unions, the Taipei County Confederation of Industrial Unions, was established. Labour received administrative support from local counties governed by the DPP and, in the case of the Taipei County Confederation of Industrial Unions, from a labour activist-turned-lawyer who headed the Bureau of Labor Affairs. County confederations of trade unions were similarly established in other DPP-governed districts. For the DPP, this was a strategy that paid off through workers' votes in local elections (Wang 2010, pp. 64–65). Thus, as the growing KMT offensive against labour exposed the precarious organisational foundations of the movement, the alliance with the DPP provided a means whereby labour could nonetheless seek to influence the political process. In the national elections of 1990 and 1992, many labour activists obtained DPP membership and joined the party's campaign in an attempt to bring labour issues into the realm of electoral politics. Although this entry of activists into the political realm did not succeed in halting KMT repression, the DPP's victory in the 1992 legislative elections did serve to intensify the KMT's internal antagonism between hardliners and reformists. Premier Hau's resignation in 1993 marked the decline of hardliner influence within the KMT and to some extent defused tension between the state and the social movements (Ho 2010, p. 10).

Certain sections of the labour movement did seek an independent path into electoral politics. As early as 1987, the Workers' Party, led by former DPP lawmaker Wang Yi-hsiung, was established in the hope of securing an independent parliamentary voice for labour. However, the party suffered from fractious internal debates whereby a moderate faction led by Wang Yi-hsiung favoured a gradualist approach of cooperation, whilst a more militant faction was led by Lou Mei-wen of the Far Eastern Chemical Factory Union and other militant labour activists, the Labour Rights Association, and a number of left-leaning intellectuals from the *dangwai* China Tide group. The latter group argued that the government's obstruction of autonomous unions meant that more confrontational tactics were needed. They also criticised Wang's opportunistic use of the party to maintain his legislative seat and, in particular, Wang's appointment of a Kaohsiung fishery businessmen as deputy secretary-general (Shim 1989). The two groups were also divided in that the former supported Taiwanese independence whilst the latter strongly supported unification. As a result, the militant faction broke away from the Workers' Party and, in March 1989, established the Labour Party. The Labour Party was based on a Marxist- and socialist-oriented pro-labour ideology; it proclaimed to struggle against capitalism, neoimperialism, and American and Japanese hegemony and emphasised the role of class struggle. However, like the Workers' Party, the Labour Party failed to make any inroads into the Legislative Yuan, suggesting little support from Taiwanese workers for both a pro-labour and pro-unification orientation (Congiu 2006, p. 15).

The mainstream independent labour movement maintained a close relationship with the DPP – a relationship that brought a number of concrete results for labour. The two Taiwan Labor Front members who were elected to parliament in 1996 successfully pushed to have the Labor Standards Law (LSL) revised to extend its coverage to more than 2 million additional workers in the service sector. In early 2000, the Taiwan Labor Front published 'Where Taiwanese Workers Stand,' a document that was for the most part adapted by the DPP as its labor policy platform in the 2000 presidential election (Chen *et al.* 2003, p. 326). Furthermore, the DPP's ascendancy opened the way for the legalisation of the independent labour movement. Chen Shui-Bian made a number of proposals aimed at dismantling the restrictive corporatist structure, including the withdrawal of political parties from union affairs and the reform of the LUL to end the ban on multiple union confederations at the national level (Chen *et al.* 2003, pp. 326–327). This latter measure paved the way for the legalisation of the Taiwan Confederation of Trade Unions (TCTU), a national centre for independent unions established in 1997. The TCTU served to break the formal monopoly of the Chinese Federation of Labour (CFL), although the labour movement in reality became more fractious than that of Korea's as a result of further breakaway factions from the CFL following the DPP's rise to power (Chen 2012, p. 23).

Nonetheless, the TCTU, consisting of 18 industrial unions with a membership of more than 280,000, represented a significant proportion of organised workers in Taiwan. Its primary political strategy was to use its linkages with the DPP to pursue a pro-labour agenda; as such, the TCTU displays some marked differences in terms of political strategy to that of Korea's KCTU. Their independent attempts at political participation notwithstanding, Korean workers were largely unable to find any meaningful political representation within the country's democratic political system and remained for the most part institutional outsiders. As a result, they displayed a greater reliance on street politics. Taiwanese workers, as we have seen, largely identified their grievances primarily as sub-ethnic injustices and consequently saw the DPP as representing their own interests (Lee 2011, p. 46). Furthermore, the TCTU has been able to achieve some significant gains through its partnership with the DPP, such as the promotion of gender equality in employment through the passage of the Equal Employment Law in 2002, the Protective Act for Mass Redundancy of Employees in 2003, the Employment Insurance Law in 2002, and the Workers Incurring Occupational Accidents Act in 2001 (Ho 2006b, pp.134–135).

Despite these important gains, however, the TCTU and organised labour more broadly were unable to prevent the DPP's shift to the right after taking power in 2000. Chen's election coincided with, and to some degree further provoked, a serious economic downturn in Taiwan. His decision to heed the environmental movement's call to scrap the island's planned fourth nuclear power station led foreign investors to question the new government's ability to honour contracts and led to a fall in Taiwan's stock market index by 50 per cent. This in turn led to a rapid collapse in the collateral of Taiwanese banks and a rise in defaults (Wu 2001, p. 47). As such, Taiwan saw an economic slowdown that was unprecedented in its post-war history. Economic growth dropped from nearly 8 per cent in early 2000 to −4 per cent at the end of 2001. Unemployment rose to 5.3 per cent and exports and imports shrank by over 20 per cent (Wu 2002, pp. 31–32). Chen thus declared the need to 'salvage the economy' as his top priority in 2001, whereby he effectively shelved his social welfare-related campaign promises and argued that economic growth should take precedence. The DPP government became increasingly critical of existing environmental regulations and the latter's alleged role in deterring investment by business. By the time of the 2004 election campaign, the DPP had abandoned its commitment to social reform and instead relied even more heavily on Taiwanese identity to mobilise voters (Ho 2010, p. 15).

One manifestation of this shift to the right was the resumption of the privatisation programme. Although the DPP had initially proposed privatisation as a means of undermining the KMT's power base, the party's close linkage with labour had led it to drop the issue in the 1990s. Indeed, Chen had been a vocal critic of the KMT's privatisation policy during his presidential campaign, and he halted further privatisations after the DPP came to power in 2000 (Chen *et al.* 2003, p. 330). However, in 2003, the DPP announced a new wave of privatisations that had significant anti-labour implications. The privatisation of China Shipbuilding Corporation, for example, led to the downsizing of the workforce by as much as 30 per cent, whilst the wages of the remaining workers were also cut by 30 per cent. At Taiwan Motor Transport, workers who wanted to keep their jobs were forced to contribute NT$ 300,000 each to form a new company. Whilst the DPP often sought to draw attention to the heightened efficiencies of these companies following privatisation, this neglects the fact that it was the workers who had shouldered most of the transformation costs (Ho 2006b, pp. 137–138).

The DPP also began to drag its feet over planned labour reforms. For example, it refused to grant union rights to teachers and public servants, despite having previously argued that this ban should be lifted. Whilst even the Council for Labor Affairs encouraged teachers and public servants to request union rights, there was considerable opposition within quarters of the DPP government itself. Plans to reform the LSL to shorten Taiwan's culture of long working hours (see Figure 5.1) also became subject to opportunistic struggles between the DPP and the KMT in the Legislative Yuan. Whilst the KMT had in 1997 proposed a shortening of the working week, it wavered in its approach due to resistance from business (Low 2000). The issue was then taken up by Chen in his presidential electoral campaign when he promised to reduce weekly working hours to 44 hours, in the first instance, and then to 40 hours from 2002. However, upon coming to power, the DPP's attempts to pass the bill in time for Labour Day were met with resistance from the KMT and business, as well as some quarters of the DPP itself (Chu 2000). However, in an unexpected turn of events, the KMT opportunistically decided to outmanoeuvre and embarrass the DPP by passing its own bill that was even more generous to workers, to which the DPP then voiced its strong opposition (Ho 2006b, p. 137). In 2002, the DPP also added further flexible provisions to the LSL to enable employers to enforce extended working hours and deprive workers of overtime during extended shifts (Lin 2000). Following the DPP's rise to power, therefore, the party's policies did little to fundamentally adjust power relations between labour and capital. As Jui-Ming Huang (2000b) of the Department of Labour Relations at National Chung Cheng University argued at the time:

> The KMT walked the extreme capitalist road in the past. The DPP, which claimed to sympathize with labour and the underprivileged, is also veering right in every step ... The new government's financial and economic policies are almost identical to those of the old regime ... The DPP is rife with factionalism, but a real leftist faction is nowhere to be seen. There is no lack of gurus well-versed in Taiwan independence theories, but socialist thinkers are unheard of.

It was paradoxically the KMT's return to power in 2007 under Ma Yingjiu that opened the path for further reform of the legal framework governing labour relations. The Protective Act for Mass Redundancy of Employees, for example, was amended in May 2008 so that employers would be subject to foreign travel restrictions if they close their business but fail to provide workers with owed salaries or redundancy money (Mo 2008). The Labour Union Law (LUL), the Collective Agreement Law, and the Labour Management Dispute Settlement Law (LMDSL) were also revised in 2010, 2007, and 2009, respectively, and were implemented simultaneously on 1st May 2011. The LUL reform allowed teachers to form and join unions and gave foreign workers more powers to pursue their rights through unions and take up positions in union management. Employers were also prohibited from firing, laying off, or reducing the salaries of workers on the grounds that they had joined unions or engaged in union activities. Union members were also given the right to take days off to take care of union business (The China Post 2010).

There remained limitations, however. The LMDSL amendment's requirement that 'rights items,' such as employment contracts and collective bargaining agreements, must be settled through judicial arbitration was criticised by labour unions because the process is often a protracted one that disadvantages workers. Furthermore, the amendment also requires that industries dealing with public safety, including water, electric, and gas utilities as well as medical institutions, set a 'minimum level' of service in the event of a strike and that this minimum level must be negotiated between management and workers before a strike begins. This clause was criticised as a requirement to 'ask for an opponent's permission before starting a fight.' By refusing to reach an agreement with the union on what constitutes a 'minimum level' of service, an employer could prevent the union from legally announcing a strike (Huang 2009b). Indeed, this increased role of judicial arbitration has not been a positive development for Taiwanese labour. The reform of the laws involved the establishment of a Labour Court, whose rulings have largely been *anti*-labour in content. There have been prominent cases in which the court has ruled that workers have a 'duty of allegiance' to their employer; therefore, any breech of such allegiance, such as engaging in union activities against the employer, constitutes legal grounds for dismissal. If such cases form a legal precedence, they will be even more stringent than the laws of the 1920s (Chen 2012, p. 24).

It should also be noted that the KMT pursued this strategy of reforming the legal framework governing trade unions whilst at the same time pushing for increased labour market flexibility. Whilst there is some difficulty in accurately examining the extent of irregular work in Taiwan due to lack of official statistics (Lee 2011, p. 24), as with other countries, there is evidence to suggest that Taiwan has recently experienced a rapid rise in the number of contingent workers, including part-time workers, temporary help-service workers, direct-hire workers, subcontracting workers (contract company workers), leased workers, independent contract workers, and self-employed workers (Ko 2007, p. 6). One 1994 study found that 33 per cent of enterprises surveyed made use of employed temporary workers, 32 per cent used subcontractors, 22 per cent used part-time workers, and 19 per cent used dispatched workers (Chen *et al.* 2003, p. 335). In the first half of the 2000s, Taiwan witnessed a steady increase in nonstandard employment, from 224,554 (2.39 per cent) in 2001 to 470,147 (4.64 per cent) in 2006. Furthermore, in the years between 2008 and 2010, the total number of nonstandard workers jumped to 924,000, accounting for 8.8 per cent of the total employed population (Hsiao 2012, p. 378). Whilst the figures are certainly not as high as in Japan and Korea, there is an unmistakable trend upwards. Furthermore, Taiwan has experienced increased levels of social inequality. Taiwan and Korea were once seen as cases of 'growth with equity,' but the Gini coefficient in Taiwan has more recently reverted to pre-industrialisation levels (Chen 2012, p. 4). In addition, as Figure 5.5 shows, Taiwan has also seen a steady rise in unemployment: 1.45 per cent in 1993 to a high of 5.21 per cent in 2010.

Despite these setbacks, Yoonkyung Lee (2011, p. 144) has argued that in comparison to Korea, Taiwan's unions have relied less on militant mobilisation and more on partisan allies in the political realm. As such, Taiwan's democratisation was

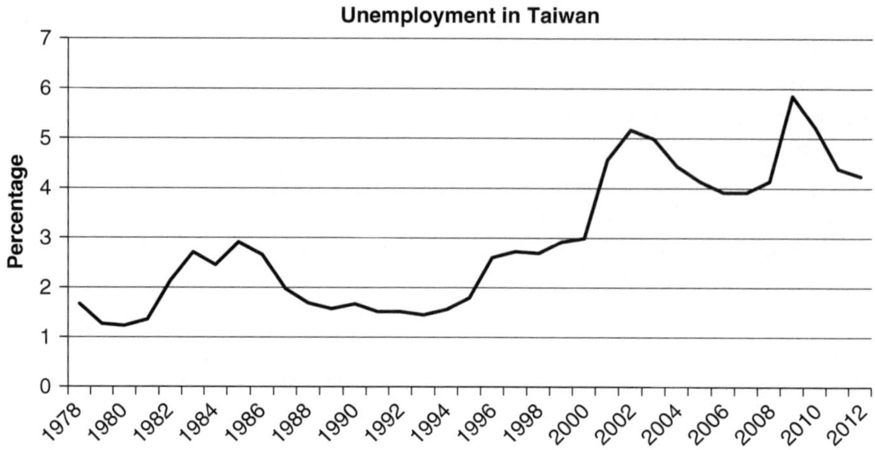

FIGURE 5.5 Unemployment in Taiwan
Source: Council for Labor Affairs, http://statdb.cla.gov.tw/html/nat/natehidx08.htm.

by and large an opportunity for labour to enhance its interests and be able to secure significant policy concessions in labour's interests. However, despite some achievements at the level of national policymaking, the labour movement in Taiwan has largely failed to achieve more basic organisational goals, such as increasing the number of unions. The number of industrial unions as well as membership levels in general has overall continued to decline. There were 1,128 industrial unions in 2000, but that number dropped to 1,104 in 2002. This trend is closely related to the continued haemorrhaging of manufacturing jobs to mainland China and the inherent difficulties involved in organising the service sector. However, the TCTU also struggled to expand its membership amongst already-unionised workers. Unions such as the Taipei County Confederation of Industrial Unions, the Taiwan Railway Labour Union, and the Chunghwa Telecom Workers' Union even went as far as leaving the TCTU. Legal recognition also did not help to improve its financial situation as a result of incessant factional infighting and difficulties in collecting membership fees from unions (Ho 2006a, pp. 124–125). Furthermore, whatever advancements Taiwanese unions have made through their political connections, they have largely failed to engage in what is arguably one of the primary functions of trade unions, namely that of collective bargaining. In 1986, there were only 285 union–management contracts in Taiwan, with the number slowly increasing to 306 in 1992, of which 38 per cent were in the public sector. Furthermore, most of these contracts were simple and consisted of items already stipulated in existing law. In the late 1980s, contracts rose in importance as the role of the independent unions became more prominent. However, as a 1991 survey showed, only 34 per cent of contracts set wages higher than those set by law; thus, union influence on employee working conditions was minimal (Lee 1994, pp. 7–8).

As a result, the TCTU has been criticised for redirecting resources and energy from workplace organisation toward parliament, elections, and local government, and for spending more time with politicians than with rank-and-file workers. Unionists have increasingly criticised their leaders for having become detached from the grassroots of the labour movement (Ho 2006a, pp. 124–126). As Yu-bin Chiu (2011, p. 59) has argued, the independent labour movement in Taiwan has turned into a fragmented set of inward-looking interest groups. The movement has lost its militancy and political significance, and it has failed to adopt a strategic response to the challenges posed by neoliberal globalisation. This has led to the criticism of the labour movement as a 'labour aristocracy' in that the movement had become merely a vehicle to advance the interests of the most secure and comfortable workers in the public sector. Whilst fighting the government's privatisation plan and bargaining for a better deal for public-sector workers, for example, criticisms were made that the movement had neglected the interests and needs of workers private-sector SMEs, alongside immigrant and middle-aged unemployed workers and others disadvantaged in the labour market (Liu 2011, p. 36). Conciliatory strategies, such as lobbying politicians and political parties, establishing friendly relations with legislators, and holding press conferences in the Legislative Yuan, have therefore provided little assistance to workers in the private sector who have experienced sudden factory closures, mass redundancies, and casualisation. Whilst the SOE unions often signed statements of support, they were unable to mobilise their members and protests were rarely effective (Chiu 2011, p. 67).

Conclusion

As noted in Chapter 1, the rise of global neoliberalism has often been regarded by labour scholars as having mixed implications for workers and unions globally. Whilst globalisation itself is seen as undermining workers' wages and livelihoods in the global North and South, it is simultaneously regarded as providing new imperatives and opportunities for labour to overcome national boundaries and establish solidarity with labour movements elsewhere. The labour movements of industrialising East Asia were often seen as offering examples of militant workers' struggles that adopted an uncompromising stance in resisting neoliberal restructuring. This was most clearly the case with regards to the Korean labour movement, which has been portrayed as one that practices grassroots 'shop-floor internationalism' (Waterman 1998, p. 120), with its leadership displaying 'remarkable self-confidence, independence, and will to resist' (Lambert 1998, p. 75) by developing alternatives to neoliberalism in the face of government and business repression (Ranald 2002). Kim Moody (1997, pp. 217–218) has similarly regarded the Taiwanese independent labour movement as part of the 'new social-movement unionism.' In contrast, the Japanese labour movement has been drawn on less as a source of progressive union strategies in an era of neoliberal globalisation. Indeed, as Hoogevelt (1995, p. 724) has argued, the internationalism of *Rengō* has consisted of an evangelical movement to spread Japan's enterprise model and its 'harmonious industrial relations' abroad, though such practices have received a much more critical stance from *Zenrōkyō* and *Zenrōren*.

Yet, as I have argued in this chapter, increased global competition and the spread of neoliberal ideology have led to a renewed passive revolution based on a strategy of *trasformismo*, whereby the upper echelons of the labour movement have been co-opted into the structures of liberal democracy. The Japanese labour movement had, of course, already been subordinated by state and capital in the immediate post-war years. Following the early 1970s oil crisis and transition to the medium growth path, it sought consolidation and an increased presence in national-level policymaking. Despite gains in terms of labour's political presence, Japanese unions have been largely unable to make decisive interventions in national-level policymaking or temper the impact of restructuring on wages and working conditions. In Korea and Taiwan, the democratic transition brought a much greater degree of discontinuity in the labour regime. The militant labour struggles of the late 1980s invited repression by the state and capital and the search by labour for a new strategy based on participation in the liberalised political sphere. This was also a deliberate strategy on the part of the state as a means of co-opting labour into the broader project of raising 'international competitiveness' through neoliberal restructuring. The direct mechanisms whereby labour sought to participate differed in the two countries, however, and were closely influenced by the specificities of their post-war passive revolutions. In Korea, it took the form of labour's independent participation in formal tripartite institutions following the financial crisis, whereas in Taiwan, unions established more pluralistic relationships with the mainstream political parties. The results have broadly been similar, however. As in Japan, gains have been made in Korea and Taiwan in terms of organisation at the national level, but these have failed to temper the impact of neoliberal restructuring.

In Japan, many of the key institutions of labour subordination have remained in place. Wages have failed to keep up with productivity increases and enterprise unionism has become weaker as the number of irregular workers has grown. Taiwan has similarly seen a decline in unionisation and expansion of contingent work. This latter process has been most marked in Korea, however, where contingent workers have come to account for more than half of the country's workforce. Such processes have had a negative impact on the role and structural position of the trade union movement. The continued relocation of Japanese, Korean, and Taiwanese production to offshore locations, and especially to China, has further undermined the structural power of labour to challenge its own subordination. However, as the framework established in Chapter 1 suggests, this relocation of production poses the question of the emergence of new working-class movements elsewhere, particularly in mainland China. Whilst one might expect a similar process of class formation followed by workers' consciousness and militancy followed by repression and perhaps co-optation, there is reason to suggest that the specificities of China's own post-war passive revolution may mean a response that diverges from the repression of East Asia's developmental path. It is to China now that the analysis will finally turn.

Notes

1 For a more in-depth discussion of these debates, see Gray (2008a, Chap. 4).
2 For further discussions on labour and social agreement politics in Korea, see Gray (2008b).
3 The UPP was formed by the DLP, the People's Participatory Party (a party established by Rhyu Shi-min following the death of former president Roh Mu-hyun), and a faction of the New Progressive Party led by Shim Sang-Jeong.

6

CHINESE WORKERS' CHALLENGE TO LABOUR SUBORDINATION

China's extraordinary economic growth since the onset of economic reform in the late 1970s has been central to the broader fate of labour under contemporary global economic restructuring. A key argument in the globalisation literature has been that the emergence of China as 'workshop of the world' has facilitated a global 'race to the bottom' in workers' wages and working conditions. Rather than representing the latest in the flock of Asian 'flying geese' (Akamatsu 1962), China has now come to serve as a final production platform for the region's broader export-oriented production networks. At the same time, East Asian countries have narrowed their industrial bases to the production and trade of parts and components. As such, it has been argued that this process has served to pit different workers in different countries against each other to the benefit of transnational capital and its local subordinates, intensifying competition and uneven development (Hart-Landsberg and Burkett 2007, p. 13). This process is not limited to East Asia, however. The so-called 'China price' (Harney 2008) has had a devastating impact on the livelihood of workers globally. As William Greider (2001) has argued, 'it is [no longer] Mexico sucking away American jobs. It is China sucking away Mexico's jobs. And jobs from Taiwan and South Korea, Singapore and Thailand, Central and South America, and even from Japan .... In the "race to the bottom," China is defining the new bottom.'

The role that China plays in this race to the bottom conforms to the overall pattern of catch-up industrialisation presented in this book in that it has been based upon a comprehensive system of labour subordination designed to make Chinese wages particularly low in comparison with other countries at similar stages of development. Anita Chan (2003, p. 5) argues that the structural weakness of Chinese labour and the low wages paid to workers is a result of the fact that the country has an 'almost inexhaustible supply of cheap labour from the countryside.' Yet, this driving down of wages in China is also a result of a number of institutions unique to the country, thus suggesting that cheap labour is by no means 'natural' for a country at

China's level of development but is deliberately created by government policy. On the supply side, it is actively brought about by the Chinese state's rural-agricultural policies, which bankrupt the countryside and create a continuous exodus toward the urban areas. China's 'inexhaustible' supply of labour is thus predicated upon a net transfer of resources from the rural areas to the urban areas through fiscal policies and the financial system. This repression of consumption in the countryside has thereby deepened China's dependence on consumption in the West (Hung 2009, pp. 10–14).

Furthermore, after having relocated to the urban areas, the *hukou* residency permit system effectively makes migrant workers foreigners in their own country by denying them access to education and other government services (Solinger 1999). In the workplace, labour is denied collective rights through strict proscription of free trade unions and denial of the right to strike (Chen 2007); as a result, workers experience a form of 'managerial despotism' at the point of production (Lee 1999), with local authorities failing to enforce the labour laws and minimal wage standards that do exist. In addition, the prospects for reform of China's labour conditions are not considered to be bright because it is precisely low wages and export-oriented industrialisation (EOI) that have underpinned the country's impressive economic growth in recent years (Morgan 2008, p. 418). In any case, any concrete measures taken by the central government to improve labour conditions are likely to be ineffectual as a result of the decentralised governance structure and the fact of competition among local governments to attract foreign investment (Hart-Landsberg and Burkett 2007, p. 25).

However, this rather static depiction of China's labour regime fails to consider possible countervailing processes that might challenge and seek to reverse China's lead in the global race to the bottom and neglects the comparative significance of the transformations that have taken place in labour regimes elsewhere in East Asia. As argued in the preceding chapters, Korea and Taiwan's experiences of EOI were underpinned by their distinctive systems of authoritarian labour subordination. However, catch-up industrialisation conferred upon workers the structural power with which to challenge this system of state-mandated hyper-exploitation. Taiwan in the late 1960s and Korea in the mid-1970s experienced Lewisian turning points whereby they underwent transitions from 'unlimited' to limited labour supplies (Fei and Ranis 1975, Bai 2007). This led to the rise of labour movements in both countries in the 1980s and to workers' struggles for further improvements in wages and working conditions. Indeed, it was these structural changes in the labour market and the rise of labour as a social force, alongside aggressive US exchange rate policies, that led to the relocation of low-wage manufacturing away from Taiwan and Korea toward Southeast Asia and, above all, to mainland China. Their experience shows, therefore, that even the most repressive labour regimes are vulnerable to challenges from within and without. The question addressed in this final chapter therefore is the extent to which China may also see the emergence of a strong working-class movement that will contest the country's comprehensive system of labour subordination and, as a result, challenge one of the key social underpinnings of the global race to the bottom. The first stage in answering the question is to examine the spatial and temporal specificities of China's own history of passive revolution.

The Chinese party-state and capitalist restoration

With the rise of US dominance in the East Asian region following the end of the Second World War, Japan, Korea, and Taiwan all underwent a repression of independent labour movements and the establishment of a comprehensive system of labour subordination. As the previous chapters have argued, it was this political weakness of labour that underpinned the region's rapid catch-up industrialisation in the latter part of the twentieth century. China lay on the margins of this US-centred regional order, but it experienced a process whereby workers were elevated to a nominally privileged position whilst at the same time were effectively stripped of their independent organisations (Harris 1978, pp. 103–107). China's labour regime thus came to resemble the state-corporatism particularly of Taiwan (Chang and Bain 2006), partly as a result of the structural similarities of the Chinese and Taiwanese party-states. China's decision to embark upon an outward turn toward the path of economic liberalisation has commonly been interpreted as the response of the post-Mao leadership to endemic domestic problems that were undermining the Chinese Communist Party's (CCP) legitimacy. These problems include the systematic inefficiency and waste associated with Soviet-style central planning, as well as the failure of developmental Maoism to establish a viable alternative accumulation regime based on mass mobilisation. By the late 1970s, there was as a result a widespread social mandate for change, particularly amongst those who had suffered under the political mobilisations of the Cultural Revolution, or those who worked in the agricultural collectives or SOEs and were subject to often irrational and stifling administrative direction from above (White 1993, pp. 21–50).

More broadly, however, the economic reform programme can be seen as a broader response to the geopolitical challenge posed by the economic miracles on China's immediate periphery – namely, Japan, Korea, and the most challenging for China of all, Taiwan. Indeed, Deng Xiaoping would go on to make explicit reference to the imperative of catching up with these countries during his Southern Tour of 1992, and in the mid-1990s, the Chinese state sought to directly borrow elements of the Korean model in its reform of the state-owned enterprise (SOE) sector (Fewsmith 2001, pp. 56, 203). This borrowing from the experience of the East Asian developmental states was driven more specifically by the failure following the death of Mao Zedong and the end of the Cultural Revolution to return to the heavy industrialisation strategy of the 1950s. In particular, the failure to effectively exploit the country's own oil resources led the Chinese government to pursue an outward-oriented strategy of enmeshment within the international division of labour. This strategy was, however, given added impetus by the dynamics of the Cold War and the Sino–Soviet split, as China came to view a closer alliance with the United States as a counterpoint to the perceived Soviet threat. From the perspective of the United States, China's outward turn could be welcomed because it could potentially lead to long-term dependence on the United States for defence, resources, and high technology (Cumings 1989).

In the absence of an indigenous bourgeoisie, the Chinese state took upon itself the leading 'Piedmont-type role' (Gramsci 1971, pp. 104–106) in the reorganisation of social relations commensurate with a restoration of capitalism. This took place through three key 'social' interventions from above. First, the state sought to create a nascent capitalist class out of the ranks of the party-state bureaucracy itself. Cadres turned local state and collective enterprises into township and village enterprises, and later, when the state adopted a policy of privatisation of small and medium state enterprises, the assets of these companies were placed directly in the hands of the cadres who managed them. Second, the state sought to bring about a proletarianisation of workers by dismantling the socialist enterprise system and creating a capitalist labour market. From the mid-1990s, the government abandoned its long-held commitment to SOEs as the central anchor of the economy, leading to the creation of a massive sector of laid-off or 'off-post' (*xiagang*) workers. Third, the state's de-collectivisation of agriculture in the early 1980s played a key role in bringing about the semi-proletarianisation of the rural workforce to supply the export-oriented sector in the coastal areas, the latter of which had emerged as a result of the liberalisation of foreign direct investment.

As noted in Chapter 1, Gramsci elaborated his concept of passive revolution to explain Italian state formation within the context of the continent-wide spread of capitalist social relations of production and the accompanying threat of bourgeois revolution to the old established classes. It became a means by which bourgeois revolution could be forestalled through a series of reforms designed to quell more radical popular demands, thereby encapsulating the manner in which 'revolution' occurs through state intervention and the inclusion of new social groups within the hegemony of an emergent political order without an expansion of mass-producer control (Sassoon 1987, p. 210). China's passive revolution can similarly be understood in the dual context of the global spread of capitalist industrial relations and the nascent rise of subaltern demands. Whilst industrialisation in the broader East Asian region provided the context for China's own capitalist restoration, the accompanying rise of labour and movements for democratisation posed a direct challenge to ongoing attempts by the CCP to preserve its own primacy. In response, from the 1980s, a trend within Chinese intellectual circles known as 'neo-authoritarianism' explicitly sought to borrow the model of rapid economic development amidst the absence of political freedoms. This concept was endorsed by Deng Xiaoping in 1989 as justification for a state that would take the lead in establishing a strong economy and stable society (Fewsmith 2001, p. 63). Ultimately, however, the CCP was only able to establish its 'exceptionalism' vis-à-vis the collapse of communist states in 1989 through repression. The task of achieving a more stable societal consent to the one-party state has proved somewhat elusive in the context of the unequal development brought by the CCP's economic reform policies.

The restoration of capitalism and associated emergence of endemic albeit scattered and largely spontaneous social unrest has led to a crisis of legitimacy and the corresponding search for a perennial 'mandate of heaven' for the CCP (Lam 2006, pp. 34–62). Within the context of increasing marketisation and privatisation, the challenge faced by the CCP has been that of incorporating potentially subversive social classes into the ruling bloc. Responses to the question of the means by which such incorporation is to be achieved have been varied. Deng Xiaoping approached the task through the espousal of a 'trickle-down' theory of neoliberal economics; indeed, the reforms of the 1980s did initially succeed in raising the living standards of a considerable portion of the population, particularly in the rural areas (Huang 2008). However, the exact method whereby the emergent social forces were to be incorporated was not made explicit. In reality, linkages between the state and the nascent capitalist class were largely achieved through a corrupt relationship between private entrepreneurs and party cadres, with many cadres themselves becoming entrepreneurs. At the same time, workers and peasants increasingly fell outside the state's purview as a result of the SOE reforms and the de-collectivisation of agriculture. As inequality worsened and these groups failed to enjoy the fruits of economic growth, there emerged a growing disjuncture between, on the one hand, the CCP's theoretical claim to be representative of the working and rural classes, and on the other, the reality of the growing inequality brought by the economic reforms. In order for the state to re-establish its hegemonic position vis-à-vis the nascent capitalist class and workers/peasants, the importance of a legitimising ideology that seeks to integrate new groups into the ruling bloc became all the greater.

The Jiang Zemin administration, building upon the revisions to official Marxist thought made by Deng Xiaoping, thereby developed the theory of the 'Three Represents.' This theory stresses the central role of the CCP in the country's modernisation; at the same time, it seeks to strengthen social support of the regime through increased representation of three key constituencies, defined as the development of advanced social productive forces, the direction of advanced culture, and the fundamental interests of the greatest majority of the people. Although these categories were not clearly defined, they can be understood as representing respectively the new capitalist strata of private entrepreneurs, intellectuals and technical experts, and the public in general. By emphasising the 'development of productive forces,' the Three Represents implies a redefinition of the working class to include private entrepreneurs, described as 'workers who have changed their jobs.' The association of capitalism with exploitation is thereby avoided, and official Marxist theory is accordingly revised to exclude any recognition of classes and class struggle (Holbig 2006). As a result, the Three Represents amounts to an attempted shift in the social basis of the party toward the 'progressive' elements of the nascent capitalist society. At the same time, however, the CCP's claim to be representative of workers and peasants has become even weaker than before. As Dorothy Solinger (2003, pp. 951–954) has argued, despite reference to the 'fundamental interests of the greatest majority of the people,' the poverty-stricken, the new urban poor, and those who are without steady jobs appear to be completely excluded from these newly represented strata.

The formulation of the Three Represents theory under the Jiang Zemin administration is a compelling example of a strategy of *trasformismo* toward potential oppositional groups, in this case the 'advanced social productive forces.' Indeed, the Three Represents can be understood as an elaborate theoretical justification for the CCP's decision to allow private entrepreneurs to become party members, announced at the Sixteenth Party Congress in 2002. This extension of party membership to private entrepreneurs was designed to facilitate the development of party networks throughout the organisational hierarchy of emerging private enterprises (Morgan 2003, p. 70). Of course, the publicity surrounding the admittance of capitalists into the CCP overlooks the fact that a significant number of those who can be termed 'beneficiaries' were already part of the ruling elite. Many of the newly rich and more prominent managers had long ago joined the party and its more powerful councils. Yet, their rising status and wealth had lacked legal or ideological sanction, and entrenched conservatives could easily find lawful justification for expelling them from the party, blocking their business activities, or confiscating their property. Thus, the need for *de jure* protection of the beneficiaries was becoming an urgent requirement for securing and legitimising their ongoing contributions (Lewis and Xue 2003, pp. 933–934). This revision of state ideology has transformed the basis of linkages between the state and the nascent capitalist class from a dysfunctional one of corruption to one that is at least ideologically sanctioned by a revised official Marxist theory. That this strategy of *trasformismo* toward the 'advanced social productive forces' has been reasonably successful is evident in the manner in which the middle class now largely exhibits conservative tendencies and prefers gradual reforms to radical change. Whilst the middle class is able to articulate its own interests, its political preferences are based solely on its class interests and thus is unlikely to fulfil expectations a democratising role (Lui 2005, p. 478; Unger 2006). This offers a marked contrast to the cases of Korea and Taiwan whereby the middle classes, whilst benefiting materially from catch-up industrialisation, were also a key constituency in opposition to authoritarianism (Koo 1991, Hsiao and Koo 1997).

The 'legalisation' of labour relations

In relation to the working class, the Jiang Zemin administration in practice continued to adhere to the basic principles of Deng Xiaoping's brand of 'trickle down' neoclassical economics and sought to contain grassroots social tensions through a more even combination of coercion and consent. Coercion was directed to workers' protests (particularly those making explicitly political demands), the individuals who took on a leadership role, and attempts at independent organisation. In terms of eliciting consent, the Chinese state sought to regulate labour–capital relations through the enforcement of the *rule by law* (依法治国). This 'legalisation' of labour relations and accompanying implementation of new social policies has taken place amidst an explosive growth in law-making activities that reflects the Chinese leadership's broader insistence on the law's function in maintaining political stability (Lee 2002, p. 195). This rise of rule by law can be seen as a concomitant aspect of the transition from authoritarianism to a more liberalised capitalism. As in Korea and Taiwan, a deepening enmeshment within the global market has involved a relative decline in the state's paternalistic management of labour relations and a shift toward greater regulation of social forces through legal frameworks. Given the context of the restoration of capitalism, the introduction of rule by law into the labour regime should thus be understood more in terms of its social control function. Furthermore, as Ching Kwan Lee (2008a) has argued, this strategy can be viewed as one of 'decentralised legal authoritarianism' – a dual strategy of decentralised accumulation and legalistic legitimation of authoritarian rule. Thus, alongside financial and administrative decentralisation, there has also been a shift of the ground of political legitimation from utopian ideology and personal rule toward the legal measures. This decentralisation aspect has the effect of making local government responsible for both economic development, as well as for implementing relevant labour laws and maintaining social stability. As a result, rural and workers' protests are for the most part directed at local government rather than at the central state.

A key feature of rule by law has been the manner in which the Chinese state has conferred a renewed role on the hitherto moribund trade union structure. Instead of lifting restrictions on the freedom of association in China, the CCP has established a system of state-corporatist labour relations resembling the authoritarian labour regimes of post-war Korea and Taiwan. The All-China Federation of Trade Unions (ACFTU) has been given a new role in the representation of workers' interests, and the organisation itself has played a greater role in the design of reform policies (White *et al.* 1996, p. 53). This has been combined with a top-down strategy of deliberately strengthening local trade unions and shifting to them the function of mediating labour–management disputes in the hope of appeasing an increasingly discontented workforce (Zhang 1997, p. 144). At the grassroots level, therefore, unions have taken on a greater role in addressing workers' grievances. It is important to recognise here that the state-corporatist structure nonetheless constitutes a decisive constraint on unions' claims, options, and strategies in their representation efforts; thus, unions cannot fulfil a representative role that is at odds with state policy and priorities. Instead, they accommodate workers to the state's development strategy and are responsible for forestalling spontaneous organising from below (Chen 2003, p. 1011). As such, the Chinese trade union structure does not in any sense belong to the workers and it is unlikely that Chinese official unions themselves will play any kind of democratising role. Nonetheless, it is necessary to recognise the significance of their revival in the era of economic reform. The CCP has attempted to restructure civil society so that social organisations such as trade unions serve to mediate social tensions, and their revival as part of a wider legalisation of industrial relations can be seen as a key element of the CCP's passive revolution.

However, by reforming the country's labour regime in this manner, the Chinese state may be unwittingly facilitating the very molecular changes it seeks to forestall because, in the long run, the legalisation of labour relations can serve to increase workers' sense of their own rights vis-à-vis capital. The labour law, for example, seeks to incorporate workers into a market and contract-driven system by conceding them certain legal rights and interests as contract-based, individualistic, industrial citizens. Indeed, this notion of 'legal rights' has become increasingly apparent in the labour struggle in China (Lee 2002, p. 197), as workers engaged in struggle take the rights and protections provided by these laws seriously. As such, from the perspective of the CCP, rule by law can be seen as a double-edged sword in that it contains elements conducive to both hegemony as well as resistance. It is important, therefore, to note the contradiction that this legalisation of labour relations brings in terms of the reality of government- and management-controlled unions. Whilst the legalisation of labour relations may seek to confer legitimacy on China's official trade union structure, the history of labour resistance in Korea, Taiwan, and elsewhere suggests that government and management-controlled unions may in fact serve to intensify workers' opposition by serving as a negative example and departure point for a nascent independent labour union movement.

Formidable barriers to the formation of working-class identity notwithstanding, the Chinese case would therefore confirm the established trend of the regional dynamics of capitalist restructuring in East Asia. In accordance with the spatial unevenness of global capitalist development, the Chinese labour regime has come to resemble the soft authoritarianism that formed the basis of the late-industrialisation drives elsewhere in the region. This is not a surprising development as it follows the logic of China's enmeshment into the global political economy as a final-stage low-value-added manufacturer, occupying a position in the international division of labour similar to that of earlier industrialising countries. Thus, as the labour shortages and workers' struggles in Korea and Taiwan during the late 1980s led to the relocation of production to mainland China, in a sense, these countries also exported their authoritarian state-corporatist system of industrial relations. The case of the Chinese labour regime thereby stresses the congruence between EOI and repressive labour–capital relations.

The harmonious socialist society?

The attempted restructuring of labour relations notwithstanding, the CCP has largely failed to establish a position of hegemony vis-à-vis those emergent social classes. This failure can be seen as an inevitable outcome of a reform process that has produced many more losers than winners. According to one estimate, the 'winners' of the economic reforms – namely the state administrators, managers, private entrepreneurs, professionals, and technicians – amount to approximately 9 per cent of the entire population. The 'losers,' on the other hand – the production workers, service workers, farmers, the unemployed, and the underemployed – amount to about 82 per cent of the population (Li 2013). In contrast to the conservative tendencies displayed by the middle class, the reaction to this coercive marketisation of social relations by workers and peasants has been expressed through the rising frequency and scale of social protest. In 2004, officials reported 74,000 mass incidents in China, including both peasants and workers, up from 10,000 in 1994, with the number of participants rising from 730,000 to 3.8 million (Macartney 2006), although actual figures are likely to be higher. Workers' protests have taken the form of direct collective actions, such as strikes, sit-down demonstrations, protests outside government offices, traffic blockades, and riots. Laid-off workers have generally been the most desperate of all workers, and indeed, they have had little to lose through open protest. However, as a report on labour protests between 2000 and 2004 has shown, workers in SOEs and collective enterprises facing privatisation and downsizing were also increasingly prone to engage in collective action. Their demands were mostly concerned with job security, wages, and the punishment of corrupt managers. A further significant development was that in coastal areas there was an increased propensity for migrant workers to engage in collective action. Most disputes were related to wages, particularly the non-payment of wages owned by the enterprise, demands for wage increases in general, and the payment of overtime wages. Indeed, the export-oriented coastal areas had seen stagnation in wages. In the Pearl River Delta, for example, monthly wages for migrant workers had only risen by only 68 yuan between 1992 and 2004 (China Labour Bulletin 2007).

What is noteworthy, however, is the way in which this unrest has failed to develop into an organised movement. Protests have remained largely sporadic and spontaneous, and a genuine national working-class movement has so far not emerged. Marc Blecher (2002, pp. 285–288) has argued that the spontaneous and uncoordinated nature of workers' protest in China suggests 'the political passivity of Chinese workers and the hegemony of state and market.' However, such analysis may underestimate the role of state coercion in manufacturing this apparent political passivity. The apparent 'consent' owes much to the lack of freedom of association in China and the highly repressive approach of the government with regards to any attempts at establishing independent unions outside of the official state-corporatist structure. This somewhat undermines the claim that the present system of accumulation is based on the tacit support of the working class. Gramsci's understanding of hegemony refers to a situation whereby the implications of transformations in the social relations of production are fully worked out in the political sphere, which is clearly not the case in China. As such, the manifest failure of the state's attempts to quell grassroots social tension and establish hegemony has led to further initiatives at establishing a new ideological basis for the state that is more inclusive of the interests of workers and, more generally, those left behind in China's economic growth. The coming to power of Hu Jintao in 2002 led to a reinterpretation of the Three Represents that gave greater emphasis to the impoverished majority. Increased social instability had general given a relatively stronger hand to those who opposed the neoliberal content of Jiang's policies. The fear was that Jiang's attempt at bringing about a fusion of elites into a new historical bloc was tantamount to an abandonment of the working and peasant classes at a time of growing unemployment and economic inequality (Dittmer 2003, p. 916). The decision to allow capitalists into the CCP and the addition of the Three Represents to the party constitution alongside provisions to protect private property provoked some quite considerable public dissent, drawing attention to the obvious contradiction of allowing capitalists to become members of a self-avowed communist party, and of the legal moves to protect illegal property gains (Holbig 2006, p. 23).

The Hu Jintao administration thus sought to present itself as more concerned with the plight of those left behind in China's march toward prosperity, on clean and transparent government and the rooting out of corruption, and on the rule of law (Miller 2003). This involved a redefinition of the content of the Three Represents, placing more emphasis on the 'third represent'—that of representing the needs of the majority of ordinary people. More specifically, the Hu leadership displayed more concern with the plight of poor farmers, unemployed urban workers, miners in unsafe working conditions, and elders without pensions. Various economic initiatives included the reallocation of resources from the coast to the inland; the reduction of the tax burden upon farmers; the acceleration of infrastructural development, particularly in the more backward western and inland regions; improvement of the natural environment in the western provinces; absorption of millions of surplus rural labourers in the newly expanding urban centres; stimulation of demand in the domestic market; attraction of both foreign direct investment and domestic firms from the coastal region to China's interior regions; and the establishment of a social safety net (Li 2003, pp. 339–341).

This approach was in marked contrast to the Jiang administration, which had been seen as responsible for the increasing economic gap between urban and rural areas, coastal and inland regions, and the traditional and new economic sectors. Jiang disproportionately allocated economic resources toward Shanghai and other coastal cities whilst allowing many inland provinces to lag behind. Hu and other fourth-generation leaders had their power bases in the poorer inland and Western provinces, and they appeared to better understand the daunting challenges that China faces than their predecessors (Li 2003, p. 340). These two approaches form the bases of the two main factions in Chinese politics: the 'Shanghai gang, (上海邦), as represented by Jiang Zemin, and the informal political coalition centred around the Communist Youth League, known as *Tuanpai* (团派), as represented by Hu Jintao and Wen Jiabao (Li 2001). As Solinger (2003, p. 957) has argued, '[I]t does seem possible that now that forebears Mao and Deng have both departed, their respective legacies may be legitimating the adoption of two different political stances, one more akin to the preferences of the former and one more aligned with the policies of the latter.' This manoeuvring of political factions in response to the perceived challenge posed by subaltern classes as a whole demonstrates that there is no single strategy toward passive revolution as the incorporation of new social classes emergent in the course of capitalist restoration is an inherently contested process. However, the continued relationship between coercion and consent is nonetheless apparent in both these approaches. Indeed, despite the greater emphasis on ameliorative measures, the Hu Jintao administration appeared even more willing than the Jiang Zemin administration to deploy physical repression of rural protests (Walker 2006, p. 13).

It is important to note, however, that the threat to the continuation of the present Chinese regime of accumulation and mode of enmeshment with the capitalist world economy does not necessarily come from an explicitly counterhegemonic, politically conscious organised labour movement. The everyday resistance of migrant workers has unwittingly served to undermine the highly exploitative model of coastal export-led growth to an extent to which protests have as yet failed to achieve. It has been argued, for example, that a migrant worker shortage in the

Pearl River Delta has increasingly served to hamper local economic development. Whilst the increased demand for migrant workers and the continued restrictions placed on migration by the household registration system are cited as playing a key role in the shortages, the report also cites low wages and a failure to protect labour rights as leading potential rural migrants to expect higher living standards, with many workers returning to the countryside. Of the companies surveyed, 45.9 per cent believed that job applicants were overly picky, whereas 13.1 per cent thought that low wages were the main reason that it was difficult to recruit workers (Li 2005). Though there are a number of reasons for the increased unwillingness of peasants to work in the coastal sweatshop factories, the labour shortages should also be understood in the context of the government's agricultural reforms. Endemic rural protests served to provoke responses from the government directed at ameliorating the burden of tax on rural peasants. These rural reforms have been more than cosmetic, and they have brought about genuine improvements in the situation in the countryside. As a result, both younger peasant workers and more experienced migrants are no longer willing to accept the exploitative conditions of the coastal factories (Weil 2006), and as Giovanni Arrighi has argued, these rural reforms 'have combined to create labour shortages that are undermining the foundations of the super-exploitation of migrant labor' (Arrighi 2008, pp. 360–361).

Difficulties in recruiting labour have been compounded by ongoing shifts in the structure of the Chinese labour market of the kind that preceded wage rises and the emergence of labour movements elsewhere in East Asia. As Fang Cai (2010) of the Chinese Academy of Social Sciences has argued, China itself may now be approaching or may even have already passed its Lewisian turning point (see also Das and Diaye 2013). Together, these trends have further slowed migration to the cities and intensified the labour shortages in the export-oriented manufacturing sector (Hung 2009, p. 20). Although low wages had been cited as a key factor in the increasing reluctance of workers to migrate to the coastal sweatshop factories in the early 2000s, these labour shortages have unsurprisingly led to rising wages in recent years. Their impact has been felt differentially across the country, however, and have been particularly high in the coastal manufacturing regions such as Guangzhou and Shenzhen and the urban centres of Beijing and Shanghai, and have been higher for skilled workers (Yang *et al.* 2010).

Chinese workers and the global financial crisis

The days of China's repressive labour regime may be numbered, not only due to domestic social processes but also as a result of China's changing position within the broader international political economy. Whilst a sizeable body of literature has emerged in recent years predicting the rise of China as the world's next superpower or global hegemon (Overholt 1994, Fishman 2005, Kynge 2007), scholars within the field of international political economy have, for the most part, been more sceptical of such claims, arguing that they are based on unfounded judgements regarding China's growing economic strength. They argue that the more hyperbolic accounts of China's rise commonly rely on aggregate national data, such as bilateral trade statistics that fail to gauge the nature of China's integration into global commodity chains. Chinese industrialisation, according to this latter view, should be viewed not so much as portending the rise of a new economic powerhouse so to speak but rather as reflecting the country's dependent role within global capitalist production. In 2003, for example, foreign-invested enterprises accounted for 55.8 per cent of all Chinese exports. If domestic Chinese producers, who are largely engaged in original equipment manufacturing under contract for export, are included, then 70 per cent of all Chinese exports are made by or for foreign companies (Breslin 2005, p. 743). East Asian as well as Western corporations have also increasingly relocated manufacturing to China, the latter often through subcontracting via Taiwanese, Hong Kong, and overseas Chinese firms that have established a niche role managing labour-intensive production. The failure of national aggregate statistics to capture the realities of global commodity chains thereby serves to overstate Chinese 'power' in the global economy (Breslin 2005, p. 746; see also Moore 2008, p. 514). China's foreign direct investment-driven rise therefore has been viewed as a 'workshop of the world' – a final production platform that is heavily dependent not only on external demand but also on imports of components and machinery. James Petras goes as far in this respect to question even what it means to speak of 'China' when the manufacturing taking place within the country's territory is increasingly dominated by foreign corporations that are increasing their share of exports, profits, royalty payments, and control over the more dynamic sectors of the economy (Petras 2006, p. 425).

Yet, this more pessimistic view, centred on China's integration into global production networks, runs the risk of underestimating the nuances of the international dimensions of China's political economy. Whilst it has been noted that the Chinese economy is highly dependent on overseas markets – particularly that of the United States – it is also important to recognise the mutual nature of this dependence. The other side of the coin to China's dependence on the US market is the high level of US dependence on the import of cheap Chinese-made consumer goods. Indeed, as a Centre for Strategic and International Studies report shows, China's cheap exports make the United States approximately $70 billion better off per year by maintaining low-cost consumption growth (cited in Morgan 2008, p. 419). As a result of these massive exports to the United States, however, by April 2011, China's foreign exchange reserves reached the value of $3 trillion US dollars (People's Daily 2011), of which $1.15 trillion had been invested in US treasury bonds, making China the largest holder of US government debt (US Treasury 2012). As such, China is effectively financing the US government's budget deficit and underpinning a key market for the country's exports. This accumulation of foreign exchange reserves has been more than simply an unintended consequence of EOI. Rather, it has been part of a deliberate strategy within a broader commitment to 'reserve adequacy' within the context of a broader 'grand reserves system' of grain, energy, and material supplies (Chin 2010, pp. 698–701). This imperative for foreign exchange reserve adequacy was highlighted by the failure of international financial institutions to provide any form of collective insurance during the East Asian financial crisis of the late 1990s.

The opportunistic use of the crisis by the International Monetary Fund (IMF)–Wall Street–US Treasury nexus (Wade and Veneroso 1998) in order to impose Washington consensus policies onto the former Asian 'miracle economies' led China to pursue a strategy of self-insurance. This involved the intensification of export-led development as a means of accumulating the foreign exchange reserves necessary to maintain the dollar peg in the face of speculative attacks.

There is much debate, however, as to the extent to which these arrangements are an expression of China's structural power in the global political economy. As the largest holder of US government debt, China has a theoretical ability to cause a crash in the dollar's value by abandoning its policy of purchasing US treasury bonds. Large foreign exchange reserves not only serve to deter international speculators but also serve to prevent the United States from taking action against China's alleged currency manipulation beyond vague threats of economic sanctions (Chin 2010, p. 701). However, whilst China's theoretical ability to crash the US dollar certainly exists, it has been argued that such an approach would be self-defeating because it would both undermine the value of China's remaining dollar-denominated assets as well as cause a collapse in China's primary export market (Breslin 2005, p. 741; Moore 2008). Thus, the consequences of the strategy of the accumulation of foreign exchange reserves have often been presented as negative for China and as an indicator of the 'superimperialism' of the United States (Hudson 2003). Viewed in this light, the subjugation of labour and repression of consumption in China is a deliberate strategy of both underpinning consumerism in the United States and pursuing a strategy for self-insurance against financial instability.

It has been argued, therefore, that China's export dependence means that any rise in wages is likely to have a deleterious impact on the Chinese economy and that any failure to quell labour unrest is likely to have serious implications for the broader global political economy (Morgan 2008, pp. 417–420). China is thus faced with a dilemma: on the one hand, if it fails to address the causes underpinning social unrest, China could see a snowball effect in social conflict across the country. However, any attempts to solve the problem of social conflict may cause capital flight which may in any case negatively affect economic growth and induce further unrest (Morgan 2008, p. 431). Nonetheless, as noted above, the government had, even prior to the global financial crisis, sought to create institutions that were able to represent workers more effectively by channelling unrest into bureaucratic forms of dispute resolution (Clarke and Pringle 2009, p. 93). Such initiatives are not simply limited in their aims to eliciting consent from workers. There has been an explicit concern with upgrading labour conditions within China. The passing of the new Labour Contract Law (LCL) in 2008 was aimed at compelling companies to sign contracts with their workers, stipulating that employees who have been with a company for more than ten years are automatically entitled to contracts, thereby protecting them against dismissal without cause. In addition, the law stipulates that employers must contribute to employee's social security funds and set new wage standards for employees on probation and those working overtime (National People's Congress 2009).

Whilst the primary motivation behind the LCL was tackling the increased social tensions that threaten the rule of the CCP, the task of shifting the balance of class forces toward labour was given added impetus by the global financial crisis. The crisis served to expose the inherent vulnerabilities of the Chinese model of growth and its reliance on developed country markets, particularly that of the United States. The Chinese government has, as a result, increasingly signified the need to facilitate a shift away from EOI toward a model oriented more toward domestic consumption. This imperative was made more explicit in the twelfth Five-Year Plan, which called for a doubling of workers' wages (Xinhua News 2010). In reality, however, the central government's measures to deal with the fallout of the global financial crisis appeared to be at cross-purposes with its aims of raising domestic consumption. Its US $585 billion stimulus package placed more emphasis on investment in infrastructure than on boosting household spending. As a result, China saw a sharp decrease in the share and consumption in gross domestic product (GDP) between 2007 and 2010 (Foster and McChesney 2012). Whilst the fall in China's current account surplus to GDP ratio in 2011 suggests a possible shift in the weight of the economy toward domestic consumption, as the IMF pointed out, this was more a result of high levels of investment, a weak global economy, and an increase in the costs of commodity imports (Yu 2012). Furthermore, when China saw its weakest growth for three years in the second quarter of 2012, Premier Wen Jiabao called for greater investment, suggesting again a preference for increasing export capacity rather than a shift toward household consumption (Bradsher 2012).

There were also real weaknesses in the way that the LCL was implemented. As Feng Chen has argued, the law aims to strengthen individual rather than collective labour rights through the provision of mechanisms by which workers as individuals are able to seek redress for their grievances through arbitration commissions and courts. Enforcement of the law's stipulations concerning wages and working conditions remains weak, and, without the freedom of association, workers lack an effective means with which to collectively ensure the enforcement of the law (Chen 2007, pp. 63–64). The state-sanctioned ACFTU claims to represent all workers in China, but when faced with labour unrest, it seeks to channel grievances into institutional channels through legislation and administration. As such, it plays no role in facilitating collective bargaining, and the right to strike was removed entirely from the 1982 constitution and has not been reinstated. Despite these manifest weaknesses, the LCL still managed to provoke vocal resistance when it was first proposed from foreign business interests in China. Furthermore, prior to the law's implementation, companies sought to avoid the requirement to offer permanent contracts to workers with over ten years of service by asking workers to 'voluntarily' resign and then offer new temporary contracts (China.org.cn 2007). When the law came into effect, some employers provided workers with contracts in English (a language few could understand), forced them to sign two separate documents with two different company seals, or used other methods to get around the provision of the law (China Labour Bulletin 2009, pp. 18–19). Labour administration authorities have also lacked the economic and political incentives to supervise and inspect employers' compliance with the laws. Punitive measures that can be applied for noncompliance are limited to fines, and there is a national shortage of labour inspectors (Zheng 2009, p. 608).

At the same time, the LCL has done little to reverse trends toward increased labour unrest or of labour shortages that lead to heightened labour costs. Whilst the onset of the crisis saw a brief wave of mass layoffs (Chan 2010, pp. 666–667), anecdotal evidence suggests the return to an upward trend in labour shortages and wage costs. A survey of 200 Hong Kong-based manufacturers operating in the Pearl River Delta found that in the first three months of 2012 alone, labour shortages and stricter enforcement of social insurance contributions had led to an increase in wages of 10 per cent (Standard Chartered 2012). The global financial crisis also saw a rapid rise in the number of 'mass incidents' of unrest. Whilst the government stopped releasing official figures after 2005, unofficial reports suggest that 2008 saw as many as 120,000 incidents, declining only slightly in 2009 (Friedman 2012, p. 464). Furthermore, whereas migrant workers had hitherto been relatively quiescent compared to laid-off SOE workers, the crisis saw a marked shift in the locus of workers' struggles toward the coastal manufacturing regions. This grassroots movement for improved living standards led by migrant workers has raised further questions about the social instability generated by China's export-oriented model.

Thus, despite the weaknesses of labour reform, parallels with the experience of labour reform elsewhere in East Asia suggest that China is nonetheless potentially on the verge of a significant transformation in the realm of labour relations. As argued in Chapter 4, in the midst of the kinds of broader structural changes in the labour market outlined previously, the KMT adopted a strategy of pre-emptive labour legislation vis-à-vis increasingly restless social forces through the passing of the LSL in 1984. The KMT's strategy of labour reform arose from a concern about a potential alliance between labour and the emerging *dangwai* political opposition movement. As with China's LCL, Taiwan's LSL suffered from a number of shortcomings, which facilitated evasion by employers, and poor enforcement, and it failed to provide any actual mechanisms whereby unions could negotiate matters within its remit. Nonetheless, it was precisely these shortcomings that led to struggles for proper implementation of the law – a strategy known as 'fight for what the law offers' (顺法斗争) – and, as such, marked the rise of the independent labour movement. Similarly in China, most labour rights advocates agree that the passing of the LCL has led to workers becoming more aware of the importance of gaining a contract and of the provisions of the new legal regime. The introduction of the laws has seen an upsurge in litigation by workers, suggesting that workers are indeed becoming more conscious of their rights (Wang *et al.* 2009, p. 492). Structural labour market changes and historical precedent do not, of course, determine agency. The forms that workers' struggles take and their impact is an empirical question. Indeed, Silver's (2003, pp. 71–73) analysis of world-historical patterns of labour unrest cite the case of Japan, which, whilst apparently possessing the conditions for the emergence of a strong labour movement, in fact saw the transition towards cooperative labour relations and the subordination of organised labour. Even between Korea and Taiwan, as I have argued in this book, there are significant differences in terms of the intensity of their respective strike waves in the late 1980s and the degree to which organised labour development remained an influential actor in the post-authoritarian era (Lee 2008b).

However, since the onset of the global financial crisis, workers' struggles show no signs of abating. An intensification of workers' consciousness could also be seen in the anti-privatisation struggle of July 2009 at the Tonghua Steel Mill, where workers were successful in halting plans to privatise the company. Furthermore, in November 2011, workers at Pepsi bottling plants resisted attempts to have their contracts terminated and renegotiated with the company's new owner. The strike was unprecedented in that the industrial action involved workers at different bottling plants in five different cities (Au and Bai 2012, pp. 226–230). However, the 2010 strike wave in China, particularly the strike that took place at Nanhai Honda for 17 days in the early summer of that year, suggests that China may be following the Korean path of the rise of a more militant class-conscious labour movement. The workers' struggle at Nanhai Honda suggested a qualitative shift toward a militant workers' consciousness capable of challenging Chinese labour subordination to the degree that notions of the 'race to the bottom,' particularly those predicated on the subordination of Chinese labour in particular, should be rethought. Based not only on reactive issues concerned with the infringement of workers' rights, the workers at Nanhai Honda engaged in a more proactive struggle for material gains and union democracy.

Conclusion

This chapter has sought to examine the extent to which the kind of passive revolution seen in the East Asian states of Japan, Korea, and Taiwan can also be witnessed in mainland China following the onset of economic reforms in the late 1970s. As the analysis has suggested, there are signs that EOI in China's coastal regions has indeed led to the nascent emergence of collective subjectivity, which threatens to disrupt the accumulation strategies of the Chinese state and capital. However, the CCP's response to this increased unrest has also been shaped by the specificities of China's external relations as well as the instructive examples of labour struggles elsewhere in East Asia and even further afield. As such, it has sought to adopt pre-emptive strategies of reform from above that seek to co-opt the new social forces emerging out of the restoration of capitalism. Specifically, this has involved a sustained attempt to re-establish an organic relationship between the state and certain sections of society. The CCP has opened its own doors to the new 'progressive' class of private entrepreneurs, thus seeking to establish its roots in the new capitalist economy. Yet, the losers in the capitalist restoration vastly outnumber the winners, and they have become increasingly vocal about their grievances. As such, the threat of widespread social unrest has forced the state in China to attempt to redefine its relationship with the subaltern classes of workers, peasants, and those generally left behind by the economic development.

The emerging social unrest that has accompanied the restoration of capitalism has, as a result, forced the government to anticipate many of the changes it seeks to forestall. Thus, even without the emergence of a militant, politically conscious, organised labour movement in China, many of the nascent institutional features of capitalist industrial society have been introduced through a process of top-down reform. This has involved the establishment of a legal basis for the mediation of labour–capital relations alongside ostensibly neutral trade unions, thus forming the institutional basis for the defence of workers' rights, albeit on an individualised basis. Whilst state ideology has moved away from the theoretical recognition of class struggle, many of the recently created institutions nonetheless represent recognition of the divergence of interests between capital and labour. Furthermore, there is evidence to suggest that the dynamics of China's workers' movement may be following the path of earlier industrialisers in East Asia. In Korea and Taiwan, for example, the state-dominated unions and the failure to enforce labour standards laws and offer a minimum of protection to workers became key grievances for the workers' movement there.

Whilst the CCP has placed a great deal of emphasis on controlling social unrest, the contradictory effects of its passive revolution suggest that the CCP's efforts have to date largely failed, and that social unrest in China will remain a significant dynamic in years to come. The state's attempts to forestall social unrest have also, however, provided the basis for the undermining of China's low-wage export-manufacturing model. Reforms in the countryside have somewhat reduced the disciplining role of the reserve army of labour in the countryside, thereby threatening the low-wage EOI model. China's role as 'workshop of the world' may therefore come under increasing threat, particularly because the Chinese state lacks the industrial upgrading capabilities common to the earlier generation of East Asian developmental states. Whilst there is evidence that multinationals are beginning to relocate to sites with cheaper labour, the importance of China as a spatial fix for global capital, as well as the mutual dependence of the United States and China predicated on low-road labour relations, mean that the implications of these developments are likely to have a wider significance for profitability in the capitalist world economy as a whole. The question may be raised, therefore, as to whether this outcome confirms Silver's argument (2003) that 'where capital goes, militancy goes.' If low-wage manufacturers relocate to lower-wage countries where labour is also politically weak, then China would seem to fulfil its role in the continuous global search by capitalists for cheaper labour. However, the analysis presented here shows that the actual actors and processes involved are quite different than that portrayed by Silver. The state has played a much more central role in instituting certain reforms that, whilst designed to appease a potentially rebellious working class, ultimately serve to introduce institutions that may undermine the contemporary mode of China's insertion into the international political economy. Thus, the role of the state in carrying out a passive revolution plays a large part in ensuring that capital can find no permanent solution to its crisis of profitability through the spatial fix alone.

CONCLUSIONS

Few would deny that the rise of East Asia constitutes one of the most significant geopolitical developments of the late twentieth and early twenty-first centuries. The global financial crisis that engulfed the heartlands of advanced industrial capitalism in 2008 seemed to accelerate this East Asian challenge to Western global dominance. Prior to this crisis, a number of observers had argued that East Asia's industrialisation strategy, based as it was upon the repression of workers' rights and domestic consumption in order to promote low-cost production for Western markets, was testament to the region's subservient position within the global economic order. This dependence on external demand meant, it was argued, that there was little likelihood that East Asian governments would adopt concrete measures aimed at upgrading wages and working conditions because to do so would serve to price the region's manufacturers out of those external markets. Yet, as I have argued in this book, the position of the East Asian countries within the hierarchy of world capitalism has remained anything but static, and that a key but often neglected factor in shaping the trajectory of East Asian development has been precisely that of domestic social struggles in which workers have played a central role. This dynamic can be seen most recently in the case of China. Despite a seemingly inexhaustible supply of labour within the country, Chinese capitalism is now coming under significant internal social pressures that suggest a potential shift away from a low-wage economy based on labour subordination toward one in which domestic consumption plays a more central role. Furthermore, the confluence of these domestic social struggles with tectonic shifts in the international political economy serves to confirm the broader narrative put forward in this book regarding the manner in which workers' agency has historically exerted a profound influence on the rise of East Asia.

As I have argued, the underexplored nexus between labour, development, and the international political economy warrants a re-theorisation of the politics of late development itself. For the most part, theories of East Asian development have either focused on the relative role of states and markets in underpinning catch-up industrialisation, or they have sought to explain such processes with reference to the favourable geopolitical context provided by the Cold War – a process that has been referred to as one of 'development by invitation.' In these approaches, labour is at best viewed as a largely passive actor; as such, it is not recognised let alone theorised as one of the key sources of transformation within the international political economy. In more recent debates concerning transitions toward neoliberalism in East Asia, a handful of writers have paid more attention to the role of ongoing transformations in domestic social relations of production. A more common view, however, has been that of neoliberal transition as stemming from international factors, such as the global dominance of neoliberal ideology and/or the coercive manoeuvrings of the United States in concert with the international financial institutions. Yet, the argument put forward in this book has been not simply that both levels of analysis are important in terms of explaining the rise of East Asian national developmentalism and its subsequent transition toward neoliberalism, but rather that 'the social' and 'the geopolitical' need to be understood as interrelated dynamic processes and as mutually constitutive. The dual neglect present in these explanations of historical change in East Asia thus calls for a single integrative theory of development that incorporates the dialectical relationship between the social underpinnings of development and the inter-societal dynamics of the global geopolitical order.

I have argued that Gramsci's concept of passive revolution provides a means of achieving this aim by elucidating how processes of state–society contestation are situated within the wider dynamics of the interstate system. In this sense, passive revolution can be understood as the political counterpart to the rise of state-led developmentalism amidst heightened geopolitical pressures and resulting imperatives to industrialise. As Gramsci (1971, p. 132) argued, 'All history from 1815 onwards shows the efforts of the traditional classes to prevent the formation of a collective will … and to maintain "economic-corporate" power in an international system of passive equilibrium.' Of course, the East Asian experience of late development differed from the Italian case analysed by Gramsci in several important respects. The landowner class in East Asia, for example, was thoroughly dispossessed in the late 1940s and early 1950s – a process which removed from the equation a social class that had historically acted as a significant fetter on capitalist development. More broadly, however, Gramsci's framework of passive revolution can shed light on the manner whereby governments in the East Asian region have been highly active in reorganising social relations in a manner commensurate with catch-up industrialisation and in forestalling the emergence of a 'collective will' from below. Thus, rather than representing an 'overextension' of the concept (Callinicos 2010), the application of passive revolution to more contemporary processes of state-led development captures a more general phenomenon accompanying the global spread of capitalism.

Using this framework, this book sought to address several key questions concerning the role of labour in East Asia's experience of late development. The first of these questions was related to the origins of East Asia's labour subordination, specifically the role of the post-war geopolitical conjuncture in establishing the foundations for export-oriented industrialisation (EOI) based on the subordination of labour. How did industrialisation under US auspices impact upon processes of working class formation and what were the implications of such processes for East Asia's position within the international hierarchy of capitalist production? The region's experience of state-mandated catch-up development can in the first instance be seen as the long-term outcome of the clash between East and West in the nineteenth century and the subsequent emergence of nascent nationalisms aimed at the emulation of Western industrialism and militarism as a means of national survival. However, in Japan, Korea, and Taiwan, American intervention following the Second World War further paved the way for a thoroughgoing process of passive revolution, which served to re-impose aspects of the pre-war order against popular opposition combined with new institutional features specific to the US post-war hegemonic geopolitical project.

In Japan, the 1945 surrender led to heightened social unrest and a burgeoning labour movement, which posed a significant challenge to the strategic aims of the ascendant power in East Asia, the United States. In the early stages of the occupation, Supreme Commander for the Allied Powers (SCAP) policies were largely of a punitive nature, aimed at imposing 'democracy from above' as a means of eradicating the roots of militarism in Japanese society. These democratising reforms included the dissolution of the *zaibatsu* and liberalisation of the legal code governing labour relations so as to encourage the growth of an autonomous trade union movement. However, the economic hardships faced by workers in the aftermath of the surrender led to increased militancy on the part of Japanese workers. Furthermore, the growing global dollar gap frustrated US policymakers' attempts to reconstruct the world economy along liberal lines. Thus, by 1947, SCAP shifted from a policy of democracy promotion toward one of facilitating the revival of Japanese industry and the subordination of labour. This so-called 'reverse course' involved a purge of public employees associated with the Japanese Communist Party, as well as the promotion of 'democratisation leagues' aimed at competing with the communist-oriented *Sanbetsu* trade union. By the late 1950s, the US occupation authorities, in partnership with the Japanese state and capital, had succeeded in reversing the gains made by the left-leaning labour movement in the immediate post-war years and had effectively re-established the pre-war system of enterprise unionism as the basis of labour–management relations. As such, the post-war passive revolution laid the foundations for the 'miracle years' of Japanese growth and for the centrality of the country's political economy within the broader East Asian regional production system.

This understanding of the repressive character of Japanese labour relations runs counter to the mainstream view of the Japanese employment system as not only underpinning the extraordinary competitiveness of Japanese industry but also as constituting an altogether more humane worker-friendly form of employment relations. As I have argued, 'lifetime employment' and the 'seniority wage system' are more limited than the terms themselves suggest, and in any case cover only approximately 20–30 per cent of the country's workforce. Enterprise unions should be regarded as serious impediments to working-class solidarity and are in fact expressions of the weakness of organised labour rather than its strength. This more critical interpretation of Japanese labour institutions thus provides a rather different interpretation of the relationship between Japan's traditional Confucian culture and the country's extraordinary success in meeting the challenges of late development. Whilst mainstream accounts have focused on how the influence of Confucian values have helped to nurture a culture of harmony and cooperation in the workplace, the analysis offered in this book has drawn attention to the selective and instrumental use of traditional cultural values by management for the purposes of subordinating workers to the rule of capital.

In contrast to Japan, neither Korea nor Taiwan were made the subject of any initial democratic experiment. Post-war labour policy in both countries was immediately of a more repressive nature. The greater social upheaval in Korea following independence meant that the occupying US forces in the southern half of the peninsula gave strong support to Korean conservative elites in facilitating the violent repression of labour. Taiwan also experienced widespread popular resistance against the mainlander Kuomintang (KMT), to which the latter responded through a brutal crackdown in 1947. Though the role of the United States in Taiwan's repression was less direct than in the Korean case, the continued existence of the KMT regime on Taiwan was ultimately secured by massive US military and economic aid following the outbreak of the Korean war. By the onset of EOI in the 1960s, the repression of labour had meant that both the Korean and Taiwanese developmental states were uniquely well situated to embark upon a rapid programme of industrialisation, albeit in the context of a position of economic dependency vis-à-vis Japan. This comprehensive subordination of labour under US auspices thereby underpinned both a significant comparative advantage in terms of production costs, as well as an extraordinary ability on the part of the Korean and Taiwanese developmental states to facilitate industrial upgrading and thereby make rapid advances in the hierarchy of world capitalism.

A further question that this book raised was that of how the origins of divergent labour regimes across the East Asian region can be explained. As I have argued, the regional political economy of East Asia is perhaps uniquely hierarchical in its organisation, highly uneven in terms of levels of development across the region, and has allowed for a significant degree of upward mobility on the part of its constituent states. As the Japanese, Korean, and Taiwanese developmental states upgraded their industries and relocated the most labour-intensive stages of production offshore, they also to a certain degree upgraded their labour regimes. However, the comparative cases of Korea and Taiwan pose a particularly intriguing question that requires a closer examination of how unevenness and historical specificity serve to produce divergent labour regimes and patterns of working-class formation. Though the two cases share in many respects a quite similar developmental trajectory, it is nonetheless clear that since the colonial era, Korea has witnessed comparatively greater social turmoil and labour militancy than in Taiwan, a contrast that is still visible in the present day. The first factor in this divergence is the differential impact of colonial industrialisation. Korea witnessed a greater degree of social dislocation and working-class formation under colonialism as a result of the country's geographical proximity to the Asian mainland. As a result, the country saw a more intense wave of labour unrest following the Japanese surrender.

However, Korea and Taiwan's divergent experiences of working-class formation were also closely shaped by the specificities of the post-war passive revolution. The higher concentration of capital in the Korean case created conditions that were more conducive to the development of class consciousness and the emergence of strong working-class organisations. Taiwan's more fractious industrial structure, on the other hand, was in many respects an outcome of the KMT's strategy of reserving the more privileged employment opportunities in the state-owned enterprise sector for mainlanders, whilst restricting employment for local Taiwanese workers to the small and medium enterprise (SME) sector. The more diffuse nature of the SME sector in Taiwan meant that local Taiwanese workers enjoyed less structural power with which to establish strong labour organisations and to challenge the rule of capital. Furthermore, the sub-ethnic grievances that resulted from this discriminatory industrial structure were powerful enough to militate against the formation of working-class consciousness. Indeed, this prevalence of sub-ethnic over class cleavages was characteristic of Taiwanese labour politics; it would become all the more pronounced following the democratic transition of the late 1980s.

A further question that this book has raised concerns the manner in which East Asia's catch-up industrialisation, based as it was on the subordination of labour, subsequently impacted upon the structure of post-war US hegemony itself. As I have argued, successful catch-up industrialisation intensified certain contradictions that were to increasingly challenge the underpinnings and rationale of the US hegemonic project in East Asia. As the United States was faced with increased economic competition from East Asian manufacturers alongside the spiralling costs of its military campaigns in Southeast Asia, it began in the 1970s to reassess the premises of its role in the region and sought to restrict East Asian exports to the US domestic market, as well as shift the burden of maintaining security in the region onto the Asian countries themselves. In Korea and Taiwan, this shift in US strategy led to a shift in development policy toward heavy and chemical industrialisation (HCI), with significant implications for working-class formation in the two countries.

This then leads us to the further question of the role of labour in the decline of national developmentalism and the transition toward neoliberalism. Whilst HCI can be seen as a strategic response to the challenges posed by the changing US strategy toward East Asia, as noted previously, it also served to expand the size of the industrial working class in Korea and Taiwan and confer greater structural power on labour with which it could challenge the autonomy of the developmental state. The rise of labour as a collective actor occurred in tandem with the emergence of a broad pro-democracy movement. Following the democratic aperture in the late 1980s, Korean and Taiwanese movements were able to make significant organisational advancements and push for reforms to the broader legal framework governing labour relations. As such, the rise of Korean and Taiwanese labour should be seen as a revolt against the post-war developmental passive revolution. However, whilst democratisation had a strong internal impetus, it should also be understood as part of a global transition toward neoliberalism and democracy that also came about as a result of the changing nature of US policy toward its authoritarian allies.

Indeed, the longer-term response of the United States to the decline of capital profitability was the project of global neoliberalism. US democracy promotion was integral to this project as the economic nationalism of authoritarian strongmen regimes remained a significant impediment to the reach of global, and especially Wall Street, financial capital. Thus, far from tempering the global spread of neoliberalism, formal democratisation in East Asia ultimately served to facilitate ongoing liberalisation, privatisation, and the thoroughgoing commodification of society. This dual transition to neoliberalism and democracy posed a formidable set of material as well as ideational challenges to East Asian labour movements. Indeed, the transition from national developmentalism toward neoliberalism can be understood as a renewed strategy of passive revolution on the part of political and economic elites aimed at co-opting labour and dispelling potential resistance to the anti-labour thrust of neoliberal reform.

Japanese labour's response to the economic slowdown of the 1970s involved seeking increased participation in policymaking at the national level, although this is a strategy that has met with mixed results. Whilst the relative continuity of lifetime employment, seniority wages, and enterprise unionism has been taken by some as evidence of the continuity of Japan's distinctive model of capitalism in the face of global neoliberalism, as I have argued, these institutions were already expressions of the comprehensive subordination of labour in Japan; as such, their resilience is not surprising. However, in line with ongoing hollowing-out of manufacturing in Japan, the country has in recent years witnessed a secular decline in the organisational strength of labour. In Korea, organised labour has sought to establish an independent presence in the formal political arena as well as facilitate a shift from enterprise to industrial-level unionism. However, any achievements made in these goals have largely failed to temper the deepening of the dualistic labour market and expansion of the contingent labour force. In Taiwan, unions have largely failed to establish collective bargaining with employers, and labour politics have for the most part remained subordinated to the identity-oriented party political system. As such, in all three countries, increased opportunities for labour to participate in formal politics emerged at the same time as neoliberal restructuring increasingly undermined the organisational basis of labour. Furthermore, rising labour costs in Japan, Korea, and Taiwan have led to the further spatial expansion of the East Asian regional production system to offshore locations such as China, with the result of further increasing competitive pressures on workers in the former countries.

This process of sustained regional restructuring and spatial reorganisation of production led to the increased importance of Chinese labour in the international political economy. Beverly Silver (2003, p. 65) has argued that 'where capital goes, militancy goes' and that, as a consequence, China is likely to become the next big centre of labour unrest. The analysis presented in this book thus raised the question of to what extent China will in fact follow the other East Asian countries and see the development of a class-conscious labour movement aimed at challenging labour subordination. Given its heightened concern with the destabilising effects of social unrest, the

Chinese Communist Party (CCP) has pre-emptively enacted a series of top-down reforms that are designed to enable workers to protect themselves from the worst forms of capitalist exploitation. Whilst it is true that these reforms are problematic in that they allow for only an individualised notion of labour rights and still effectively proscribe freedom of association, these reforms are nonetheless significant given that in the pre-reform era the very notion of rights was largely nonexistent. The significance of the reforms is evidenced by the increased recourse by workers to the labour courts to address their grievances.

In addition, the experience of the global financial crisis has served to increase the Chinese leadership's sense of the vulnerabilities inherent within the EOI model. As such, the CCP has explicitly stated the need to facilitate a transition toward a model based on domestic consumption. Whilst doubts can be raised as to the extent to which the Chinese leadership will indeed enact the reforms necessary for this transition to take place, deeper changes in the Chinese labour market and the ongoing conferment of structural power on workers may make this transition inevitable. As such, whereas China has previously played a key role in driving a broader regional and indeed global race to the bottom, a tentative conclusion offered by this book is that we may now be witnessing the beginnings of a shift away from a model of development based on labour subordination

This analysis of the Chinese case also confirms the argument put forward in this book that understanding contemporary labour struggles through a framework of global capital pitted against global labour unduly neglects the importance of 'the international' in explaining transformations in specific state–society complexes. At the same time, however, the emphasis on the role of the state in establishing developmental labour regimes should not be taken to indicate prevalence of the national over the global level of analysis. As we have seen, relations *between* states play a constitutive role in the dynamics of passive revolution. State strategies of capital accumulation are conditioned by interstate rivalry, as well as by historically specific patterns of state–society contestation. Geopolitical events such as the Sino–Soviet rivalry, transformations in US hegemony in the 1970s, and the rise of the East Asian developmental states have played key roles in China's capitalist restoration. Furthermore, the international system, characterised as it is by nations and regions at differing levels of development, plays an important role in mediating forms of class struggle. Again, the Chinese case shows that the demonstrative effects of class struggles in newly industrialising countries such as Korea and Taiwan, as well as that of former socialist countries such as Poland, have shaped the contemporary response of the state toward emergent labour unrest. Thus, even in the absence of a politically conscious organised working-class movement, Chinese state strategies are profoundly shaped by these processes of class formation and class agency; as such, class struggle can still be seen as occupying a central position within the international political economy. This observation further underlines the argument that the study of the role of labour in the changing international political economy cannot simply be reduced to the activities of a few labour bureaucracies acting in a 'global civil society,' to isolated incidents of cross-border organisation and solidarity, or to a general conviction that at some unspecified point in the future workers will play a distinctive transformatory and emancipatory role globally.

As noted, there is evidence to suggest that the last great 'spatial fix' of global capitalism may now be coming to an end as a result of the agency of labour. However, seeking to chart the future direction of East Asian capitalism is, of course, a speculative activity. The rise of labour in Korea and Taiwan led to counter-movements on the part of the state and capital that sought to repress wages in the name of international competitiveness, although structural trends in the economy and the emergence of labour as an organised political force meant that there was little chance that these countries could return to the repressive low-wage regimes of the past. The Chinese government also appears to have accepted that repression alone is not a viable option in dealing with the country's growing worker restiveness and rising wages. An important question, however, is how employers will react to the increasing challenges to capital accumulation. One response of employers in the labour-intensive sector has been to relocate production to China's inland provinces and thus move closer to supplies of labour. Companies targeting China's domestic market have also relocated within the country in order to avoid the rising costs of the coastal areas. Foxconn, for example, has opened new factories in the Northern provinces of Hebei and Shaanxi, where the average salary is more than 60 per cent lower than in Shenzhen (IHLO 2008). This response is, in fact, in line with the government's strategy of achieving more geographically equitable development. As such, it is by no means self-evident that wage rises in the coastal areas will undermine the Chinese government's attempts to strengthen labour regulations.

It may be that manufacturers are successful in facilitating a new spatial fix by seeking out exploitable reserves of labour beyond China. There are untapped reserve armies of labour in other countries, such as Vietnam and Bangladesh, with the demographic and political pre-conditions for insertion into the lower end of global production networks. Yet, these countries also have experienced waves of labour unrest in recent years that raise doubts regarding any possibility of a permanent spatial fix. Vietnam, for example, saw a sharp increase in strike activity in 2006, and with similarities to the Chinese experience, this led to attempts by the Vietnamese government to address the problem through legislative reform, though without any legal framework whereby Vietnamese trade unions could effectively represent their members (Clarke 2006). The conditions endured by textile workers in Bangladesh, on the other hand, attracted the world's attention following the fire and collapse of the Tazreen Fashions building in Dhaka, which led to the 'avoidable' death of more than 100 workers (Young 2013). In the autumn of 2013, Bangladeshi textile workers launched a wave of strikes affecting a fifth of the country's textile factories in seeking to raise the country's minimum wage. Combined with international pressure over working conditions in the country, Bangladeshi employers were forced to respond to the workers' demands (Asokan 2013).

As such, a number of different paths appear possible for East Asia's workers. Rapid industrialisation is likely to continue to strengthen workers' structural power to the point at which they are able to collectively engage in strategies of 'anti-passive revolution' and challenge their own subordination. However, political and economic elites are likely to continue to adopt strategies aimed at containing labour militancy through the strategies of repression, pre-emptive reforms aimed at appeasing workers, and co-opting organised labour into the institutions of formal democracy. It is also clear that the future trajectory of East Asian development will remain highly contingent upon the mutual relations between labour struggles at the grassroots level and broader international dynamics. By analysing how these dynamics have shaped the broader developmental experience in East Asia, it is hoped that this book has offered an important insight into the role of labour in late development through the framework of passive revolution. Gramsci's understanding of passive revolution enables the analysis of the social struggles underpinning state formation; as such, it helps to elucidate how political and economic elites in specific national contexts are exposed to the geopolitical imperative to facilitate catch-up development and, as part of that process, are compelled to take measures to contain the emergence of labour as a collective subjectivity. Given the considerable social restiveness that continues to characterise production in the East Asian region, such processes of passive revolution are likely to continue to characterise late development in the twenty-first century.

BIBLIOGRAPHY

Abegglen, J., 1959. *The Japanese Factory: Aspects of Its Social Organisation*. Bombay: Asia Publishing House.

Adesnik, A.D. and Kim, S., 2008. If at first you don't succeed: The puzzle of South Korea's democratic transition. *Centre on Democracy, Development, and the Rule of Law Working Paper Series*. Available online at http://cddrl.stanford.edu/publications/if_at_first_you_dont_succeed_the_puzzle_of_south_koreas_democratic_transition/ (accessed 12 March 2014).

Akamatsu, K., 1962. A historical pattern of economic growth in developing countries. *The Developing Economies*, 1 (S1), 3–25.

Allinson, G.D., 2004. *Japan's Postwar History*. Ithaca: Cornell University Press.

Allinson, J.C. and Anievas, A., 2010. The uneven and combined development of the Meiji restoration: A passive revolutionary road to capitalist modernity. *Capital and Class*, 34 (3), 469–490.

Amin, S., 1993. The issue of democracy in the contemporary third world. *In*: B. Gills, J. Rocamora, and R. Wilson, eds. *Low Intensity Democracy*. London: Pluto, 59–79.

Amsden, A.H., 1979. Taiwan's economic history: A case of etatisme and a challenge to dependency theory. *Modern China*, 5 (3), 341–379.

Amsden, A.H., 1989. *Asia's Next Giant: South Korea and Late Industrialization*. Oxford: Oxford University Press.

Amsden, A.H., 1990. Third world industrialization: 'Global Fordism' or a new model? *New Left Review*, 182, 5–31.

Amsden, A.H., 1994. Why isn't the whole world experimenting with the East Asian model to develop? Review of the East Asian miracle. *World Development*, 22 (4), 627–633.

Amsden, A.H. and Chu, W., 2003. *Beyond Late Development: Taiwan's Upgrading Policies*. Cambridge, MA: The MIT Press.

Anon, 1990. December election victory in Taiwan. *Taiwan Communique*, 43, 1–23.

Appelbaum, R.P., Parker, R., and Cao, C., 2011. Developmental state and innovation: Nanotechnology in China. *Global Networks*, 11 (3), 298–314.

Armstrong, P., Glyn, A., and Harrison, J., 1991. *Capitalism Since 1945*. Oxford: Basil Blackwell.

Arrighi, G., 1996. The rise of East Asia: World systemic and regional aspects. *International Journal of Sociology and Social Policy*, 16 (7/8), 6–43.

Arrighi, G., 2003. The social and political economy of global turbulence. *New Left Review*, 20 (March), 5–71.

Arrighi, G., 2008. *Adam Smith in Beijing: Lineages of the 21st Century*. London: Verso.

Arrighi, G., Hui, P., Hung, H., and Selden, M., 2003. Historical capitalism, east and west. *In*: G. Arrighi, T. Hamashita, and M. Selden, eds. *The Resurgence of East Asia: 500, 150 and 50 Year Perspectives*. London: Routledge, 259–333.

Arrighi, G., Ikeda, S., and Irwan, A., 1993. The rise of East Asia: One miracle or many? *In*: R.A. Palat, ed. *Pacific-Asia and the Future of the World-System*. Westport, CT: Greenwood Press, 41–65.

Arrighi, G. and Silver, B.J., 2000. Workers north and south. *In*: L. Panitch and C. Leys, eds. *Socialist Register*. London: Merlin Press, 53–72.

Asokan, S., 2013. Bangladesh poised to hike garment wages, but may not end strikes. Available online at: http://www.reuters.com/article/2013/10/21/us-bangladesh-garments-wage-idUSBRE99K02M20131021 (accessed 12 March 2014).

Au, L.Y. and Bai, R., 2012. New signs of hope: Resistance in China today. *In*: L.Y. Au, ed. *China's Rise: Strength and Fragility*. Pontypool: Merlin Press, 225–237.

Augelli, E. and Murphy, C., 1988. *America's quest for supremacy and the third world: A Gramscian analysis*. London: Pinter Publishers.

Ayusawa, I.F., 1966. *A History of Labor in Modern Japan*. Honolulu: East-West Center Press.

Bae, J., 2009. The South Korean left's 'northern question.' *In*: R. Frank and P. Kollner, eds. *Korea Yearbook*. Leiden: Brill, 87–116.

Baek, S.-W., 2005. Does China follow 'the East Asian development model'? *Journal of Contemporary Asia*, 35 (4), 485–498.

Bai, M.-K., 2007. The turning point in the Korean economy. *The Developing Economies*, 20 (2), 117–140.

Bailey, D., 2003. Explaining Japan's Kūdōka: A case of government and strategic failure? *Asia Pacific Business Review*, 10 (1), 1–20.

Baker, D., 1965. The trade union movement in Japan. *International Socialism*, 23 (Winter), 19–26.

Balassa, B., 1988. The lessons of East Asian development: An overview. *Economic Development and Cultural Change*, 36 (S3), S273–S290.

Barrett, R.E., 1988. Autonomy and diversity in the American state in Taiwan. *In*: E.A. Winckler and S.M. Greenhalgh, eds. *Contending Approaches to the Political Economy of Taiwan*. Armonk, NY: M. E. Sharpe, 121–137.

Beasley, W.G., 1990. *The Rise of Modern Japan: Political, Economic, and Social Change Since 1850*. London: George Weidenfield & Nicholson.

Beeson, M., 2003. Japan's reluctant reformers and the legacy of the developmental state. *In*: A. Cheung and I. Scott, eds. *Governance and Public Sector Reform in Asia: Paradigm Shifts or Business as Usual?* London: Curzon Press, 57–91.

Beeson, M., 2004. The rise and fall (?) of the developmental state: The vicissitudes and implications of East Asian interventionism. *In*: L. Low, ed. *Developmental States: Relevancy, Redundancy or ....* Hauppauge, NY: Nova Science, 29–40.

Beeson, M., 2009. Developmental states in East Asia: A comparison of the Japanese and Chinese experiences. *Asian Perspective*, 33 (2), 5–39.

Bello, W., 2005. *Dilemmas of Domination: The Unmaking of the American Empire*. London: Zed Books.

Bello, W. and Rosenfield, S., 1992. *Dragons in Distress: Asia's Miracle Economies in Crisis*. London: Penguin.

Berger, M.T., 2004. *The Battle for Asia: From Decolonization to Globalization*. London: RoutledgeCurzon.

Bernard, M. and Ravenhill, J., 1995. Beyond product cycles and flying geese: Regionalization, hierarchy, and the industrialization of East Asia. *World Politics*, 47 (2), 171–209.

Bhagwati, J.N., 1978. *The Anatomy and Consequences of Exchange Control Regimes*. Cambridge, MA: Ballinger for the National Bureau of Economic Research.

Bieler, A., Lindberg, I., and Pillay, D., 2008. *Labour and the Challenges of Globalization: What Prospects for Transnational Solidarity?* London: Pluto Press.

Bieler, A. and Morton, A.D., 2008. The deficits of discourse in IPE: Turning base metal into gold? International Studies Quarterly, 52 (1), 103–128.

Blecher, M.J., 2002. Hegemony and workers' politics in China. *The China Quarterly*, 170 (June), 283–303.

Bolesta, A., 2007. China as a developmental state. *Montenegrin Journal of Economics*, 3 (5), 105–111.

Bond, P., 2005. *Elite Transition: From Apartheid to Neoliberalism in South Africa*. Scotsville: University of KwaZulu-Natal Press.

Borden, W.S., 1984. *The Pacific Alliance: United States Foreign Economic Policy and Japanese Trade Recovery, 1947–1955*. Madison: University of Wisconsin Press.

Bradsher, K., 2012. Facing a slowing economy, China turns to American exports. Available online at http://www.nytimes.com/2012/07/14/business/global/chinese-exports-to-us-surge-as-the-domestic-economy-cools.html (accessed 19 April 2013).

Brecher, J., 1972. *Strike: The True History of Mass Insurgency from 1877 to the Present*. San Francisco: Straight Arrow.

Brenner, R., 1998. The economics of global turbulence. *New Left Review*, I/229.

Breslin, S., 2005. Power and production: rethinking China's global economic role. *Review of International Studies*, 31 (4), 735–753.

Broadbent, K., 1990. Shin-rengo: Recent developments in the Japanese trade-union movement. *Japanese Studies*, 10 (2), 41–47.

Bruff, I., 2010. European varieties of capitalism and the international. *European Journal of International Relations*, 16 (4), 615–638.

Buci-Glucksmann, C., 1979. State, transition and passive revolution. *In*: C. Mouffe, ed. *Gramsci and Marxist Theory*. London: Routledge.

Budd, A., 2007. Gramsci's Marxism and international relations. *International Socialism*, 114 (April), 125–136.

Burkett, P. and Hart-Landsberg, M., 2000. *Development, Crisis, and Class Struggle: Learning from Japan and East Asia*. New York: St. Martins Press.

Burkett, P. and Hart-Landsberg, M., 2003. Progressive capitalism, crisis, and class struggle: Lessons from Japan's production control and democracy movements, 1945–1947. *Capital and Class*, 79, 25–54.

Cai, F., 2010. Demographic transition, demographic dividend, and Lewis turning point in China. *China Economic Journal*, 3 (2), 107–119.

Callinicos, A., 2010. The limits of passive revolution. *Capital and Class*, 34 (3), 491–507.

Candland, C. and Sil, R., 2001. Introduction. *In*: C. Candland and R. Sil, eds. *The Politics of Labor in Late-industrializing and Post-socialist Economies: New Challenges in a Global Age*. Oxford: Oxford University Press.

Carlile, L., 1994a. Party politics and the Japanese labor movement: Rengo's 'new political force.' *Asian Survey*, 34 (7), 606–620.

Carlile, L., 1994b. Sōhyō versus Dōmei: Competing labour movement strategies in the era of high growth in Japan. *Japan Forum*, 6 (2), 145–157.

Cerny, P.G. and Germain, R., 2000. *Restructuring the Polictical Arena: Globalization and the Paradoxes of the Competition State*. Basingstoke: Macmillan, 117–137.

Chan, A., 2003. A 'race to the bottom': Globalisation and China's labour standards. *China Perspectives*, 46 (March–April), 1–12.

Chan, K.W., 2010. The global financial crisis and migrant workers in China: 'There is no future as a labourer; returning to the village has no meaning.' *International Journal of Urban and Regional Research*, 34 (3), 659–677.

Chang, C. and Bain, T., 2006. Employment relations across the Taiwan Strait: Globalization and state corporatism. *Journal of Industrial Relations*, 48 (1), 99–115.

Chang, D.-O., 2009. *Capitalist Development in Korea: Labour, Capital and the Myth of the Developmental State*. London: Routledge.

Chang, D.-O., 2001. Bringing class struggle back into the economic crisis: Development of crisis in class struggle in Korea. *Historical Materialism*, 8 (1), 185–213.

Chang, H.-J., 1998a. Korea: The misunderstood crisis. *World Development*, 26 (8), 1555–1561.

Chang, H.-J., 2002. *Kicking Away the Ladder: Development Strategy in Historical Perspective*. London: Anthem.

Chang, H.-J., 2007. *Bad Samaritans: Rich Nations, Poor Policies and the Threat to the Developing World*. London: Random House Business.

Chang, H.-J., Park, H.-J., and Yoo, C.-G., 1998. Interpreting the Korean crisis: Financial liberalisation, industrial policy and corporate governance. *Cambridge Journal of Economics*, 22 (6), 735–746.

Chang, Y.-S., 1998b. The progressive Christian church and democracy in South Korea. *Journal of Church and State*, 40 (2), 437–465.

Chang, Y.-S., 2008. Industrial workers, corporate employers and the government in South Korea. *In*: Y. Chang, H. Seok, and D.L. Baker, eds. *Korea Confronts Globalization*. London: Routledge, 95–117.

Chen, F., 2003. Between the state and labour: The conflict of Chinese trade unions' double identity in market reform. *The China Quarterly*, 176 (December), 1006–1028.

Chen, F., 2007. Individual rights and collective rights: Labor's predicament in China. *Communist and Post-Communist Studies*, 40 (1), 59–79.

Chen, H.-H., 2012. How did democracy lose its green? Taiwan's democratization and its social content. Presentation at *People Power and the Globalisation of Democracy – ISA Workshop*, San Diego.

Chen, S.-J., Ko, J.-J.R., and Lawler, J., 2003. Changing patterns of industrial relations in Taiwan. *Industrial Relations*, 42 (3), 315–340.

Chen, Y. and Wong, M., 2002. *New Bondage and Old Resistance: Realities of the Labour Movement in Taiwan*. Hong Kong: Hong Kong Christian Industrial Committee.

Cheng, T., 1990. *Political Regimes and Development Strategies: South Korea and Taiwan*. Princeton, NJ: Princeton University Press.

Chin, G.T., 2010. Remaking the architecture: The emerging powers, self-insuring and regional insulation. *International Affairs*, 86 (3), 693–715.

China Labour Bulletin, 2007. Standing up: The workers movement in China, 2000–2004. Available online at http://www.clb.org.hk/en/content/standing-workers-movement-china-2000-2004 (accessed 19 April 2013).

China Labour Bulletin, 2009. Going it alone: The workers' movement in China (2007–2008). *China Labour Bulletin*. Available online at http://www.china-labour.org.hk/en/files/share/File/research_reports/workers_movement_07-08_print_final.pdf (accessed 12 March 2014).

China.org.cn, 2007. Huawei urges thousands of employees to resign. Available online at http://www.china.org.cn/english/news/230662.htm (accessed 19 April 2013).

Chiu, Y., 2011. Old constraints and future possibilities in the development of Taiwan's independent labor movement. *Capitalism Nature Socialism*, 22 (1), 58–75.

Cho, H., 2008. [A re-examination of modern Korea's political transformation] *Marŭkŭsŭjuŭi yŏn'gu [Marxist Research]*, 5 (1), 90–133. (In Korean.)
Cho, H. and Kim, E.M., 1998. State autonomy and its social conditions for economic development in South Korea and Taiwan. *In*: E.M. Kim, ed. *The Four Asian Tigers: Economic Development and the Global Political Economy*. San Diego: Academic Press.
Choi, J.-J., 1984. A corporatist control of the labor union in South Korea. *Korean Social Science Journal*, 11, 25–55.
Choi, J.-J., 1989. *Labor and the Authoritarian State: Labor Unions in South Korean Manufacturing Industries, 1961–1980*. Seoul: Korea University Press.
Choi, J.-J., 1992. [For the search for a new direction of the labour movement]. *Sahoep'yŏngnon [Social Critique]*, June, 232–246.
Chŏng, S., 1992. [A criticism of the present understanding of militant labour unionists]. *Sahoep'yŏngnon [Social Critique]*, March, 290–293. (In Korean.)
Chu, M., 2000. Bill on reduction to work week gets bogged down during third reading. *Taipei Times*. Available online at http://www.taipeitimes.com/News/local/archives/2000/05/31/38179 (accessed 12 March 2014).
Chu, Y.-W., 1996. Democracy and organised labor in Taiwan: The 1986 transition. *Asian Survey*, 36 (5), 495–510.
Chun, J.J., 2009. Legal liminality: The gender and labour politics of organising South Korea's irregular workforce. *Third World Quarterly*, 30 (3), 535–550.
Chun, S., 2003. *They Are Not Machines: Korean Women Workers and Their Fight for Democratic Trade Unionism in the 1970s*. Aldershot: Ashgate.
Clarke, S., 2006. The changing character of strikes in Vietnam. *Post-Communist Economies*, 18 (3), 345–361.
Clarke, S. and Pringle, T., 2009. Can party-led trade unions represent their members? *Post-Communist Economies*, 21 (1), 85–101.
Cohen, T., 1987. *Remaking Japan: The American Occupation as New Deal*. New York: The Free Press.
Cole, D.C. and Lyman, P.N., 1971. *Korean Development: The Interplay of Politics and Economics*. Cambridge, MA: Harvard University Press.
Cole, R.E., 1978. The late-developer hypothesis: An evaluation of its relevance for Japanese employment practices. *Journal of Japanese Studies*, 4 (2), 247–265.
Colignon, R.A. and Usui, C., 2003. *Amakaduri: The Hidden Fabric of Japan's Economy*. Ithaca: ILR Press.
Congiu, F., 2006. National identity and the weakness of Taiwanese organised labour. *In*: *3rd Conference of the European Association of Taiwan Studies*. London: SOAS, 1–18.
Cooney, S., 1996. The new Taiwan and its old labour law: Authoritarian legislation in a democratised society. *Comparative Labor Law Journal*, 18, 1–61.
Cotton, J., 1989. From authoritarianism to democracy in South Korea. *Political Studies*, 37 (2), 244–259.
Council for Economic Planning and Development (CEPD), 2009. *Taiwan Statistical Yearbook 2009*. Taipei: CEPD.
Cox, R., 1981. Social forces, states and world orders: Beyond international relations theory. *Millennium: Journal of International Studies*, 10 (2), 126–155.
Cox, R., 1987. *Production, Power and World Order: Social Forces in the Making of History*. New York: Columbia University Press.
Cox, R. W. (1992). Global perestroika. In R. Miliband & L. Panitch (Eds.), Socialist Register 1992 (pp. 26–43). London: Merlin Press.
Cronin, J.E., 1979. *Industrial Conflict in Modern Britain*. London: Croom Helm.
Crotty, J., 1999. Turbulence in the world economy. *Challenge*, 42 (3), 108–130.

Cumings, B., 1981. *The Origins of the Korean War: Liberation and the Emergence of Separate Regimes 1945–1947*. Princeton, NJ: Princeton University Press.

Cumings, B., 1984. The origins and development of the Northeast Asian political economy: Industrial sectors, product cycles, and political consequences. *International Organization*, 38 (01), 1–40.

Cumings, B., 1989. The political economy of China's turn outward. *In*: S.S. Kim, ed. China and the World: Foreign Policy in the Post-Mao Era. Boulder, CO: Westview Press.

Cumings, B., 1998. The Korean crisis and the end of 'late' development. *New Left Review*, (231), 43–72.

Das, M. and Diaye, P.N., 2013. Chronicle of a decline foretold: Has China reached the Lewis turning point? *IMF Working Paper*. Available online at http://www.imf.org/external/pubs/ft/wp/2013/wp1326.pdf (accessed 12 March 2014).

Delbridge, R., Turnbull, P., and Wilkinson, B., 1992. Pushing back the frontiers: Management control and work intensification under JIT/TQM factory regimes. *New Technology, Work and Employment*, 7 (2), 97–106.

Dent, C.M., 2003. Taiwan's foreign economic policy: The 'liberalization plus' approach of an evolving developmental state. *Modern Asian Studies*, 37 (2), 461–483.

Deyo, F.C., 1987. State and labor: Modes of political exclusion in East Asian development. *In*: F.C. Deyo, ed. *The Political Economy of New Asian Industrialisation*. Ithaca: Cornell University Press, 182–202.

Deyo, F.C., 1989. *Beneath the Miracle: Labor Subordination in the New Asian Industrialism*. Berkeley: University of California.

Dittmer, L., 2003. Leadership change and Chinese political development. *The China Quarterly*, 176 (December), 903–925.

Dohse, K., Jurgens, U., and Nialsch, T., 1985. From 'Fordism' to 'Toyotism'? The social organization of the labor process in the Japanese automobile industry. *Politics and Society*, 14 (2), 115–146.

Dore, R., 1973. *British Factory – Japanese Factory: The Origins of National Diversity in Industrial Relations*. Berkeley: University of California Press.

Dower, J., 1999. *Embracing Defeat: Japan in the Wake of World War II*. New York: W.W. Norton & Co.

Duménil, G. and Lévy, D., 2004a. The neoliberal (counter) revolution. *In*: A. Saad Fihlo and D. Johnson, eds. *Neoliberalism: A Critical Reader*. London: Pluto Press.

Duménil, G. and Lévy, D., 2004b. *Capital Resurgent: Roots of the Neoliberal Revolution*. Cambridge, MA: Harvard University Press.

Dunn, B., 2004. *Global Restructuring and the Power of Labour*. Basingstoke: Palgrave Macmillan.

Evans, P., 1995. *Embedded Autonomy: States and Industrial Transformation*. Princeton, NJ: Princeton University Press.

Fei, J.C.H. and Ranis, G., 1975. A model of growth and employment in the open dualistic economy: The cases of Korea and Taiwan. *The Journal of Development Studies*, 11 (2), 32–63.

Femia, J., 2005. Gramsci, Machiavelli and international relations. *The Political Quarterly*, 76 (3), 341–349.

Ferhat-Dana, S., 1998. The Democratic Progressive Party and independence: An issue on the back burner? *China Perspectives*, 19, 30–36.

Fewsmith, J., 2001. *China Since Tiananmen: The Politics of Transition*. Cambridge, UK: Cambridge University Press.

Fishman, T.C., 2005. *China, Inc.: How the Rise of the Next Superpower Challenges America and the World*. London: Simon & Schuster.

Foster, J.B. and McChesney, R.B., 2012. The global stagnation and China. *Monthly Review*, 63 (9), 1–28.

Friedman, E., 2012. Getting through the hard times together? Chinese workers and unions respond to the economic crisis. *Journal of Industrial Relations*, 54 (4), 459–475.

Garon, S., 1987. *The State and Labor in Modern Japan*. London: University of California Press.

Germain, R.D. and Kenny, M., 1998. Engaging Gramsci: International relations theory and the new Gramscians. *Review of International Studies*, 24 (1), 3–21.

Gerschenkron, A., 1962. *Economic Backwardness in Historical Perspective*. Cambridge, MA: Harvard University Press.

Giddens, A., 2000. *The Third Way and Its Critics*. London: Polity Press.

Gill, S. and Law, D., 1988. *The Global Political Economy*. London: Harvester Wheatsheaf.

Gills, B.K., 1993. Korean capitalism and democracy. *In*: B.K. Gills, J. Rocamora, and R. Wilson, eds. *Low Intensity Democracy: Political Power in the New World Order*. London: Pluto Press, 226–257.

Gills, B.K., 1996. Economic liberalisation and reform in South Korea in the 1990s: A 'coming of age' or a case of 'graduation blues'? *Third World Quarterly*, 17 (4), 667–688.

Gills, B.K., 2000. The crisis of postwar East Asian capitalism: American power, democracy and the vicissitudes of globalization. *Review of International Studies*, 26 (3), 381–403.

Gills, B.K., Rocamora, J., and Wilson, R., 1993. Low intensity democracy. *In*: B.K. Gills, J. Rocamora, and R. Wilson, eds. *Low Intensity Democracy: Political Power in the New World Order*. London: Pluto, 3–34.

Glassman, J., 1999. State power beyond the 'territorial trap': The internationalization of the state. *Political Geography*, 18 (6), 669–696.

Glyn, A., 2006. *Capitalism Unleashed: Finance Globalization and Welfare*. New York: Oxford University Press.

Gold, T.B., 1986. *State and society in the Taiwan miracle*. New York: ME Sharpe.

Gold, T.B., 1988. Colonial origins of Taiwanese capitalism. *In*: E.A. Winckler and S.M. Greenhalgh, eds. *Contending Approaches to the Political Economy of Taiwan*. Armonk, NY: M. E. Sharpe, 101–117.

Gordon, A., 1985. *The Evolution of Labor Relations in Japan: Heavy Industry, 1853–1955*. Cambridge, MA.: Harvard University Press.

Gordon, A., 2003. *The Modern History of Japan: From Tokugawa Times to the Present*. Oxford, UK: Oxford University Press.

Gordon, D.M., Edwards, R., and Reich, M., 1982. *Segmented Work, Divided Workers: The Historical Transformation of Labor in the United States*. Cambridge, UK: Cambridge University Press.

Gordon, M.E. and Turner, L., 2000. *Transnational Cooperation Among Labor Unions*. London: ILR Press.

Graham, L., 1994. How does the Japanese model transfer to the United States? A view from the line. *In*: T. Elger and C. Smith, eds. *Global Japanization? The Transnational Transformation of the Labour Process*. London: Routledge, 123–151.

Gramsci, A., 1971. *Selections from the Prison Notebooks of Antonio Gramsci*. London: Lawrence and Wishart.

Gray, K., 2008a. *Korean Workers and Neoliberal Globalization*. London: Routledge.

Gray, K., 2008b. The global uprising of labour? The Korean labour movement and neoliberal social corporatism. *Globalizations*, 5 (3), 483–499.

Greider, W., 2001. A new giant sucking sound. *The Nation*. Available online at http://www.thenation.com/article/new-giant-sucking-sound# (accessed 12 March 2014).

Grinberg, N. and Starosta, G., 2009. The limits of studies in comparative development of East Asia and Latin America: The case of land reform and agrarian policies. *Third World Quarterly*, 30 (4), 761–777.

Haberman, C., 1987. In Korea strike, tension but hope of harmony. *The New York Times*. Available online at http://www.nytimes.com/1987/09/04/world/in-korea-strike-tension-but-hope-of-harmony.html (accessed 12 March 2014).

Halliday, J., 1975. *A political history of Japanese capitalism*. New York: Pantheon.

Hamaaki, J., Hori, M., Maeda, S., and Murata, K., 2012. Changes in the Japanese employment system in the two lost decades. *Industrial and Labor Relations Review*, 65 (4), 810–846.

Harari, E., 1973. *The Politics of Labor Legislation in Japan*. Berkeley: University of California Press.

Harney, A., 2008. *The China Price: The True Cost of Chinese Competitive Advantage*. London: Penguin.

Harris, N., 1978. *The Mandate of Heaven: Marx and Mao in Modern China*. London: Quartet.

Harrod, J. and O'Brien, R., 2002. *Global Unions? Theory and Strategies of Organized Labour in the Global Political Economy*. London: Routledge.

Hart-Landsberg, M., 1993. *The Rush to Development: Economic Change and Political Struggle in South Korea*. New York: Monthly Review Press.

Hart-Landsberg, M. and Burkett, P., 1998. Contradictions of capitalist industrialization in East Asia: A critique of 'flying geese' theories of development. *Economic Geography*, 74 (2), 87–110.

Hart-Landsberg, M. and Burkett, P., 2007. China and the dynamics of transnational accumulation: Causes and consequences of global restructuring. *Historical Materialism*, 14 (3), 3–43.

Harvey, D., 1982. *Limits to Capital*. London: Verso.

Harvey, D., 2003. *The New Imperialism*. Oxford: Oxford University Press.

Harvey, D., 2005. *A Brief History of Neoliberalism*. Oxford: Oxford University Press.

Hayashi, S., 2010. The developmental state in the era of globalization: Beyond the Northeast Asian model of political economy. *The Pacific Review*, 23 (1), 45–69.

Held, D., McGrew, A., Goldblatt, D., and Perraton, J., 1999. *Global Transformations: Politics Economic and Culture*. Cambridge: Blackwell.

Hersh, J., 1993. *The USA and the Rise of East Asia Since 1945: Dilemmas of the Postwar International Political Economy*. Basingstoke, UK: Macmillan.

Hewes, L.I., 1955. *Japan – Land and Men: An Account of the Japanese Land Reform Program – 1945–51*. Ames: Iowa State College Press.

Hirashima, K., 2004. Regime shift in Japan? Two decades of neoliberal reforms. *Swiss Political Science Review*, 10 (3), 31–54.

Ho, M., 2006a. Challenging state corporatism: The politics of Taiwan's labor federation movement. *The China Journal*, 56 (56), 107–127.

Ho, M., 2006b. Neo-centrist labour policy in practice: The DPP and the Taiwanese working class. *In*: D.J. Fell, H. Klöter, and B.-Y. Chang, eds. *What Has Changed? Taiwan Before and After the Change in Ruling Parties*. Wiesbaden: Harrassowitz, 129–146.

Ho, M., 2007. The rise and fall of Leninist control in Taiwan's industry. *The China Quarterly*, 189, 162–179.

Ho, M., 2010. Understanding the trajectory of social movements in Taiwan (1980–2010). *Journal of Current Chinese Affairs*, 39 (3), 3–22.

Ho, S.P.S., 1978. *Economic Development of Taiwan, 1860–1970*. New Haven: Yale University Press.

Ho, S.Y., 1990. *Taiwan – After a Long Silence: The Emerging New Unions of Taiwan*. Hong Kong: Asia Monitor Research Center.

Holbig, H., 2006. Ideological reform and political legitimacy in China: Challenges in the post-Jiang era. *German Institute of Global and Area Studies Working Paper*. Available online at http://www.giga-hamburg.de/en/system/files/publications/wp18_holbig.pdf (accessed 12 March 2014).

Hoogevelt, A., 1995. Review essay: Japan and the world. *Review of International Political Economy*, 2 (4), 719–727.

Houseman, S.N. and Abraham, K.G., 1993. Female workers as a buffer in the Japanese economy. *The American Economic Review*, 83 (2), 45–51.

Hsiao, F.S.T. and Sullivan, L.R., 1983. A political history of the Taiwanese communist party, 1928–1931. *The Journal of Asian Studies*, 42 (2), 269–289.

Hsiao, H.-H.M., 1992a. The labor movement in Taiwan: A retrospective and prospective look. *In*: D.F. Simon and M.Y.M. Kau, eds. *Taiwan: Beyond the Economic Miracle*. London: M. E. Sharpe, 151–167.

Hsiao, H.-H.M., 1992b. The rise of social movements and civil protests. *In*: T. Chen and S. Haggard, eds. *Political Change in Taiwan*. Boulder, CO: Lynne Rienner, 57–72.

Hsiao, H.-H.M., 2012. Precarious work in Taiwan: A profile. *American Behavioral Scientist*, 57 (3), 373–389.

Hsiao, H.-H.M. and Koo, H., 1997. The middle classes and democratization. *In*: L. Diamond, ed. *Consolidating the Third Wave Democracies: Themes and Perspectives*. Baltimore: Johns Hopkins University Press, 312–333.

Hsu, C.K., 1989. Corporatist control and labor movement in Taiwan. *Conference on North-East Asia in the World Perspective*. Available online at http://www.sinica.edu.tw/ioe/chinese/staff/c9105/ethck-0018.pdf (accessed 16 September 2011).

Hsu, J., 2009. The spatial encounter between neoliberalism and populism in Taiwan: Regional restructuring under the DPP regime in the new millennium. *Political Geography*, 28 (5), 296–308.

Hsueh, L., Hsu, C., and Perkins, D.H., 2001. *Industrialization and the State: The Changing Role of the Taiwan Government in the Economy, 1945–1998*. Cambridge, MA: Harvard University Press.

Huang, C., 2009a. Bilateralism and multilateralism: Taiwan's trade liberalization trajectory. *The Hague Journal of Diplomacy*, 4 (1), 37–59.

Huang, C.-L., 2000a. Neo-mercantilist policies and sectoral politics: Taiwan's acquiescent working class. *Anthropology of Work Review*, 21 (3), 15–18.

Huang, C.-L., 2002. The politics of reregulation: Globalization, democratization, and the Taiwanese labor movement. *The Developing Economies*, 40 (3), 305–326.

Huang, J., 2000b. No leftist voice in Taiwan politics. *Taipei Times*. Available online at http://www.taipeitimes.com/News/editorials/archives/2000/12/29/0000067492 (accessed 12 March 2014).

Huang, S., 2009b. Critics pan amendment to labor law. *Taipei Times*, June. Available online at http://www.taipeitimes.com/News/taiwan/archives/2009/06/08/2003445630 (accessed 11 July 2014).

Huang, Y., 2008. *Capitalism with Chinese Characteristics: Entrepreneurship and the State*. Cambridge: Cambridge University Press.

Hudson, M., 2003. *Super Imperialism: The Origin and Fundamentals of US World Dominance*. London: Pluto Press.

Hung, H., 2009. America's head servant? The PRC's dilemma in the global crisis. *New Left Review*, 60 (Nov–Dec), 5–25.

Huntington, S.P., 1991. *The Third Wave*. Norman: University of Oklahoma Press.

Hyman, R., 1971. *Marxism and the Sociology of Trade Unionism*. London: Pluto Press.

IHLO (International Trade Union Confederation/Global Union Federations Hong Kong Liaison Office) 2008. New labour contract law: Myth and reality six months after implementation. *ITUC/GUF Hong Kong Liaison Office*. Available online at http://www.ihlo.org/LRC/WC/270608.html (accessed 17 April 2013).

Ikeda, S., 2004. Japan and the changing regime of accumulation: A world-system study of Japan's trajectory from miracle to debacle. *Journal of World-Systems Research*, 10 (2), 363–394.

Im, H., 1992. State, labor and capital in the consolidation of democracy: A search for post-authoritarian industrial relations in South Korea. *Korean Social Science Journal*, 18, 7–25.

Inagami, T., 1996. The death of 'labour movement' and the 'Japanization' of industrial relations.' *Industrielle Beziehungen*, 3 (2), 173–186.

Inoue, S., 2002. Japanese trade unions and their future: Opportunities and challenges in an era of globalization. *In*: A.V. Jose, ed. *Organized Labour in the 21st Century*. Geneva: International Institute for Labour Studies, 23–62.

Itoh, M., 1994. Is the Japanese economy in crisis? *Review of International Political Economy*, 1 (1), 29–51.

Ives, P. and Short, N., 2013. On Gramsci and the international: A textual analysis. *Review of International Studies*, 39 (3), 621–642.

Jacoby, N.H., 1966. *US aid to Taiwan: A study of foreign aid, self-help, and development*. London: Frederick A. Praeger.

Jeong, S., 2005. *Marŭk'ŭsŭwa han'guk kyŏngje [Marx and the Korean Economy]*. Seoul: Ch'aeggalp'i.

Johnson, C., 1982. *MITI and the Japanese Miracle: The Growth of Industrial Policy, 1925–1975*. Stanford: Stanford University Press.

Johnson, C., 1999. The Developmental State: Odyssey of a Concept. *In*: M. Woo-Cumings, ed. *The Developmental State*. Ithaca: Cornell University Press, 32–60.

Johnson, C., 2002. *Blowback: The Costs and Consequences of American Empire*. London: Time Warner.

Joll, J., 1977. *Gramsci*. London: Fontana.

Jones, S., 2006. *Antonio Gramsci*. London: Routledge.

Jung, E. and Cheon, B., 2006. Economic crisis and changes in employment relations in Japan and Korea. *Asian Survey*, 46 (3), 457–476.

Kalinowski, T. and Cho, H., 2009. The political economy of financial liberalization in South Korea: State, big business, and foreign investors. *Asian Survey*, 49 (2), 221–242.

Kang, D.C., 2012. Bad loans to good friends: Money politics and the developmental state in South Korea. *International Organization*, 56 (1), 177–207.

Katsiaficas, G., 2012a. *Asia's Unknown Uprisings: South Korean Social Movements in the 20th Century*. Oakland, CA: PM Press.

Katsiaficas, G., 2012b. *Asia's Unknown Uprisings: People Power in the Philippines, Burma, Tibet, China, Taiwan, Bangladesh, Nepal, Thailand and Indonesia*. Oakland, CA: PM Press.

Kay, C., 2002. Why East Asia overtook Latin America: Agrarian reform, industrialisation and development. *Third World Quarterly*, 23 (6), 1073–1102.

Kelly, J.E., 1998. *Rethinking Industrial Relations: Mobilization, Collectivism, and Long Waves*. London: Routledge.

Kenny, M. and Florida, R., 1988. Beyond mass production: Production and the labour process in Japan. *Politics and Society*, 16 (1), 121–158.

Kiely, R., 2005. Globalization and poverty, and the poverty of globalization theory. *Current Sociology*, 53 (6), 895–914.

Kihl, Y.W., 1991. South Korea in 1990: Diplomatic activism and a partisan quagmire. *Asian Survey*, 31 (1), 64–70.

Kim, A.E. and Park, I., 2006. Changing trends of work in South Korea: The rapid growth of underemployment and job insecurity. *Asian Survey*, 46 (3), 437–456.

Kim, E.M., 1997a. *Big Business, Strong State: Collusion and Conflict in South Korean Development, 1960–1990*. Albany, NY: State University of New York Press.

Kim, H., 1997b. *[The Political Economy of Korean Labor-Management Relations]*. Seoul: Hanul Academy. (In Korean).

Kim, H.-A., 2013. Industrial warriors: South Korea's first generation of industrial workers in post-developmental Korea. *Asian Studies Review*, 37 (4), 577–595.

Kim, J.K., 2000a. Rethinking the new beginning of the democratic union movement in Korea: From the 1987 Great Workers' Struggle to the construction of the Korean Trade Union Council (Chunnohyup) and the Korean Confederation of Trade Unions (KCTU). *Inter-Asia Cultural Studies*, 1 (3), 491–502.

Kim, M., 2000b. National memory and the identity of the working class in Korea (1910–1950). *International Journal of Korean History*, 1 (December), 63–88.

Kim, S., 1997c. State and civil society in South Korea's democratization: Is the battle really over? *Asian Survey*, 37 (12), 1135–1145.

Kim, S.-K., 2002. [The Korea 'democratic' labour movement: Critique and outlook.] *Chinbop'yŏngnon [The Radical Review]*, 13, 11–53. (In Korean.)

Kim, Y., 2004. *[Labour Market Flexibilisation and Irregular Labour]*. Seoul: Korea Labor Society Insititute. (In Korean.)

Klein, N., 2007. *The Shock Doctrine: The Rise of Disaster Capitalism*. London: Penguin Books.

Kleingartner, A. and Peng, H. (Shara), 1991. Taiwan: An exploration of labour relations in transition. *British Journal of Industrial Relations*, 29 (3), 427–445.

Knafo, S., 2010. Critical approaches and the legacy of the agent/structure debate in international relations. *Cambridge Review of International Affairs*, 23 (3), 493–516.

Ko, J.-J.R., 2007. Labor dispatching and the transformation of the employment relationship in Taiwan. *American Sociological Association Conference Presentation*. Available online at http://citation.allacademic.com/meta/p21049_index.html (accessed 12 March 2014).

Kolko, J. and Kolko, G., 1972. *The Limits of Power: The World and United States Foreign Policy, 1945–1954*. New York: Harper & Row.

Kondratieff, N.D., 1979. The long waves in economic life. *Review*, 2 (4), 519–562.

Kong, T.Y., 2005. Labour and neo-liberal globalization in South Korea and Taiwan. *Modern Asian Studies*, 39 (1), 155–188.

Kong, T.Y., 2013. Between late-industrialisation and globalisation: The hybridisation of labour relations among leading South Korean firms. *New Political Economy*, 18 (5), 625–652.

Koo, H., 1991. Middle classes, democratization, and class formation: The case of South Korea. *Theory and Society*, 20 (4), 485–509.

Koo, H., 2001. *Korean Workers: The Culture and Politics of Class Formation*. Ithaca: Cornell University Press.

Korean National Statistical Office. "Statistical Database." Available online at http://kosis.kr/eng/statisticsList/statisticsList_01List.jsp?vwcd=MT_ETITLE&parentId=B (accessed 11 July 2014).

Krugman, P., 1994. The myth of Asia's miracle. *Foreign Affairs*, 73 (6), 62–78.

Kume, I., 1988. Changing relations among the government, labor, and business in Japan after the oil crisis. *International Organization*, 42 (4), 659–687.

Kwon, H., 2004. Japanese employment relations in transition. *Economic and Industrial Democracy*, 25 (3), 325–345.

Kynge, J., 2007. *China shakes the world: A titan's rise and troubled future – and the challenge for America*. Boston: Houghton Mifflin.

Lai, S.-Y., 1993. *The Politics of State–Labour Relations in Taiwan, 1949–1989: From Passivity to Unrest*. PhD Thesis, University of Sussex.

Lall, S. and Albaladejo, M., 2004. China's competitive performance: A threat to East Asian manufactured exports? *World Development*, 32 (9), 1441–1466.

Lam, W.W.-L., 2006. *Chinese politics in the Hu Jintao era: New leaders, new challenges*. London: M. E. Sharpe.

Lambert, R., 1998. Globalisation: Can unions resist? *South African Labour Bulletin*, 22 (6), 72–77.

Large, S., 1979. Perspectives on the failure of the labour movement in pre-war Japan. *Labour History*, 37 (November), 15–27.

Lee, B.-H. and Frenkel, S.J., 2004. Divided workers: Social relations between contract and regular workers in a Korean auto company. *Work, Employment and Society*, 18 (3), 507–530.

Lee, B.-H. and Yi, S., 2012. Organizational transformation towards industry unionism in South Korea. *Journal of Industrial Relations*, 54 (4), 476–493.

Lee, C.-H., 1998. New unionism and the transformation of the Korean industrial relations system. *Economic and Industrial Democracy*, 19 (2), 347–373.

Lee, C.K., 1999. From organized dependence to disorganized despotism: Changing labour regimes in Chinese factories. *The China Quarterly*, 157 (157), 44–71.

Lee, C.K., 2002. From the spectre of Mao to the spirit of the law: Labor insurgency in China. *Theory and Society*, 31 (2), 189–228.

Lee, C.K., 2008a. *Against the Law: Labour Protests in China's Rustbelt and Sunbelt*. Berkeley: University of California Press.

Lee, E., 1997. *The Labour Movement and the Internet: The New Internationalism*. London: Pluto.

Lee, F., 2007a. The rise and fall of the Taiwanese Party-State: Its implications and impacts on the development of trade unionism. *Employment Research Unit Annual Conference, Cardiff Business School.*

Lee, H.Y., 2004. South Korea in 2003: A question of leadership? *Asian Survey*, 44 (1), 130–138.

Lee, J.S., 1994. *Is There a Bona Fide Labor Movement in Taiwan?* Taipei: Chung-Hua Institution for Economic Research.

Lee, J.-T., 1987. *Economic Development and Industrial Order in South Korea*. PhD Thesis: University of Hawaii.

Lee, J.-T., 1988. Export-oriented industrialization, labor control and the labor movement in South Korea. *Korean Social Science Journal*, 14, 103–119.

Lee, N., 2007b. *The Making of Minjung: Democracy and the Politics of Representation*. Ithaca: Cornell University Press.

Lee, W. and Lee, B., 2005. *Industrial Relations: Recent Changes and New Challenges*. Seoul: Korean Labor Institute.

Lee, Y., 2008b. Divergent outcomes of labor reform politics in democratized Korea and Taiwan. *Studies in Comparative International Development*, 44 (1), 47–70.

Lee, Y., 2011. *Militants or Partisans: Labor Unions and Democratic Politics in Korea and Taiwan*. Stanford: Stanford University Press.

Lee, Y., Chung, S., and Jang, H., 2008. Labor and politics in East Asia: The case of failure of the encompassing labor organization in Korea. *Asian Perspective*, 32 (3), 111–138.

Lee, Y. and Lim, Y.-J., 2006. The rise of the Labor Party in South Korea: Causes and limits. *The Pacific Review*, 19 (3), 305–335.

Leftwich, A., 1995. Bringing politics back in: Towards a model of the developmental state. *Journal of Development Studies*, 31 (3), 400–427.

Lewis, J.W. and Xue, L., 2003. Social change and political reform in China: Meeting the challenge of success. *The China Quarterly*, 176 (December), 926–942.

Li, C., 2001. The 'Shanghai Gang': Force for stability or cause for conflict? *China Leadership Monitor*, 1 (2), 1–18.

Li, C., 2003. The 'New Deal': Politics and policies of the Hu administration. *Journal of Asian and African Studies*, 38, 329–346.

Li, J., 2005. The Pearl River Delta migrant labour shortage. *CSR Asia Weekly*, 1 (9), 2.

Li, M., 2013. [China's social structure from a world systems perspective]. *Hongse Wenhuawang [Red Culture Website]*. Available online at http://www.hswh.org.cn/wzzx/llyd/zx/2013-05-02/17912.html (accessed 17 December 2013). (In Chinese.)

Lim Jie-Hyun, 2002. From hard history to soft history: Cultural histories of the Korean working class. *International Labor and Working-Class History*, 61, 169–172.

Lin, I., 2000. Flexitime causes labor ruckus. *Taipei Times*. Available online at http://www.taipeitimes.com/News/local/archives/2000/08/23/0000049173 (accessed 12 March 2014).

Little, I.M.D., Scitovsky, T., and Scott, M., 1970. *Industry and Trade in Some Developing Countries: A Comparative Study*. Oxford: Oxford University Press.

Liu, H., 2012. Comparing organized labor, comparing Korea and Taiwan. *Taiwanese Sociology*, 24 (December), 207–219.

Liu, H.-J., 2011. When labor and nature strike back: A double movement saga in Taiwan. *Capitalism Nature Socialism*, 22 (1), 22–39.

Low, S., 2000. Workers will get reduction in workweek. *Taipei Times*. Available online at http://www.taipeitimes.com/News/front/archives/2000/06/17/0000040291 (accessed 12 March 2014).

Lui, T., 2005. Bringing class back in: China re-stratified. *Critical Asian Studies*, 37 (3), 473–480.

Lundestad, G., 1986. Empire by invitation? The United States and Western Europe, 1945–1952. *Journal of Peace Research*, 23 (3), 263–277.

Macartney, J., 2006. China admits social unrest threatens party's iron grip. *The Times*, 9 December, p. 49.

Mandel, E., 1995. *Long waves of capitalist development: A Marxist interpretation: Based on the Marshall lectures given at the University of Cambridge*. London: Verso Books.

Marx, K. and Engels, F., 1967. *The Communist Manifesto*. Harmondsworth, Middlesex: Penguin Books.

McBeath, G.A., 1997. Taiwan privatizes by fits and starts. *Asian Survey*, 37 (12), 1145–1162.

McIlroy, J. and Croucher, R., 2013. The turn to transnational labor history and the study of global trade unionism. *Labor History*, 54 (5), 491–511.

Miller, H.L., 2003. Hu leadership focuses on compassionate conservative governance. *China Leadership Monitor,* 6 (Spring), 65–74.

Minns, J. and Tierney, R., 2003. The labour movement in Taiwan. *Labor History*, 85, 103–128.

Minns, J. and Tierney, R., 2005. Class and class struggle in Taiwan. *National Chengchi University Bulletin of Labour Research*, 18 (July), 79–117.

Mo, Y.-C., 2008. Legislature passes amendment on protection of labor. *Taipei Times*. Available online at http://www.taipeitimes.com/News/taiwan/archives/2008/05/03/2003410931 (accessed 12 March 2014).

Moody, K., 1997. *Workers in a Lean World: Unions in the International Economy*. London: Verso.

Moon, C. and Jun, B., 2011. Modernization strategy: Ideas and influences. *In*: B.-K. Kim and E.F. Vogel, eds. *The Park Chung Hee Era: The Transformation of South Korea*. Cambridge, MA: Harvard University Press.

Moore, B.J., 1966. *Social Origins of Dictatorship and Democracy: Lord and Peasant in the Making of the Modern World*. Harmondsworth, Middlesex: Penguin University Books.

Moore, J., 1983. *Japanese Workers and the Struggle for Power, 1945–1947*. Madison: University of Wisconsin Press.

Moore, J., 1988a. Summer of discontent. *Far Eastern Economic Review*, 141 (36), 116–117.

Moore, J., 1988b. Cloudy growth prospects. *Far Eastern Economic Review*, 139 (1), 51.

Moore, J., 1997. *Production Control: Workers' Control in Early Postwar Japan. The Other Japan: Conflict, Compromise and Resistance Since 1945*. London: M. E. Sharpe.

Moore, P., 2005. Revolutions from above: Worker training as trasformismo in South Korea. *Capital and Class*, 86 (2), 39–72.

Moore, T.G., 2008. China as an economic power in the contemporary era of globalization. *Journal of Asian and African Studies*, 43 (5), 497–521.

Morgan, J., 2003. Contemporary China, anachronistic Marxism: The continued explanatory power of Marxism. *Critical Asian Studies*, 36 (1), 65–90.

Morgan, J., 2008. China's growing pains: Towards the (global) political economy of domestic social instability. *International Politics*, 45 (4), 413–438.

Morton, A.D., 2007a. *Unravelling Gramsci: Hegemony and Passive Revolution in the Global Political Economy*. London: Pluto Press.

Morton, A.D., 2007b. Waiting for Gramsci: State formation, passive revolution and the international. *Millenium: Journal of International Studies*, 35 (2), 597–621.

Morton, A.D., 2010a. The geopolitics of passive revolution. *In*: A. Anievas, ed. *Marxism and World Politics: Contesting Global Capitalism*. London: Routledge, 215–230.

Morton, A.D., 2010b. Reflections on uneven development: Mexican revolution, primitive accumulation, passive revolution. *Latin American Perspectives*, 37 (1), 7–34.

Morton, A.D., 2010c. The continuum of passive revolution. *Capital and Class*, 34 (3), 315–342.

Munck, R., 2002. *Globalisation and Labour: The New Great Transformation*. New York: Zed Books.

Munck, R., 2010. Globalisation, labour and development: A view from the South. *Transformation: Critical Perspectives on Southern Africa*, 224 (72), 205–224.

Nakakita, K., 2008. Incorporating Japanese labor into the Free World: Cold War diplomacy and economic interdependence, 1949–1964. *Labor History*, 49 (2), 199–222.

Nakamura, K., 2007. Decline or revival? Japanese labor unions. *Japan Labor Review*, 4 (1), 7–22.

Nakano, Y., 1998. *Japan's Wartime Use of Colonial Labor: Taiwan and Korea (1937–1945)*. PhD Thesis, University of British Columbia.

National People's Congress, 2009. Labor Contract Law of the People's Republic of China [online]. Available online at http://www.npc.gov.cn/englishnpc/Law/2009-02/20/content_1471106.htm (accessed 11 July 2014).

Nayar, B.R., 2005. *The Geopolitics of Globalization: The Consequences for Development*. Oxford: Oxford University Press.

Ngo, T.-W., 2005. The political bases of episodic agency in the Taiwan state. *In*: R. Boyd and T.-W. Ngo, eds. *Asian States: Beyond the Developmental Perspective*. London: Routledge Curzon, 83–109.

Nichols, T., Cam, S., Chou, W.G., Chu, S., Zhao, W., and Feng, T., 2004. Factory regimes and the dismantling of established labour in Asia: A review of cases from large manufacturing plants in China, South Korea and Taiwan. *Work, Employment and Society*, 18 (4), 663–685.

Noh, J., 2002. [Corporatism and Korea's social agreement]. *Chinbop'yŏngnon [Progressive Critique]*, 13 (Autumn), 84–105. (In Korean).

O'Brien, R., 2000. Workers and world order: The tentative transformation of the international union movement. *Review of International Studies*, 26 (4), 533–555.

O'Brien, R., Goetz, A.M., Scholte, J.A., and Williams, M., 2000. *Contesting Global Governance: Multilateral Economic Institutions and Global Social Movements*. Cambridge: Cambridge University Press.

Ogle, G.E., 1990. *South Korea: Dissent Within the Economic Miracle*. Guildford and King's Lynn: Zed Books.

Ohmae, K., 1990. *The Borderless World: Power and Strategy in the Interlinked World Economy*. London: Collins.

Ok, W. and Yang, J., 2011. The Korean economy between two economic crises: Hybridization or convergence towards a market-led economy? *In*: R. Boyer, H. Uemura, and A. Isogai, eds. Diversity and Transformations of Asian Capitalisms. London: Routledge, 209–228.

Organisation for Economic Co-operation and Development (OECD), 2000. *International Trade and Core Labour Standards*. Paris: OECD.

Organisation for Economic Co-operation and Development, 2014. *StatExtracts*. Available online at http://stats.oecd.org/Index.aspx?DataSetCode=ANHRS (accessed June 19, 2014).

Otake, H., 1999. Developments in the Japanese political economy since the mid-1980s: The second attempt at neoliberal reform and its aftermath. *Government and Opposition*, 34 (3), 372–396.

Overholt, W., 1994. *The Rise of China: How Economic Reform Is Creating a New Superpower*. London: W.W. Norton & Co.

Pak, S., 1992. [Korea's labour movement: is it really in crisis?]. *Ch'anggaggwa pip'yŏng [Creation and Criticism]*, 76 (Summer), 214–226. (In Korean).

Pan, S.W., 2006. Kuomintang's trade union policy: From state control to societal control. *National Policy Foundation*. Available online at http://old.npf.org.tw/PUBLICATION/SS/095/SS-B-095-010.htm (accessed 6 January 2011).

Park, B.-G., 2001. Labor regulation and economic change: A view on the Korean economic crisis. *Geoforum*, 32 (1), 61–75.

Park, M., 2008. *Democracy and Social Change: A History of South Korean Student Movements, 1980–2000*. Oxford: Peter Lang.

Park, S.-I., 1992. Role of the state in industrial relations: The case of Korea. *Comparative Labor Law Journal*, 14, 321–338.

Park, S.-W., 1999. *Colonial Industrialization and Labor in Korea: The Onoda Cement Factory*. Cambridge, MA: Harvard University Asia Center.

Park, Y.C., 2005. *A Tale of Two Crises: Korea's Experience with External Debt Management 1979–80 and 1997–98*. Available online at http://vi.unctad.org/debt/debt/m3/documents/Country%20case%20Korea%20%5B1%5D.PDF (accessed 11 July 2014).

Patrick, H. and Rosovsky, H., 1976. *Asia's New Giant: How the Japanese Economy Works*. Washington, DC: Brookings Institution.

Pempel, T.J., 1999. The developmental regime in a changing world economy. *In*: M. Woo-Cumings, ed. *The Developmental State*. London: Cornell University Press, 137–181.

Pempel, T.J. and Tsunekawa, K., 1979. Corporatism without labor? The Japanese anomaly. *In*: P. Schmitter and G. Lehmbruch, eds. *Trends Towards Corporatist Intermediation*. London: Sage Publications, 231–270.

People's Daily, 2011. China's forex reserves pass 3 trillion USD for first time. *People's Daily*. Available online at http://english.peopledaily.com.cn/90001/90778/90862/7351620.html (accessed 17 April 2011).

Petras, J., 2006. Past, present and future of China: From semi-colony to world power? *Journal of Contemporary Asia*, 36 (4), 423–441.

Pieterse, J., 2011. Global rebalancing: Crisis and the east–south turn. *Development and Change*, 42 (1), 22–48.

Pirie, I., 2005. The new Korean state. *New Political Economy*, 10 (1), 25–42.

Pirie, I., 2008. *The Korean Developmental State: From Dirigisme to Neo-liberalism*. London: Routledge.

Price, J., 1997. *Japan Works: Power and Paradox in Postwar Industrial Relations*. London: Cornell University Press.

Ranald, P., 2002. Social movement unionism in East Asia? Regional and South Korean union responses to the crisis. *In*: M. Beeson, ed. *Reconfiguring East Asia: Regional Institutions and Organisations after the Crisis*. London: RoutledgeCurzon.

Reitan, R., 2012. Narratives of 'equivalence': Neoliberalism in contemporary Japan. *Radical History Review*, 2012 (112), 43–64.
Rice, J., 2006. The emergence of an industrial relations system in Taiwan: Historical and contextual challenges. *Asia Pacific Business Review*, 12 (2), 163–174.
Robinson, W.I., 1996. *Promoting Polyarchy*. Cambridge, UK: Cambridge University Press.
Robinson, W.I., 2004. *A Theory of Global Capitalism: Production, Class, and State in a Transnational World*. Baltimore: Johns Hopkins University Press.
Robinson, W.I., 2008. *Latin America and Global Capitalism: A Critical Globalisation Perspective*. Baltimore: Johns Hopkins University Press.
Rosenberg, J., 2002. *The Follies of Globalisation Theory: Polemical Essays*. London: Verso Books.
Rosenberg, J., 2006. Why is there no international historical sociology? *European Journal of International Relations*, 12 (3), 307–340.
Roy, D., 2003. *Taiwan: A Political History*. Ithaca: Cornell University Press.
Ruggie, J.G., 1982. International regimes, transactions and change: Embedded liberalism in the postwar economic order. *International Organisation*, 36 (2), 117–137.
Sassoon, A.S., 1982. Passive revolution and the politics of reform. *In*: A.S. Sassoon, ed. *Approaches to Gramsci*. London: Writers and Readers, 127–148.
Sassoon, A.S., 1987. *Gramsci's Politics*. Mineapolis: University of Minnesota Press.
Scholte, J., 2005. *Globalization: A Critical Introduction*. Basingstoke: Palgrave MacMillan.
Screpanti, E., 1984. Long economic cycles and recurring proletarian insurgencies. *Review, A Journal of the Fernand Braudel Center for the Study of Economies, Historical Systems, and Civilizations*, 7 (2), 509–548.
Screpanti, E., 1987. Long cycles in strike activity: an empirical investigation. *British Journal of Industrial Relations*, 25 (1), 99–124.
Selwyn, B., 2011. Trotsky, Gerschenkron and the political economy of late capitalist development. *Economy and Society*, 40 (3), 421–450.
Sen, Y.-S. and Koo, H., 1992. Industrial transformation and proletarianization in Taiwan. *Critical Sociology*, 19 (1), 45–67.
Shilliam, R., 2004. Hegemony and the unfashionable problematic of 'primitive accumulation.' *Millenium: Journal of International Studies*, 32 (1), 59–88.
Shim, J.H., 1989. To the left, march! Labour Party radicals plan a more militant grouping. *Far Eastern Economic Review*, 143 (9), 19.
Shim-Han, Y., 1987. Social control and industrialization in Korea – On the corporatist control of labor. *Korean Social Science Journal*, 13, 95–123.
Shin, J.-S., 2002. The East Asian industrialisation in the Gerschenkronian mirror: Catching-up strategies and institutional transition. *National University of Singapore Departmental Working Papers*. Available online at http://www.fas.nus.edu.sg/ecs/pub/wp/wp0208.pdf (accessed 1 December 2010).
Shin, K., 2012. The dilemmas of Korea's new democracy in an age of neoliberal globalisation. *Third World Quarterly*, 33 (2), 293–309.
Shin, K.-Y., 2000. The discourse of crisis and the crisis of discourse. *Inter-Asia Cultural Studies*, 1 (3), 427–442.
Shin, K.-Y., 2011. Globalization and social inequality in South Korea. *In*: J. Song, ed. *New Millennium South Korea: Neoliberal Capitalism and Transnational Movements*. London: Routledge, 11–28.
Shorrock, T., 1986. The struggle for democracy in South Korea in the 1980s and the rise of anti-Americanism. *Third World Quarterly*, 8 (4), 1195–1218.
Shorter, E. and Tilly, C., 1974. *Strikes in France, 1830–1968*. Cambridge: Cambridge University Press.

Silver, B.J., 1992. Class struggle and Kondratieff waves, 1870 to the present. *In*: A. Kleinknecht, E. Mandel, and I.M. Wallerstein, eds. *New Findings in Long Wave Research*. London: Macmillan, 279–296.

Silver, B.J., 2003. *Forces of Labor: Workers' Movements and Globalization since 1870*. Cambridge, UK: Cambridge University Press.

Sklair, L., 1998. Transnational corporations as political actors. *New Political Economy*, 5 (2), 284–287.

Skocpol, T., 1979. *States and Social Revolutions: A Comparative Analysis of France, Russia, and China*. Cambridge, UK: Cambridge University Press.

Solinger, D.J., 1999. *Contesting Citizenship in Urban China: Peasant Migrants, the State and the Logic of the Market*. Berkeley: University of California Press.

Solinger, D.J., 2003. State and society in urban China in the wake of the 16th Party Congress. *The China Quarterly*, 176 (December), 943–959.

Song, H.-Y., 2011. Theorising the Korean state beyond institutionalism: Class content and form of a 'national' development. *New Political Economy*, 16 (3), 281–302.

Sonn, H., 1997. The 'late blooming' of the South Korean labour movement. *Monthly Review*, July-August, 117–129.

Sonn, H., 2006. The post-Cold-War world order and domestic conflict in South Korea: Neoliberal and armed globalization. *In*: V.R. Hadiz, ed. *Empire and Neoliberalism in Asia*. London: Routledge.

Standard Chartered, 2012. China – More than 200 clients talk wages in the PRD. *Global Research*. Available online at https://research.standardchartered.com/configuration/ROW Documents/China_%E2%80%93_More_than_200_clients_talk_wages_in_the_PRD_05_03_12_05_52.pdf (accessed 29 April 2013).

Steinberg, D.I., 1985. Foreign aid and the development of the Republic of Korea: The effectiveness of concessional assistance. *US AID Report*. Available online at http://pdf.usaid.gov/pdf_docs/pnaal075.pdf (accessed 19 June 2014).

Steinberg, D.I. and Shin, M., 2006. Tensions in South Korean political parties in transition: From entourage to ideology? *Asian Survey*, 46 (4), 517–537.

Steven, R., 1990. *Japan's New Imperialism*. London: Macmillan.

Stevis, D. and Boswell, T., 2008. *Globalisation and Labour: Democratising Global Governance*. Lanham: Rowman and Littlefield.

Strange, S., 1996. *The Retreat of the State: The Diffusion of Power in the World Economy*. Cambridge, UK: Cambridge University Press.

Stubbs, R., 2005. *Rethinking Asia's Miracle*. Basingstoke: Palgrave Macmillan.

Taira, K., 1988. Labor confederation in Japan. *Current History*, 87 (528), 161–165.

Taira, K., 1997. Factory labour and the industrial revolution in Japan. *In*: K. Yamamura, ed. *The Economic Emergence of Modern Japan*. Cambridge, UK: Cambridge University Press, 239–293.

Takahashi, Y., 1997. The labor market and lifetime employment in Japan. *Economic and Industrial Democracy*, 18 (1), 55–66.

The China Post, 2010. New labor law prohibits teachers from striking. *The China Post*. Available online at http://www.chinapost.com.tw/taiwan/national/national-news/2010/06/02/258979/New-labor.htm (accessed 12 March 2014).

The Hankyoreh, 2006. S. Korean junta punished civilians with military camp in early 1980s: report. *The Hankyoreh*. Available online at http://www.hani.co.kr/arti/english_edition/e_national/171123.html (accessed 12 March 2014).

Thelen, K. and Kume, I., 1999. The effects of globalization on labor revisited: Lessons from Germany and Japan. *Politics and Society*, 27 (4), 477–505.

Thomas, K.P., 1997. *Capital beyond Borders: States and Firms in the Auto Industry 1960–94*. Basingstoke: Macmillan.

Thompson, E.P., 1963. *The Making of the English Working Class*. Harmondsworth: Penguin.

Thurbon, E., 2001. Two paths to financial liberalization: South Korea and Taiwan. *The Pacific Review*, 14 (2), 241–267.

Tilly, C., 1995. Globalization threatens labor's rights. *International Labor and Working-Class History*, 47 (Spring), 1–23.

Tolentino, P.E., 2000. *Multinational Corporations: Emergence and Evolution*. London: Routledge.

Totten, G.O., 1960. Labor and agrarian disputes in Japan following World War I. *Economic Development and Cultural Change*, 9 (1), 187–212.

Trotsky, L., 1997. *The History of the Russian Revolution*. London: Pluto Press.

Tsai, M.-C., 2001. Dependency, the state and class in the neoliberal transition of Taiwan. *Third World Quarterly*, 22 (3), 359–379.

Tsuru, S., 1993. *Japan's Capitalism: Creative Defeat and Beyond*. Cambridge, England: Cambridge University Press.

Tsuru, T. and Rebitzer, J.B., 1995. The limits of enterprise unionism: Prospects for continuing union decline in Japan. *British Journal of Industrial Relations*, 33 (3), 459–492.

Tung, C., 2005. Trade relations between Taiwan and China. *In*: J. Luo, ed. *China Today: An Encyclopedia of Life in the People's Republic*. Westport: Greenwood Press, 625–628.

Unger, J., 2006. China's conservative middle class. *Far Eastern Economic Review*, 169 (3), 27–31.

US Treasury, 2012. Major foreign holders of treasury securities. *Department of the Treasury*. Available online at http://www.treasury.gov/resource-center/data-chart-center/tic/Documents/mfh.txt (accessed 17 April 2013).

Van Hoesel, R., 1998. The emergence of Korean and Taiwanese multinationals in Europe: prospects and limitations. *Asia Pacific Business Review*, 4 (2-3), 109–129.

Veltmeyer, H., 2005. Development and globalization as imperialism. *Canadian Journal of Development Studies*, 26 (1), 89–106.

Wade, R., 1990. *Governing the Market: Economic Theory and the Role of Government in East Asian Industrialization*. Princeton, NJ: Princeton University Press.

Wade, R., 1992. East Asia's economic success: Conflicting perspectives, partial insights, shaky evidence. *World Politics*, 44 (January), 270–320.

Wade, R., 1998. From 'miracle' to 'cronyism': Explaining the great Asian slump. *Cambridge Journal of Economics*, 22, 693–708.

Wade, R., 2003. What strategies are viable for developing countries today? The World Trade Organization and the shrinking of 'development space.' *Review of International Political Economy*, 10 (4), 621–644.

Wade, R. and Veneroso, F., 1998. The Asian crisis: The high debt model versus the Wall Street–Treasury–IMF complex. *New Left Review*, 231 (5), 3–22.

Walker, K.L.M., 2006. Gangster capitalism' and peasant protest in China: The last twenty years. *The Journal of Peasant Studies*, 13 (1), 1–33.

Wang, H., Appelbaum, R.P., Degiuli, F., and Lichtenstein, N., 2009. China's new labour contract law: Is China moving towards increased power for workers? *Third World Quarterly*, 30 (3), 485–501.

Wang, J., 2010. The political economy of collective labour legislation in Taiwan. *Journal of Current Chinese Affairs*, 39 (3), 51–85.

Watanabe, S., 2000. The Japan model and the future of employment and wage systems. *International Labour Review*, 139 (3), 307–333.

Waterman, P., 1998. *Globalisation, Social Movements and the New Internationalisms*. Washington, DC: Mansell.

Waterman, P., 2001. Trade union internationalism in the age of Seattle. *Antipode*, 33 (3), 312–336.

Waterman, P. and Wills, J., 2001. *Place, Space and New Labour Internationalism*. Oxford: Blackwell.

Weathers, C., 2008. Shunto and the shackles of competitiveness. *Labor History*, 49 (2), 177–197.

Webster, E., Lambert, R., and Beziudenhout, A., 2008. *Grounding Globalization: Labour in the Age of Insecurity*. Hoboken, NJ: Wiley-Blackwell.

Weil, R., 2006. Conditions of the working classes in China. *Monthly Review*, 58 (1), 25–48.

Weiss, L., 1997. Globalization and the myth of the powerless state. *New Left Review*, I/225 (September/October), 3–27.

Weiss, L., 1998. *The Myth of the Powerless State: Governing the Economy in a Global Era*. Cambridge, UK: Polity Press.

Weiss, L., 2003. Guiding globalisation in East Asia: new roles for old developmental states. *In:* Linda Weiss, ed. *States in the Global Economy: Bringing Domestic Institutions Back In*. Cambridge, UK: Cambridge University Press, 245–270.

Westphal, L., 1990. Industrial policy in an export-propelled economy: Lessons from South Korea's experience. *Journal of Economic Perspectives*, 4 (3), 41–59.

White, G., 1993. *Riding the Tiger: The Politics of Economic Reform in Post-Mao China*. Basingstoke: Macmillan.

White, G., Howell, J., and Shang, X., 1996. Chinese trade unions: The road to corporatism? *In*: G. White, J. Howell, and X. Shang, eds. *In Search of Civil Society: Market Reform and Social Change in Contemporary China*. Oxford: Clarendon Press.

Whittaker, D., 2003. Labour unions and industrial relations in Japan: Crumbling pillar or forging a 'third way'? *Industrial Relations Journal*, 29 (4), 280–294.

Wiegersma, N. and Medley, J.E., 2000. *US Economic Development Policies Towards the Pacific Rim: Successes and Failures of US Aid*. Basingstoke: Macmillan.

Woo, J.-E., 1991. *Race to the Swift: State and Finance in Korean Industrialization*. New York: Columbia University Press.

Wright, E.O., 2000. Working-class power, capitalist-class interests, and class compromise. *American Journal of Sociology*, 105 (4), 957–1002.

Wu, Y.S., 2001. Taiwan in 2000: Managing the aftershocks from power transfer. *Asian Survey*, 41 (1), 40–48.

Wu, Y.S., 2002. Taiwan in 2001: Stalemated on all fronts. *Asian Survey*, 42 (1), 29–38.

Wu, Y.-S., 2007. Taiwan's developmental state: After the economic and political turmoil. *Asian Survey*, 47 (6), 977–1001.

Xinhua News, 2010. CPC sets targets for 12th Five-Year Program. Available online at http://www.china.org.cn/china/2010-10/27/content_21214648.htm (accessed 17 April 2013).

Yamamura, K., 1977. Success illgotten? The role of Meiji militarism in Japan's technological progress. *The Journal of Economic History*, 37 (1), 113–135.

Yang, D.T., Chen, V.W., and Monarch, R., 2010. Rising wages: Has China lost its global labor advantage? *Pacific Economic Review*, 15 (4), 482–504.

Yi, P., Kim, Y., Chông, Y., Chông, K., and Kim, Y., 2003. [Report on the Polarisation of the Quality of Labour: On the Regular and Irregular Segmentation]. Seoul: Ingangwa pokji, 313–334. (In Korean).

Yiu, C., 2004. Pioneer labor activists celebrate 20 years' work. *Taipei Times*. Available online at http://www.taipeitimes.com/News/taiwan/archives/2004/05/30/2003157505 (accessed 17 April 2013).

Yoshino, M.Y., 1968. *Japan's Managerial System: Tradition and Innovation*. Cambridge, MA: MIT Press.

Yoshitomi, M., 1976. The recent Japanese economy: The oil crisis and the transition to medium growth path. *The Developing Economies*, 14 (4), 319–340.

Young, E., 2013. Bangladesh textile workers' deaths 'avoidable.' *BBC News*. Available online at http://www.bbc.co.uk/news/business-22296645 (accessed 12 March 2014).

Yu, H., 1997. Labor relations in the new world economy: The Korean experience. *In*: H. Kwon, ed. *Contemporary Korea: Democracy, Economic Development, Social Change, Re-Unification Process*. Chicago: North Park University, 101–131.

Yu, Y., 2012. China's rebalancing act: Between exports and domestic demand. *East Asia Forum*. Available online at http://www.eastasiaforum.org/2012/10/24/chinas-rebalancing-act-between-exports-and-domestic-demand/ (accessed 17 April 2013).

Yun, J.-W., 2009. Labor market polarization in South Korea: The role of policy failures in growing inequality. *Asian Survey*, 49 (2), 268–290.

Zhang, X., 2002. Domestic institutions, liberalization patterns, and uneven crises in Korea and Taiwan. *The Pacific Review*, 15 (3), 409–442.

Zhang, Y., 1997. From state corporatism to social representation: Local trade unions in the reform years. *In*: T. Brook and M.B. Frolic, eds. *Civil Society in China*. London: M. E. Sharpe.

Zheng, Y.L., 2009. It's not what is on paper, but what is in practice: China's new labor contract law and the enforcement problem. *Washington University Global Studies Law Review*, 8 (3), 1–24.

Zhu, Y., 2008. Trade unions in Taiwan: Confronting the challenge of globalization and economic restructuring. *In*: J. Beeson and Y. Zhu, eds. *Trade Unions in Asia: An Economic and Sociological Analysis*. London: Routledge, 63–80.

Zolberg, A.R., 1995. Response: Working-class dissolution. *International Labor and Working-Class History*, 47 (Spring), 28–38.

INDEX